THE ART
OF
POETRY

PAUL
VALÉRY

VINTAGE BOOKS

A Division of Random House

New York

THE
ART
OF
POETRY

**TRANSLATED
FROM THE FRENCH BY
DENISE FOLLIOT**

**INTRODUCTION BY
T. S. ELIOT**

THIS IS VOLUME SEVEN OF THE
COLLECTED WORKS OF PAUL VALÉRY,
CONSTITUTING NUMBER XLV IN BOLLINGEN SERIES,
SPONSORED BY AND PUBLISHED FOR
BOLLINGEN FOUNDATION.
IT IS THE SECOND VOLUME OF THE
COLLECTED WORKS TO APPEAR.

FIRST VINTAGE EDITION, *September 1961*

VINTAGE BOOKS
are published by ALFRED A. KNOPF, INC.,
and RANDOM HOUSE, INC.

Manufactured in the
UNITED STATES OF AMERICA

CONTENTS

Introduction

AMONG the several motives which may impel a poet to write about poetry, we must not overlook those arising from necessity or obligation. A young poet may find himself writing essays on poets and poetry, simply because a young poet, if he has any talent for journalism at all, can earn more money by writing about other poets' poetry, than he can by selling his own. If he hopes that success in later years will free him from this kind of distraction, his hope is vain: he will merely, if successful, exchange one form of constraint for another. There is a banquet: he has to respond to the toast of "Poetry," or to propose the health of some distinguished foreign visitor. There is a centenary to be commemorated, a tablet to be unveiled, or the birthday of some venerable poet to be honored: it is necessary that a middle-aged poet should be present to drop the grain of incense, or fix, for the moment, a reputation. There is a young, unknown, and very promising poet to be assisted: the sale of his book will be promoted, or at least the reviewers will be more attentive, if some respected senior artisan will preface it. World conferences and congresses, European and local conferences and congresses, follow each other in endless succession: the public thirst for words about poetry, and for words from poets about almost anything— in contrast to its thirst for poetry itself—seems insatiable. In short, the compulsions and solicitations to a poet to write about poetry, and to talk about poetry, instead of writing poetry, begin early in life and continue to the end.

The life of Paul Valéry forms no exception to this rule. On the contrary: far from having purchased exemption by eminence, Valéry provides the most conspicuous confirmation of my words. He has said somewhere, that he never wrote prose except under some outside pressure or stimulus. This is surely an exaggeration: yet no poet has ever been more the victim of such molestations of fortune—to which, indeed, we owe some of his most remarkable prose, and without which we should have been deprived of much of what we know of a singularly fascinating mind. His situation in life was such that he arrived at the importunities of fame without altogether escaping the coercion of want. In his later years, he was saved from the possibility of financial embarrassment by being found a professorship at the Collège de France. There he earned his livelihood, long after the poetry which provides the solid foundation for his fame had been written, by lecturing to the public—on the Art of Poetry. His inaugural lecture, I have no doubt, drew a large and fashionable audience; but, because of the subtlety of the argument, and the indistinctness of his enunciation, it may have been difficult for the audience to follow. The irony of such a life as Valéry's is only fully apparent in retrospect.

The occasional character of most of Valéry's critical writing, of his *poétique*, must not however be allowed to suggest that there is anything perfunctory about it. He obviously enjoyed writing about poetry, still more about the process of writing poetry, and most of all about the process by which his own poetry got written. If the best of his poems are among the masterpieces, the best of his critical essays are among the most remarkable curiosities of French literature.

The writer whose critical essays have mostly been responses to particular situations is exposed, once the essays have been collected and published together, to a misunderstanding against which the prospective reader should be warned. In reading a volume of collected essays we are all, especially when approaching them for the first time, prone to expect a unity to which such work does not pretend. The essays contained in the present volume are some of them divided by many years from each other; and the French texts were published in collections assembled chronologically rather than by subject matter. The student of the *poétique* of Valéry may start in the expectation of complete coherence; and when he does not find it, he may be tempted to complain of inconsistencies and to deride repetitions. Here and there, among Valéry's writings, you will find the same passage repeated almost verbatim, without apology or explanation. I do not myself object to this: I prefer to read critical essays in their original form, not reshaped at a later date into an artificial unity. Indeed, I regard repetitions and contradictions in a man's writing as valuable clues to the development of his thought. When I have, myself, occasion to write on some subject which I have treated in different circumstances in the past, I prefer to remain in ignorance of my opinion of twenty or thirty years ago, until I have committed to paper my opinion of today. Then, and not till then, I wish to refresh my memory. For if I find a contradiction, it is evidence that I have changed my mind; if there is a repetition, it is the best possible evidence that I am of the same mind as ever. An unconscious repetition may be evidence of one's firmest convictions, or of one's most abiding interests.

I have thought it desirable to insist upon the occasional character of many of Valéry's essays; but I do not want to suggest that the choice of subject was always dictated by the occasion, or that the results, even when the subject was imposed, are ever negligible. In the main, the subjects are obviously of his own choosing; and the occasion was only the necessary stimulus to provoke a train of thought. Even when the subject may have been indifferent, or the occasion unwelcome, Valéry was skillful enough to turn it to his own account, to direct it towards one of his dominant topics of meditation.

The direction which Valéry's meditations on poetry tended to take was no doubt suggested to him by an essay of Edgar Poe's; but what was for Poe merely the theme of one literary exercise among many, a tour de force perhaps, became for Valéry almost an obsessive preoccupation. Valéry's *art poétique* is inspired by different motives, and directed to different ends, from those of any of the treatises, essays, or scattered dicta of other poets, with the single exception of Poe, from Horace to the present day. Apart from practical precepts which have been the fruit of experience, much of the best writing of poets about poetry has been written in defense of some new style or of some new attitude towards the material of poetry. Amongst such writings are the essays of Dryden, the prefaces of Wordsworth, and (in part) Coleridge's *Biographia Literaria*. Beside forensic and polemic criticism, there is the judicial: Samuel Johnson, in his *Lives of the Poets*, appears in the role of a judge, who has not himself chosen the persons to be tried in his court. Other poets have been moved to write criticism in revision of current opinion or traditional judgment, or to bring to light the work of some poet unjustly ignored, or to restore the reputation of some depreciated poet. Often, a poet is most effective as critic, when he writes about those poets whose work has influenced his own, or with whom he feels some affinity. And on the other hand, a poet may write with unusual understanding of some poet whom he admires and likes because that poet's work is utterly different from anything that he himself does or wants to do. In our time, Mr. Ezra Pound combined several of these functions of the poet as critic: the training of young writers, the education of the public taste with regard to forgotten, undervalued, or unknown poets of the past in several languages, and the advertisement of those contemporary and younger writers whose work met with his approval.

Valéry's *poétique* fits nowhere in the foregoing classification. His appreciations of earlier poetry—for instance, the charming "Concerning *Adonis*" in this volume—are all too few; his appreciations of living poets, in his occasional prefaces, are most interesting when he wanders from his subject. He is not didactic, and so has little in common with Horace or Boileau or Pound. There are valuable hints to poets; but his motive is never primarily to guide the young, or to advance the claims of a new school of poetry, or to interpret and revalue poetry of the past. There are valuable hints to readers; but Valéry is not primarily interested in teaching his readers anything. He is perpetually engaged in solving an insoluble puzzle—the puzzle of how poetry gets written; and the material upon which he works is his own poetry. In the end, the question is simply: how did I write *La Jeune Parque* (or *Le Cimetière marin*)? The questions with which he is concerned are questions which no poet of an earlier generation would have raised; they are questions that belong to the present self-conscious century. This gives to Valéry's thought a singular documentary value.

There are, of course, incidental observations which can be taken to heart by the young poet; there are observations which can help the reader towards understanding the nature of poetry. There are also, if I am not mistaken, observations dangerous for the young poet, and observations confusing for the reader. Before attempting to define Valéry's central interest, it seems proper to give a few instances of these incidental remarks of both kinds.

The insistence, in Valéry's poetics, upon the small part played, in the elaboration of a poem, by what he calls *le rêve* — what is ordinarily called the "inspiration" — and upon the subsequent process of deliberate, conscious, arduous labor, is a most wholesome reminder to the young poet. It is corrective of that romantic attitude which, in employing the word "inspiration," inclines consciously or unconsciously to regard the poet's role, in the composition of a poem, as mediumistic and irresponsible. Whenever we come across a poem (this has often happened to me in the course of reading manuscripts) which appears to have some original merit, but which has been turned out into the world in an unfinished state, or which perhaps is only a kind of note of something which might provide the material of a good poem, we suspect that the author has depended too confidently upon his "inspiration"; in other words, that he has shirked the labor of smelting what may have been payable ore. On the other hand, as any advice, literally and unintelligently applied, can lead to disastrous consequences, it is as well to point out that while the poet should regard no toil as too arduous and no application of time as too long, for bringing a poem as near perfection as his abilities will take it, he should also have enough power of self-criticism to know where to stop. As with the painting in Balzac's *Le Chef-d'œuvre inconnu*, there may be a point beyond which every alteration the author makes will be for the worse. A short poem, or a passage of a long poem, may appear in its final form at once; or it may have to go through the transformations of a dozen drafts. And my own experience is, that when the result is successful, nobody except the author himself will be able to distinguish between those passages which have undergone no alteration, and those which have been rewritten again and again. I think I understand what Valéry means when he says that a poem is never finished: at least, his words to this effect have a meaning for me. To me they mean that a poem is "finished," or that I will never touch it again, when I am sure that I have exhausted my own resources, that the poem is as good as *I* can make *that* poem. It may be a bad poem: but nothing that I can do will make it better. Yet I cannot help thinking that, even if it is a good poem, I could have made a better poem of it—the same poem, but better— if I were a better poet.

A corollary, perhaps, of Valéry's emphasis upon the fundamental "brainwork" (is not the phrase Dante Rossetti's?) is his insistence upon the value for the poet of the exercise of difficult and complicated rhyming stanza forms. No poet was ever more conscious of the benefit of working in strict forms, the advantage to be gained by imposing upon oneself limitations to overcome. Such exercises are, of course, of no use to the man who has nothing to say, except possibly that of helping him to appreciate the work of those poets who have used these forms well; but what they can teach the genuine poet, is the way in which form and content must come to terms. It is only by practicing the sonnet, the sestina, or the villanelle, that we learn what sort of content can *not* be expressed in each of these forms; and it is only the poet who has developed this sense of fitness who is qualified to attempt "free verse." No one should write "free verse"—or, at least, offer it for publication—until he has discovered for himself that free verse allows him no more freedom than any other verse.

Another important contribution by Valéry to the education of the poet is his emphasis upon *structure*. Although a poem can be made out of a succession of felicitous verses, it must nevertheless be built. This law, like others, could be made too absolute, and lead us into absurdities as deplorable as those of some eighteenth-century critics. It need not oblige us to deny all merit to FitzGerald's *Rubáiyát:* for that poem does make a total impression which is not merely the sum of the impressions of the several quatrains; but it does, I think, justify us in affirming that *The Deserted Village* approximates to a perfection that we miss in the *Elegy Written in a Country Church-yard*.

Valéry's analogy, in the matter of structure, is Architecture. Elsewhere, as we shall see presently, he compares Poetry to the Dance; and he always maintained that assimilation of Poetry to Music which was a Symbolist tenet. Between these analogies there is no contradiction, unless we are misled by the famous phrase of Walter Pater. For Music itself may be conceived as striving towards an unattainable timelessness; and if the other arts may be thought of as yearning for duration, so Music may be thought of as yearning for the stillness of painting or sculpture. I speak as one with no technical training in music, but I find that I enjoy, and "understand," a piece of music better for knowing it well, simply because I have at any moment during its performance a memory of the part that has preceded and a memory of the part that is still to come. Ideally, I should like to be able to hold the whole of a great symphony in my mind at once. The same is true, surely, of a great tragedy: the better we know it, the more fully we hold in mind, during the action, what has preceded and what is to come, the more intense is our experience. It is only in a detective thriller, or in some kinds of comedy and farce, that the *unexpected* is a contribution to, and even a necessary element of, our enjoyment.

I have considered Valéry's insistence upon hard work, upon study of prosodic and stanzaic form, and upon structure. There is, however, one direction in which Valéry's theory and practice take him, which seems to me not without its dangers. This direction is indicated, is even imposed, by the sharp distinction which he draws between poetry and prose. He supports this division by a very neat and persuasive analogy, *viz.*:

Poetry : Prose :: Dancing : Walking (or Running).

Prose, Valéry maintains, is *instrumental:* its purpose is to convey a meaning, to impart information, to convince of a truth, to direct action; once its message has been apprehended, we dismiss the means by which it has been communicated. So with walking or running: our purpose is to get to a destination. The only value of our movement has been to achieve some end that we have set ourselves. But the purpose of the dance is the dance itself. Similarly with poetry: the poem is for its own sake—we enjoy a poem as we enjoy dancing; and as for the words, instead of looking *through* them, so to speak, we are looking *at* them. This is, as I have just remarked, persuasive; or rather, it illuminates like the flash of an empty cigarette lighter in the dark: if there is no fuel in the lighter, the momentary flash leaves a sense of darkness more impenetrable than before. It would be a quibble, to point out that dancing is sometimes purposive (the purpose of a war dance, I believe, is to rouse the dormant pugnacity of the dancers); for even if dancing is always pure delight in rhythmical movement, the analogy may be misleading. I think that much poetry will be found to have the instrumental value that Valéry reserves to prose, and that much prose gives us the kind of delight that Valéry holds to be solely within the province of poetry. And if it is maintained that prose which gives that kind of delight *is* poetry, then I can only say that the distinction between poetry and prose has been completely obliterated, for it would seem that prose can be read as poetry, or poetry as prose, according to the whim of the reader.

I have never yet come across a final, comprehensive, and satisfactory account of the difference between poetry and prose. We can distinguish between prose and verse, and between verse and poetry; but the moment the intermediate term *verse* is suppressed, I do not believe that any distinction between prose and poetry is meaningful.

It is not, however, this attempt to discover some essential difference between prose and poetry that seems to me dangerous, but a tendency, which is very much favored by this account of prose and poetry, to approve a difference of vocabulary and idiom between poetry and prose. The words set free by Valéry from the restrictions of prose may tend to form a separate language. But the farther the idiom, vocabulary, and syntax of poetry depart from those of prose, the more artificial the language of poetry will become. When the written language remains fixed, while the spoken language, the vulgar speech, is undergoing changes, it must ultimately be replaced by a new written language, founded on current speech. Now the language of prose is ordinarily nearer to that of speech than is the language of poetry; so that if poetry arrogates the right to idiom, vocabulary, and syntax different from that of prose, it may eventually become so artificial as no longer to be able to convey living feeling and living thought. Speech on every level, from that of the least educated to that of the most cultivated, changes from generation to generation; and the *norm* for a poet's language is the way his contemporaries talk. In assimilating poetry to music, Valéry has, it seems to me, failed to insist upon its relation to speech. The poet can improve, indeed it is his duty to try to improve, the language that he speaks and hears. The characters in a play can, and usually should, have a much greater mastery of language than their originals in life would have. But neither the poem nor the play can afford to ignore the necessity of persuading us that this is the language we should ourselves speak, if we spoke as well as we should like to speak. It is perhaps significant that Valéry should attach so much importance as he does to the achievement of Mallarmé, and nowhere (so far as I am aware) acknowledge any indebtedness to the discoveries of Laforgue and Corbière.

Those observations of Valéry, which should be taken to heart by poets, can also be pondered with profit by readers—not for direct understanding of poetry, but as a help to understanding the kind of preparation that the poet needs, and the nature of the labor that the poet undertakes. And especially pertinent for the reader of poetry—and for the critic of poetry—is his repeated insistence that poetry must first of all be *enjoyed*, if it is to be of any use at all; that it must be enjoyed as poetry, and not for any other reason; and that most of the rest of what is written, talked, and taught is philology, history, biography, sociology, psychology. He defends the privacy, even the anonymity, of the poet, and the independence of the poem when it has been written and dismissed by the poet. At this stage, the poet's interpretation of his poem is not required: what matters is what the poem means—in the sense in which a poem may be said to have "meaning." What the poet meant it to mean or what he thinks it means now that it is written, are questions not worth the asking.

So far, however, I have not approached the essential problem, which is that of the characteristics distinguishing

Valéry's *art poétique* from that of anyone else. His purpose is not to teach the writing of poetry or to improve the understanding of it; his purpose is not primarily to facilitate the understanding of his own poetry—though it will very soon strike the attention of the perceptive reader, that much of what he predicates of "poetry" is applicable only to his own poetry. The best approach, I believe, is through a little essay, of very early date, included in this volume, entitled "On Literary Technique." The date is 1889, but this early credo gives a clue to his later development. What it announces is no less than a new style for poets, as well as a new style for poetry. The satanist, the dandy, the *poète maudit* have had their day: eleven years before the end of the nineteenth century Valéry invents the role which is to make him representative of the twentieth:

. . . a totally new and modern conception of the poet. He is no longer the disheveled madman who writes a whole poem in the course of one feverish night; he is a cool scientist, almost an algebraist, in the service of a subtle dreamer. A hundred lines at the most will make up his longest poems. . . . He will take care not to hurl on to paper everything whispered to him in fortunate moments by the Muse of Free Association. On the contrary, everything he has imagined, felt, dreamed, and planned will be passed through a sieve, weighed, filtered, subjected to *form*, and condensed as much as possible so as to gain in power what it loses in length: a sonnet, for example, will be a true quintessence, a nutrient, a concentrated and distilled juice, reduced to fourteen lines, carefully *composed* with a view to a final and overwhelming effect.

We must remember that Valéry was a very young man when he wrote these enthusiastic words; but in making this allowance, we are all the more struck by the fact that this is essentially the point of view to which he was to adhere throughout his life. The association of the "dreamer" and the "algebraist," for example, was to remain unbroken. The loyalty to Poe ("a hundred lines at the most") was to endure to the end. But what is most impressive about the passage I have just quoted, is that it discloses, behind Valéry's Idea of Poetry, another and perhaps the controlling Idea—Valéry's Idea of the Poet. It is from the conception of the poet that he proceeds to the conception of poetry, and not the other way about. Now this Idea of the Poet was a prophetic one, prophetic not only of the mature Valéry, but of the ideals and the idols of the coming age. Looked at in this way, the "cool scientist" is an alternative, rather than the antithesis to the "disheveled madman": a different mask for the same actor. Poe, to be sure, combined both roles: but it is only as the "cool scientist" that Valéry sees him, "mathematician, philosopher, and great writer." True, Valéry wrote this credo during the period of des Esseintes and Dorian Gray. The mature Valéry would not have extolled, as he did in this same manifesto of 1889, "the morbid search for the rarest pleasures"; nor would he have overworked the qualification "too" ("we love the art of this age...too vibrant, too tense, too *musical*," etc.). What is significant is not such phrases as these, but the introduction of such a substantive as "nutrient" (*osmazôme*) and such a verb as "distill" (*cohober*). In the year 1889, the young Valéry has already cast himself in the role which he was to play with such distinguished success during the years from 1917 (the publication of *La Jeune Parque*) to his death in 1945.

Valéry in fact invented, and was to impose upon his age, not so much a new conception of poetry as a new conception of the poet. The tower of ivory has been fitted up as a laboratory—a solitary laboratory, for Valéry never went so far as to advocate "teamwork" in the writing of poetry. The poet is comparable to the mathematical physicist, or else to the biologist or chemist. He is to carry out the role of scientist as studiously as Sherlock Holmes did: this is the aspect of himself to which he calls the public's attention. Our picture of the poet is to be very like that of the austere, bespectacled man in a white coat, whose portrait appears in advertisements, weighing out or testing the drugs of which is compounded some medicine with an impressive name.

What I have said above is what I may call the primary aspect of Valéry's poetics. The secondary aspect is its relation to his own poetry. Everything that he says about the writing of poetry must be read, of course, with constant reference to the poetry that he wrote. No one, I think, will find these essays fully intelligible until he has read Valéry's most important poems. To some extent, I see his essays on poetry as a kind of defense and vindication of his own poems—a justification of their being the kind of poems they are, of their being as brief as they are, and of their being as few as they are. And to some extent the essays seem to me a kind of substitute for the poems he did not write. In one respect especially I find these essays very different from Poe's "Philosophy of Composition," different and more genuine. I have never been able to believe that Poe's famous essay is an account of how *The Raven* was written: if *The Raven* was written with so much calculation, then it ought, as I have said elsewhere, to be better written than it is. But what for Poe was an ingenious exercise, was deadly earnest for Valéry, and from very early years. Therefore, one is ready to believe that Valéry's critical intelligence was active from the start, and that he had thought very deeply on how to write poetry before he composed either *La Jeune Parque* or *Le Cimetière marin:* and this, for me, gives to his notes on the writing of these poems a value greater than any that I can attach to Poe's. Certainly, one feels that Valéry's theory and practice are faithful to each other: how far his practice was the application of the theory, and how far his theory is simply a correct account of his practice, is an unanswerable question. It is this unity of the two which gives his essays a perennial fascination.

Valéry's account of the genesis, maturation, and completion of a poem cannot fail to arouse responses both of assent and of dissent from other poets. There are moments when I feel that an experience of Valéry's has some correspondence with one of my own: when he has recorded some process which I recognize and of which he makes me for the first time fully conscious. It is not in the nature of things that there should be a point-for-point correspondence between the mental processes of any two poets. Not only do poems come into being in as many ways as there are poets; for the same poet, I believe, the process may vary from poem to poem. Every poem has its own embryological pattern: and only the poem of a Valéry is attended, throughout its gestation, by an illustrious medical specialist. Sometimes, I think, Valéry allowed himself to be carried away too far by his metaphors of the clinic and the laboratory, as in the following general statement about his labors preparatory to writing a poem:

With every question, before making any deep examination of the content, I take a look at the language; I generally proceed like a surgeon who sterilizes his hands and prepares the area to be operated on. This is what I call *cleaning up the verbal situation*. You must excuse this expression equating the words and forms of speech with the hands and instruments of a surgeon.

This passage I find very obscure; but it may be the fact that I cannot identify, under the disguise of this metaphor, any experience of my own, that makes me suspect that "cleaning up the verbal situation" is, in plain English, eyewash.

The questions I have left to the end are: Why are Valéry's essays worth reading, and with what expectation should we read them? These questions would be easier to answer if the essays could be fitted into any existing category, the usefulness of which is admitted. We do not turn to Valéry's *art poétique* in the hope of learning how to write poetry or how to read it. We do not even turn to it primarily for the light it throws on Valéry's poetry: certainly we can say as truly that if the prose throws light on the poems, the poems also illuminate the prose. I think that we read these essays, and I think people will continue to read them, because we find Valéry to be a singularly interesting, enigmatic, and disturbing author, a poet who has realized in his life and work one conception of the role of the poet so amply as to have acquired also a kind of mythological status. We read the essays because, as Valéry himself says, "there is no theory that is not a fragment, carefully prepared, of some autobiography." We could almost say that Valéry's essays form a part of his poetical works. We read them for their own sake, for the delight in following the subtleties of thought which moves like a trained dancer, and which has every resource of language at its command; for the pleasure of sudden illuminations even when they turn out to be *feux follets;* for the excitement of an activity which always seems on the point of catching the inapprehensible, as the mind continues indefatigably to weave its fine logodaedal web.

There is, in the mind and work of Valéry, a curious paradox. He presents himself to the reader, not only as a tireless explorer of the labyrinths of philosophic speculation, but also, under the aegis of Leonardo da Vinci, as a man of scientific temper, fascinated by the problems of method; a ranging and restless mind; a dilettante of science but a specialist in a science of his own invention—the science of poetry. Yet, when we peruse the list of titles of his essays, we find a remarkably limited subject matter, with no evidence of omnivorous reading, or of the varied interests of a Coleridge or a Goethe. He returns perpetually to the same insoluble problems. It would almost seem that the one object of his curiosity was—himself. He reminds us of Narcissus gazing into the pool, and partakes of the attraction and the mystery of Narcissus, the aloofness and frigidity of that spiritual celibate.

The one complaint which I am tempted to lodge against Valéry's poetics, is that it provides us with no criterion of *seriousness*. He is deeply concerned with the problem of process, of how the poem is made, but not with the question of how it is related to the rest of life in such a way as to give the reader the shock of feeling that the poem has been to him, not merely an experience, but a serious experience. And by "experience" I mean here, not an isolable event, having its value solely in itself and not in relation to anything else, but something that has entered into and been fused with a multitude of other experiences in the formation of the person that the reader is developing into. I put it in this way, to avoid giving the misleading impression that I place the *seriousness* simply in the value of the materials out of which the poem is made. That would be to define one thing in terms of another kind of reality. The material of a poem is only *that* material after the poem has been made. How far the seriousness is in the subject treated, how far in the treatment to which the poet subjects it, how far in the intention of the poet, and how far it is in the poet below the level of conscious intention, we shall never agree upon with any poem that has ever been written. But in mentioning something of which I notice the absence in Valéry's poetics, I am not questioning the seriousness of his own finest poems. If some of Valéry's poems were not very serious poems indeed—if two of them, at least, were not likely to last as long as the French language— there could have been no interest for him in studying the process of their composition, and no delight for us in studying the result of his study.

T. S. ELIOT

THE ART
OF
POETRY

Preamble

THIS volume contains various essays which have appeared here and there, and which deal with the poet's state and the art of verse; but there is hardly anything to be found in it that would explain poetry itself.

Poetry, an ambiguous term, sometimes means a feeling that leads to creation, and sometimes, a production that tends to affect us.

The first case refers to an emotion whose peculiar effect is to fashion for itself in us and through us a WORLD that corresponds to it.

By the second sense of this word is meant a certain industry that may be thought about. It strives to produce and reproduce in others the creative state I spoke of, through the special means of articulate language. It tries, for example, to suggest a world that will give rise to the emotion just mentioned. The peak of this art is reached, in relation to a particular reader, when for the perfect and necessary expression of the effect produced on him by a work, he can find only that work itself.

But the first meaning signifies for us a kind of mystery. Poetry is at the very meeting point of mind and life—two indefinable essences.

3

Those in whom this mystery occurs mostly content themselves with their awareness of it. They simply accept this wonderful gift of being moved to create.

As passive or active poets, they endure or pursue pleasure without knowledge. Indeed it is commonly held that these two moods are mutually exclusive; that it is dangerous, perhaps impious, to want to unite them in one person. In the sphere of sensibility this opinion is incontestable—on condition that one labels as "sensibility" anything nonintelligent and divine.

But where are the perils by which no one is attracted?

Certain persons, then—although not very many—are not resigned to being merely favored by nature with a certain causeless gift. Not without pain and resistance do they admit that paroxysms and pleasures of such a high order are not completed and resolved in intellectual contemplation.

Far from thinking that the clear, distinct operations of the mind are opposed to poetry, these headstrong persons claim that the ambition to analyze and to grasp the poetic essence, besides being in itself in conformity with the general tendency of our will to intelligence, and exercising to the full our powers of understanding, is indeed essential to the dignity of the muse—or rather of all the muses, for at present I am speaking generally of all our powers of ideal invention.

In fact, however sensuous and passionate poetry may be, however inseparable from certain ravishments, and although at times it goes even to the point of disorder, one can easily show that it is still linked to the most precise faculties of the intelligence, for if it is in its principle a kind of emotion, it is a peculiar type of emotion, that wants to create its own figures. The mystic and the lover can remain in the sphere of the ineffable; but the poet's contemplation or transports tend to

4

fashion an exact and lasting expression within the real world.

Passion and emotions give us an intimate shock and affect us by surprise. Sometimes they release secret forces in us that suddenly disrupt the soul; sometimes they waste our energies in mad disordered impulses that are explicable only by the moment's overflow; at other times, they drive us to more or less reasonable and reasoned acts, tending to the attainment of some object whose possession or destruction will restore our peace of the moment before and our freedom for some moments after.

But sometimes these particularly deep states of disturbance or emotion give rise to inexplicable bursts of expressive activity whose immediate effects are forms produced in the mind, rhythms, unexpected relations between hidden points in the soul which, although remote from each other until that moment and, as it were, unconscious of each other at ordinary times, suddenly seem made to correspond as though they were parts of an agreement or of a pre-established event. We then feel that there is within us a certain Whole of which only fragments are required by ordinary circumstances. We also observe the initial disorder of consciousness giving birth to the beginnings of order, becoming mingled with projects and promises; a thousand potential perfections arise from imperfection, accidents provoke essences—and a whole creation or formation by contrasts, symmetries, and harmonies is revealed, takes shape in the mind, and at the same time evades thought, only allowing itself to be surmised.

But since I am speaking of emotions in connection with poetry, I may here make a remark that bears a relation to the general scheme of my reflections.

Poets—I mean those persons who are especially prone to feeling poetically—are not very different from other men in respect to the intensity of the emotions they feel in circumstances that move everyone. They are not much more profoundly touched than anyone else by what touches everyone —although, with their talents, they may quite often make one think so. But, on the other hand, they can be clearly distinguished from the majority of people by the ease with which they are extremely moved by things that move no one else, and by their faculty for providing themselves with a host of passions, amazing states of mind, and vivid feelings that need only the slightest pretext to be born from nothing and grow excited. In a way, poets possess within themselves infinitely more answers than ordinary life has questions to put to them; and this provides them with that perpetually latent, superabundant, and, as it were, irritable richness which at the slightest provocation brings forth treasures and even worlds.

This greatness of effect combined with this smallness of cause is quite simply what marks the essential poetic temperament.

But is not this the very character of our nervous system? Is it not the remarkable function of this system to substitute the controllable appearance for the unseizable, insurmountable, and inconsistent reality? Hence this agent and mysterious apparatus of life, seeing that its function is to compose all differences, to make what no longer exists act on what is, make what is absent present to us, and produce great effects by insignificant means, offers us, in short, everything needed for the beginnings of Poetry.

A poet, in sum, is an individual in whom the agility, subtlety, ubiquity, and fecundity of this all-powerful economy are found in the highest degree.

If one knew a little more about it, one could hope in consequence to form a fairly clear idea of the poetic essence. But we are far from possessing this central science. The devotees of analysis, of whom I said just now that they are not resigned to being merely the playthings of their talents, are soon aware that the problem of the invention of forms and ideas is one of the most delicate that a speculative and practiced intelligence can set itself. Everything in this field of research must be created—and not only the means, the methods, the terms, and the notions—but also, and above all, the very object of our curiosity must be defined.

A little metaphysics, a little mysticism, and much mythology will for a long time yet be all we have to take the place of positive knowledge in this kind of question.

Concerning *Adonis*

THIS *essay on "Adonis" was written in a beautiful stretch of country, so vast, and enclosed at such a distance by forests and gentle curves, that only the deepest peace seemed to come as the fruit of that expanse lying open to the sun and girded by enormous trees.*

In that favorable spot I had no difficulty in feeling everything in the way we may imagine La Fontaine felt it. There are uncounted hours in which one seems to hear the murmur of pure time flowing by; one watches a whole day melt in the sky without interrupting one's musing by the least distraction. Sometimes I roused myself from this shadowless sleep; I returned indolently to my work, and studied myself a little so as to imagine the poet at his labors.

This delicate task has hardly changed its procedure or its character since poets first existed. La Fontaine labored and idled as we do. Virgil sought, lost, and found with the same boredom and the same joys as we. Whatever the language and the prosody, this odd craft of reconciling quite different conditions is the same and is repeated in every age and almost everywhere. I have lately been astonished by recognizing in a Chinese poet who sometimes comes to see me, a strange ability to grasp and make his own many of the fine shades of our art which escape so many people here, even the well read. I hardly dare add that being well read may spoil one's right understanding of poetry; but it happens to be so—about seven times out of ten.

A poet is something of a potter. He takes a common material, he sifts it, removes the gravel, and begins to impose on it the form of his idea; he feels all the time as though he were poised between what is being made and what he wanted to make. The expectation and the unexpected both act and react on each other through him. That is the godlike in him. God Himself fashioned us from a little red earth and somewhat less wit. But that essential Poet, who

8

could create infallibly, thought it more worthy of Himself to risk under-taking a work. He did not make what He imagined, and we are like Him.

* * *

THERE hangs about La Fontaine a reputation for laziness and dreaminess, an habitual suggestion of absence of mind and perpetual distraction that naturally leads one to imagine a fictitious personage perpetually taking the easiest course through life. We see him vaguely as one of those inner images which are never far from our minds, though they were formed many years ago from the first engravings and the first stories we knew.

Perhaps the very name of La Fontaine has, from our child-hood, fixed forever upon the imagined figure of a poet some indefinable suggestion of freshness and depth, some spell derived from water. Sometimes a consonance creates a myth. Mighty gods have been born of a play on words, which is adultery of a kind.

He is, then, a creature who dreams and babbles on in the greatest possible simplicity. We naturally situate him in a park, or in a delightful countryside, whose beautiful shadows he pursues. We give him the bewitched attitude of a solitary who is never really alone: either because he is rejoicing with himself at the peace around him, or because he is talking to the fox, the ant, or another of those animals of the age of Louis XIV who spoke so pure a language.

If the beasts leave him—for even the wisest of them do not cease being restless and easily frightened by the slightest thing—he turns toward the land spread out in the sun and listens to the reed, the mill, the nymphs responding to each other. He bestows his own silence on them, which they turn into a kind of symphony.

He is faithful to nothing but the pleasures of the day (but

on condition that they yield of themselves and that he does not have to pursue them or use force to hold them), and his destiny would seem to be fulfilled in drawing out by a silken thread the sweetness of each moment: delicately deriving from it endless hours.

There is no easier comparison with this dreamer than the lazy cloud that holds his gaze: that gentle drift across the sky insensibly diverts him from himself, from his wife and child; it bears him toward forgetfulness of his own affairs, relieves him from all consequences, absolves him from all plans, for it is vain to try to outstrip the very breeze that bears you; even vainer, perhaps, to claim responsibility for the movements of a mist.

* * *

But a poem of six hundred lines in rhyming couplets like those of *Adonis;* such a prolonged sequence of graces; a thousand difficulties overcome, a thousand delights captured in an unbroken and inviolable web in which they come together and so tightly that they are forced to melt into each other, thus giving the illusion of a vast and varied tapestry— all this labor which the connoisseur sees transparently, through the magic of the work, in spite of the action of the hunt and of the vicissitudes of love, and at which he marvels as his mind reconstructs it, makes him renounce once and for all the first, crude idea he had held of La Fontaine.

* * *

We must no longer imagine that a lover of gardens, a man who runs through his time as he does through his stockings; part dazed, part inspired; a little stupid, a little quizzical, a little sententious; dispensing to the small animals around him a kind of justice entirely based on proverbs—we must no longer imagine that such a man could be the true author of *Adonis*. We should note that here the nonchalance is deliberate; the indolence is studied; the facility is the height of artistry. As for artlessness, it is entirely beside the point: to my mind such sustained art and purity exclude all sloth and all guile-lessness.

*   *   *

One cannot engage in politics with a simple heart; but still less is it by absence of mind and dreaming that one can impose on speech such precious and rare arrangements. The true condition of a true poet is as distinct as possible from the state of dreaming. I see in it only willed inquiry, suppleness of thought, the soul's assent to exquisite constraints, and the perpetual triumph of sacrifice.

It is the very one who wants to write down his dream who is obliged to be extremely wide awake. If you would give a fairly exact imitation of the oddities and self-betrayals of the helpless sleeper you have just been, would pursue in your depths that pensive fall of the soul like a dead leaf through the vague immensity of memory, do not flatter yourself that you can succeed without the utmost effort of attention; and attention's greatest achievement will be to discover that which exists only at its expense.

Whoever says exactness and style invokes the opposite of a dream; whoever meets these in a work must presuppose in its author all the labor and time he needed to resist the permanent dissipation of his thoughts. The most beautiful thoughts are shadows, as are the others; and here the ghosts precede the living. It was never an idle pastime to extract a little grace, a little clarity, a little permanence from the

II

mobility of things of the mind, or to change what passes into what endures. And the more restless and fugitive the prey one covets, the more presence of mind and power of will one needs to make it eternally present in its eternally fleeting aspect.

* * *

Even a fabulist is far from resembling that careless being we once carelessly created. Phèdre is all elegance, the La Fontaine of the *Fables* is full of artifice. It is not enough to have heard, under a tree, the chattering of the magpie or the dark laughter of the crow to make them speak so felicitously: for there is a strange abyss between the speech that birds, leaves, and ideas hold with us and that which we attribute to them: an inconceivable distance.

This mysterious difference between even the clearest impression or invention and their finished expression becomes as great as it can be—and hence most remarkable—when the writer imposes on his language the system of regular verse. This is a *convention* which has been greatly misunderstood. I shall say a few words about it.

* * *

Freedom is so seductive, particularly to poets; it presents itself to their fancy with reasons that are so plausible and, most of them, well grounded; it clothes itself so suitably in wisdom and novelty, and urges us, by so many advantages whose dark side one hardly sees, to reconsider the old rules, judge their absurdities, and reduce them to the simple observance of the natural laws of the mind and the ear, that at first one does not know what to reply. Can one even say to this charmer that she is dangerously encouraging carelessness, when she can so easily reply by showing us an appalling quantity of very bad, very facile, and terribly regular verse? It is true that one can hold against her an equal quantity of detestable free verse. Accusations hurtle between the two camps: the best supporters of one party are the weak members of the other, and they are so much alike that it is impossible to understand why they are divided.

It would therefore be extremely embarrassing to make a choice, if this were absolutely necessary. As for myself, I think that everyone is right and that one should do what one wants. But I cannot help being mystified by the kind of obstinacy with which poets of every age, up to the days of my youth, have voluntarily put themselves in chains. This subjection, which one hardly noticed before it was found to be unbearable, is a fact difficult to explain. Whence comes this immemorial obedience to commandments that appear so futile to us? Why this long-continued error on the part of such great men, who had, moreover, such a great interest in giving their minds the highest degree of freedom? Must one solve this riddle by a dissonance of terms, as is the fashion since the decline of logic, and think that there exists an instinct for the artificial? These words swear at each other.

* * *

Another thing amazes me. Our epoch has seen the birth of almost as many prosodies as it has counted poets, that is, rather more systems than persons, for some of them produced several. But, during the same period, the sciences, like industry, pursuing an altogether contrary policy, created uniform systems of measurement; they established units, they set up standards for them and imposed their use by laws and treaties; meanwhile each poet, taking himself as a collection of standards, set up his own body, the period of his personal rhythm, the interval of his breathing, as absolute types. Each made of his ear and his heart a universal diapason and time-piece.

Did they not thus risk being wrongly understood, badly read, and ill recited; or at least being taken in a totally un-expected way? This risk is always very great. I do not say that an error in interpretation always harms us and that a strangely curved mirror does not sometimes embellish us. But those who fear the uncertainty of the exchanges between author and reader undoubtedly find in the fixed number of syllables and in the more or less artificial symmetries of the old verse the advantage of limiting this risk in a very simple—one might even say crude—manner.

As for the arbitrariness of these rules, it is no greater in itself than the arbitrariness of language, whether of vocabu-lary or syntax.

*　*　*

I will go somewhat further into this apologia. I do not deem it impossible to give to convention and strictness, which are so arguable, their own individual value. To write regular verses is, no doubt, to return to a strange, somewhat senseless law, always harsh and sometimes cruel; it deprives life of an infinity of beautiful possibilities; it summons from afar a multitude of thoughts which did not expect to be conceived. (Of these latter I admit that half were not worth conceiving and that the other half, on the contrary, procure us delicious surprises and harmonies not pre-established, so that loss and gain balance each other, and I have no need to bother about them any further.) But all the innumerable beauties which will remain shut in the mind, all those whose appearance is strictly prevented by the necessity of rhyming, by meter, and by the incomprehensible rule of the hiatus, seem to us an immense loss that we may truly mourn. Let us try for once to rejoice over it: it is the business of a wise man always to force himself to change a loss into the semblance of a loss. One has only to think, to probe deeply into oneself, in order to succeed often enough in turning to ridicule the idea we first had of loss and gain in the matter of ideals.

* * *

A hundred figures of clay, however perfectly molded, do not give the mind the same noble idea as a single one of marble almost as beautiful. The former are more fragile than ourselves; the latter slightly less so. We can imagine how it resisted the sculptor; it would not leave its crystalline darkness. This mouth, these arms, cost many long days. An artist struck thousands of rebounding blows, slow questioners of the future form. The dense, pure shadow fell shattered, it fled in sparkling powder. With the help of time, man advanced against a stone; with difficulty, he felt his way toward a mistress deeply asleep in the future, and prowled round this creature, gradually overcoming her, until she was finally detached from the mass of the universe, as from the uncertainty of the idea. Behold her, a monster of grace and hardness, born, for an indeterminate time, from the duration and energy of a single thought. These rebellious alliances are the most precious of all. The sign of a great soul is the weakness of wanting to draw from itself some object at which it will wonder, which resembles it and disconcerts it by being purer, more incorruptible, and in some way more necessary than the very being from whom it came. But by itself the soul produces only the mingling of its facility and its power, which it does not easily distinguish; it revives good and evil; it does what it will, but it wills only what it can; it is free, not sovereign. You must try, Psyche, to use up all your facility against an obstacle; face the granite, rouse yourself against it, and for a while despair. See your vain enthusiasms and your frustrated aims fall away. Perhaps you lack sufficient wisdom yet to prefer your will to your ease. You find that stone too hard, you dream of the softness of wax and the obedience of clay? Follow the path of your aroused thought and you will soon meet this infernal inscription: *There is nothing so beautiful as that which does not exist.*

* * *

The exigencies of a strict prosody are the artifice that confers on natural language the qualities of a resistant matter, foreign to our soul and, as it were, deaf to our desires. If these require-ments were not half senseless and did not excite us to revolt, they would be radically absurd. Once they are accepted, one can no longer do everything, one can no longer say every-thing; and in order to say anything, it is no longer enough to conceive it strongly, to be full of it and drunk with it, nor to give off at some mystic moment a figure which has been al-most completed in our absence. To a god alone is reserved the ineffable lack of distinction between his act and his thought. But for us, we must labor; we must bitterly recognize their difference. Our task is to pursue words that do not always exist and chimeric coincidences; we must remain impotent while trying to couple sounds and meanings, while creating in full daylight one of those nightmares which exhaust the dreamer when he tries endlessly to match two phantom shapes as unstable as himself. We must, then, wait passionately,

change the hour and the day as one would change a tool—
and will, will. . . . And, moreover, not will too much.

* * *

Purged from all compulsion and from all false necessity,
these severities of the old laws have today no virtue beyond
that of defining very simply an absolute world of expression.
That, at least, is the new meaning that I find in them. We
have stopped submitting nature—by which I mean language
—to any rules other than its own, which indeed are not
necessary, but which are ours; and we even carry this firmness
to the point of not deigning to invent them: we take them as
they come.

They clearly separate what exists of itself from what
exists only through us. This is strictly human: a decree. But
neither our pleasures nor our emotions perish or suffer from
being submitted to it: they multiply, they are even born of
conventional disciplines. Consider all the trouble taken by
chess players, all the ardor inspired in them by their odd rules
and by the imaginary restraints upon their acts: they see their
little ivory horse invincibly subjected to a particular jump on
the board; they are aware of fields of force and invisible
constraints unknown to physics. This magnetism vanishes
with the match, and the extreme concentration which had
sustained it for so long loses its nature and disappears like a
dream. . . .The reality of games is in man alone.

* * *

Please understand me. I do not say that "trackless delight"
is not the principle and very aim of the poet's art. I do not
disparage the dazzling gift which our life makes to our
consciousness when it suddenly throws a thousand memories

all at once upon the fire. But up to now neither a happy stroke nor a collection of happy strokes has ever been seen to constitute a work.

* * *

I have only wished to make it understood that compulsory meters, rhymes, fixed forms, and all that arbitrariness, adopted once and for all and ranged against ourselves, have a kind of philosophic beauty of their own. Fetters that tighten at every movement of our genius remind us at that moment of all the contempt deserved, without doubt, by that familiar chaos which the vulgar call *thought*, not knowing that its *natural* conditions are no less fortuitous or futile than the conditions of a charade.

Skilled verse is the art of a profound skeptic. It presupposes an extraordinary freedom with respect to the whole of our ideas and sensations. The gods in their graciousness give us an occasional first line *for nothing;* but it is for us to fashion the second, which must chime with the first and not be unworthy of its supernatural elder. All the resources of experience and of the mind are not too much to render it comparable to the line which was a gift.

* * *

The author of *Adonis* could only be someone of a singularly alert mind, compact of delicacy and refinement. This La Fontaine, who later knew how to write admirably varied lines, was not to do so until he had devoted twenty years to symmetrical verse: exercises among which *Adonis* is the finest. During that time, he gave observers of his epoch a spectacle of simple-mindedness and laziness, whose tradition they simple-mindedly and lazily transmitted to us.

Literary history, like any other, is woven of legends more or less golden. The most fallacious of these are bound to come from the most faithful witnesses. What is more misleading than those truthful men who confine themselves to telling us what they saw, just as we might have seen it ourselves? What do I care for what can be seen? One of the most responsible men I ever knew, and with the most methodical habits of thought, ordinarily gave the impression of complete frivolity: a second nature cloaked him in nonsense. Our mind and our body are alike in this: they wrap in mystery and hide from themselves what they feel is most important; they mark and protect it by the depth at which they place it. Everything that counts is well veiled; witnesses and documents obscure it; acts and works are expressly made to disguise it.

Did Racine himself know whence he drew that inimitable voice, that delicate tone of inflection, that transparent manner of discourse which make him Racine, and without which he shrinks to that inconsiderable personage about whom the biographers tell us a great number of things that he had in common with ten thousand other Frenchmen? The so-called lessons of literary history, indeed, hardly ever deal with the mysteries of the genesis of poems. Everything takes place deep within the artist, as though the observable events of his existence had no more than a superficial influence on his works. The most important thing—the working of the Muses themselves—is independent of adventures, manner of life, incidents, and everything which might appear in a biography. Everything that history can observe is insignificant.

But it is the indefinable happenings, the hidden encounters, the facts which are visible only to one man, and others which are so familiar or so simple to that man that he ignores them, which form the essential part of the work. One can easily discover from oneself that these incessant and impalpable events are the stuff of our real person.

Every man who creates—half sure, half unsure of his strength—feels in himself a known and an unknown whose incessant relations and unexpected exchanges finally give birth to some product. I do not know what I shall do; and yet my mind thinks it knows itself; and I build on that knowledge, I count on it, calling it my *Self*. But *I shall surprise myself;* if I doubted this, I would be nothing. I know that I shall be astonished by some thought which will presently come to me—yet I look for this surprise, I build and count on it, as I count on my certainty. I hope for something unexpected, and aim towards it; I need my known and my unknown.

What, then, will give us an idea of the true maker of a fine work? He is not positively *anyone*. What is the Self, if I see it change its opinion, change sides, during the course of my work, to the point of disfiguring the work in my hands; if each change of mind can entail immense modifications; and if a thousand accidents of memory, attention, or sensation which befall my mind finally appear in the finished work as the essential ideas and original objects of my efforts? And yet the work is indeed by me, for my weakness, my strength, my repetitions, my idiosyncrasies, my light and shade are always recognizable in what falls from my hand.

We must despair of a clear vision in these matters. One must lull oneself with an image. My image of the poet is of a mind full of resources and cunning, feigning sleep at the imaginary center of his yet uncreated work, the better to await that instant of his own power which is his prey. In the vague depths of his eyes all the forces of his desire, all the springs of his instinct are taut. And there, waiting for the chance events from which she selects her food—there, most obscure in the middle of the webs and the secret harps which she has fashioned from language, whose threads are inter-woven and always vaguely vibrating—a mysterious Arachne, huntress muse, is on watch.

*　　*　　*

Predestined to be united by the soft and voluptuous euphony of their Greek* and Latin names, Venus and Adonis meet on the banks of a stream, where the one is dreaming,

Il ne voit presque pas l'onde qu'il considère;

and the other comes to rest and alights from her chariot.

Venus is fairly well known. There is no delight lacking in this entirely sensual abstraction except, perhaps, precisely that which she has hurried here to find.

It is very difficult to portray a Venus. Since she has all the perfections, it is almost impossible to make her really seduc-tive. What captivates us in a person is not that supreme degree of beauty nor such general graces: it is always some individual trait.

As for Adonis, to whom she is hastening to be loved, he shows no traces, in La Fontaine, of the mystical adolescent who was adored in Byblos. He is only a very beautiful young man about whom there is very little to say, once one has admired him. Doubtless one can get from him only pleasant and magnificent actions, which will be enough for the Muses and will satisfy the Goddess. He is here to make love, and then, to die: intelligence is not needed for these great things.

*　　*　　*

* But the Greek name, Adonis, comes from a Semitic name. (P.V.)

21

One should not be surprised at the great simplicity of these heroes: the principal personages of a poem are always the sweetness and vigor of the verse.

* * *

The happiness of our two lovers is incomparable. There is no attempt to describe it for us: one must avoid the insipid and be on guard against the crude. What then is the poet to do but trust himself to the poetry alone and make use of a deliciously combined music to touch on everything that we know and of which we need only to be reminded?

To Venus, lovely and apparently satisfied as she is, there comes, nevertheless, the subtle feeling that a touch of philosophy would not spoil this happiness. The sensual enjoyment that is shared, or rather doubled, between lovers always risks a certain monotony. Two people who accord each other almost the same delights sometimes end by finding that they are too little different. A couple, at the highest moment of their happiness, compose a kind of echo, or—which is the same thing—an arrangement of parallel mirrors—Baudelaire said: "twin mirrors."

In this the goddess shows a profundity that she gained perhaps from her brushes with Minerva. She has come to understand that love cannot be infinite if it is reduced to being finished as often as it can. With the majority of lovers, one too often sees that their minds are ignorant of each other as naturally as their bodies know each other. They have learned their likes and dislikes, which they have matched or harmoniously united; but they know nothing and indeed wish to know nothing about their metaphysics and their not immediately usable curiosities. But love without intelligence, supposing it mutual and with no obstruction, is no more than an habitual occupation. It needs misfortunes or ideas.

However that may be, Venus attempts a few reflections on permanence. She shows that she has not read very much on this serious subject. Neither Heraclitus nor Zeno had yet been born. Kant, Aristotle, and the difficult M. Minkowski lay jumbled in the anachronism of the future. However, she observes very correctly that time never returns to its source; but how great is her error when she says this fine thing:

> *Vainement pour les dieux il fuit d'un pas léger.*

She hardly foresaw the destruction of her finest temples or the decadence of her cult; I mean, of course, her public cult.

Adonis is not listening to her. They return to straightforward pleasure, of which the poet himself is somewhat weary:

> *Il est temps de passer au funeste moment*
> *Où la triste Vénus doit quitter son amant.*

This brisk platitude is a very obvious sign of fatigue. It is true that in poetry everything which *must* be said is almost impossible to say well.

*   *   *

Venus, then, must leave in order to go to Paphos to dispel rumors there that the goddess no longer cares for her worshipers. It is strange that she should care so much for being worshiped while she loves and is loved.

But vanity, and the stupidities that we imagine to be the obligations of our state, always persuade us to leave our chamber, which in this case is a beautiful forest. No one has yet been found, even among the gods, who felt powerful enough to scorn his faithful. And as for despising his altars and sanctuaries, the sacrifices consumed there, the prayers and smoke rising from them; as for detesting praises, and in disgust raining down fire and misfortune on all those heads which only fear and desperate hopes have turned toward divine things, I have never yet seen an immortal who has made up his mind to it. This taste they have for us is beyond me.

So Venus, happy as she is, and almost omnipotent, is to separate herself for a while from Adonis, so as not to upset her devout clientele. If there were none of these oddities, there would be no gods, perhaps no poems, and certainly no women.

* * *

She gives a thousand counsels to the lover whose office she is so pointlessly interrupting. The little speech she makes to put him on guard against the two imaginable dangers—his death and his infidelity—is delightfully proportioned. I notice in it this very fine line, in which all at once the great artistry and abstract power of Corneille appear, and which comes when she adjures Adonis not to become attached to the wood-nymphs. She says:

Leurs fers après les miens ont pour vous de la honte.

* * *

What farewells are theirs! They are only eight lines, but eight miracles; or rather, one miracle of eight lines, which is almost infinitely rarer and more astonishing than eight beautiful lines. It is impossible to separate two beings more voluptuously; and, by this pure affliction, to add anything to the idea we had formed of the sweetness of their union. Using a refinement of which there are not many examples in our poetry, La Fontaine here takes up again, as it were in a minor key, the motif of the delightful moments of which he had just told us. He had bestowed them upon his heroes:

Jours devenus moments, moments filés de soie....

And now he takes them back:

Moments pour qui le sort rend vos vœux superflus,
Délicieux moments, vous ne reviendrez plus!

* * *

Now Adonis suffers all the pains of absence.

In other words, he enumerates all the perfections of the happiness he has just lost. Once the bodies are separated, the soul is entirely occupied with the contrast between the two realities which contend for it; it reconstructs even those pleasures which it had hardly noticed; the past which is recalled seems richer than the vanished present from which it proceeds; and the period of separation works to tighten, with increasing cruelty, the inner bond insensibly woven by so many caresses. Adonis is like a stone halted in its fall, during which it had ceased to have any weight. If it feels anything, it must feel at that moment all the violent effects of a suddenly arrested movement; and then all its weight, which it had lost, as it were, when it was free to obey it. So the sentiment of love, which is weakened by possession, is developed by loss and deprivation. Possession means ceasing to think; but loss means possessing indefinitely in the mind.

Adonis, being unhappy, was about to become intelligent. The terrible memories left behind by a season of excessive warmth and voluptuousness were working on him, deepening him, leading him to the threshold of the most important doubts, and they were threatening to involve him in those inner difficulties which, by dividing our feelings, force us to invent our intelligence.

Adonis, about to become intelligent, hastens to order a hunt. Death rather than reflection.

* * *

It must be admitted that this unfortunate hunt is the weak part of the poem. It is almost as fatal to its singer as it will be to its hero.

How is one to manage a hunt? The authors of the seventeenth and eighteenth centuries who dealt with this fine subject have left us fragments whose vigor and precision, and hence whose language, are admirable. From one of them, not among the best known, Victor Hugo did not disdain to borrow a whole page in the finest style, which he introduced almost verbatim, and with great advantage, into the charming tale of the Beau Pécopin and the Belle Bauldour. But La Fontaine, Master Verderer though he is, gives us here only a venery of pure rhetoric. Failing an amusing and learned account of a hunt, one might have expected a kind of sylvan fantasy from this future animator of the furred and feathered tribe. One can imagine what this man, marked by the gods to write the *Fables*, could have done with all those animals in movement, some urged and lashed on, others hunted and brought to bay, all beside themselves, the hounds belling, the huntsmen galloping and winding their horns. He would have invented the conversations and thoughts of these actors; and the remarks made by the winged creatures, safely watching from their trees, would by a very natural artifice have informed us of the events of the day. All these elementary souls, the reasonings they utter, their strategies, the passions that occupy them, the figure men cut in this rude sport, all these are themes of which the *Fables* are full and whose combination would have given us a wonderfully new and diverting hunt.

But, it would seem, La Fontaine did not realize that here he was very near to what he was to become a little later. Far from feeling himself conducted by his subject to the verge of his natural kingdom, he was obviously somewhat bored by the elaboration of the three-hundred-odd lines that this hunt obliged him to write. Now yawning is not so far removed from laughter that it does not sometimes combine curiously with it. They have a common frontier, on the approaches to which the absurdity of acting against one's will easily turns into burlesque action. When, therefore, I find essentially comic lines in a sequence that does not call for anything of the kind, and is even the occasion of serious and fatal events, I feel the exasperated author suddenly taking revenge on himself, for his self-appointed task and for the trouble he is taking, by some drollery which escapes him uncontrollably. Laughter and yawns overtake us in the very act of rejection.

So the assemblage of hunters does not pass without being enlivened by various caricatures. I rather like this one in which the whole humor is in the sonority of the verse:

On y voit arriver Bronte au cœur indomptable.

* * *

The monster also had to be depicted, a very redoubtable boar; one of those solitary beasts who trust only in their tusks and whose strong teeth rip up the horses and wound the hounds "in the vitals."

However terrifying a monster may be, the task of describing him is always slightly more terrifying. It is well known that monsters, unhappy creatures, have never been able to cut any but a ridiculous figure in the arts. I can think of no painted, sung, or sculptured monster that either gives us the least fright or, moreover, fails to make us smile. The large fish that devoured the prophet Jonah and, in the same vicinity a little later, swallowed up the adventurous Sinbad; the same that, at another period of its career, was perhaps the savior and bearer of Arion; in spite of its great courtesy, and despite that scrupulous honesty which makes it punctiliously disgorge on the shore its meals of distinguished men, restoring them in such good condition to their occupations and studies, at the very place, moreover, where they had intended to go, although it is not intentionally formidable, but rather obliging and docile, cannot help being extremely comic. Consider that extravagantly composite animal which Roger, armed all in gold, pierces at the feet of M. Ingres' delightful Angelica; think of that dugong or porpoise whose sudden leaps and rough play in the foaming sea startle the horses of Hippolytus; hark to the wheezing and lamentable Fafner braying in his den—none of these has ever managed to beg from anyone the least bit of terror. They are consoled only by this observation: that the more human monsters, the Cyclopes, the Gwinplaines, the Quasimodos, have never gained a much better reputation or more authority than they themselves. The necessary complement to a monster is a child's brain.

This misfortune of being ridiculous, which for them surpasses the misfortune of being monsters, does not seem, however, to be connected so much with the incapacity of their inventors as with their own nature and their extraordinary vocation, as can be easily understood by the briefest visit to a museum. There the authentic Bicorne, the combination of wings and weight, of a supple neck with a most heavy belly; there the true dragons, the wyverns that have existed, the

Hydras traced in the slate, the gigantic tortoises with pigs' heads, all these successive populations which have lived on the uneasy levels of the earth and which have ceased to gratify this planet, offer us, as we are in the present, the grotesque part of nature. They are like illustrations of fashions in anatomy. We cannot believe we are so bizarre; and we are rescued by a feeling of improbability and by the consideration of a primitive clumsiness and stupidity measurable only in laughter.

*   *   *

Let us leave the monster and go on to the rather stilted battle which is joined. From this I would mention only one charmingly executed distich, whose mocking music has always amused me:

> *Nisus, ayant cherché son salut sur un arbre,*
> *Rit de voir ce chasseur plus froid que n'est un marbre.*

*   *   *

It is in vain that the water goddesses, vaguely resembling in their behavior and in their fluid habits and uncertain genus those mad Rhine maidens who, under other skies, tried to save the wild Siegfried, strive to protect Adonis. Knowing that heroes always run directly toward their ruin, they try to mislead this one and to make him miss his appointment with death. They oppose to the Fates the most beautiful verses in the world:

> *Les nymphes, de qui l'œil voit les choses futures.*
> *L'avaient fait égarer en des routes obscures.*
> *Le son des cors se perd par un charme inconnu....*

The Fates care nothing for poetry, without which, however, their very name would long since have dropped out of the dictionary of usage. The Naiads have no influence over the soul of this passer-by dedicated to death. Adonis must perish: every road must lead him there. He enters the thick of the hunt, eager to avenge his friend Palmire, who has just been slightly wounded; he swoops, he strikes, he is struck. The monster and the hero die; but they die in the finest style. Here is the expiring boar:

> *Ses yeux d'un somme dur sont pressés et couverts,*
> *Il demeure plongé dans la nuit la plus noire.*

And as for Adonis:

> *On ne voit plus l'éclat dont sa bouche était peinte,*
> *On n'en voit que les traits.*

* * *

Venus having been informed by the winds, Venus hurrying back affrighted, there is nothing left for her to do but to sing to us of her despair, and she does so like a goddess. There is nothing more beautiful than the attack and development of this noble closing section; but I consider these accomplished lamentations to have an importance apart from this. Nearly all the qualities that Racine will not exhibit until a few years later adorn this passage of about forty lines. If the author of *Phèdre* had thought of leading her to the body of Hippolytus and of making her express her regrets, I do not think he could have given them a purer sound or made the despairing queen utter a more harmonious complaint.

It must be observed that *Adonis* was written in 1657, about ten years before Racine's full flowering, and that in the funeral oration with which I am concerned, the tone, the development, the monumental shape, and even the sonority are sometimes indistinguishable from those which are admired in his best tragedies.

Whose lines are these?

> *Mon amour n'a donc pu te faire aimer la vie!*
> *Tu me quittes, cruel! Au moins ouvre les yeux,*
> *Montre-toi plus sensible à mes tristes adieux;*
> *Vois de quelles douleurs ton amante est atteinte!*
> *Hélas! J'ai beau crier: il est sourd à ma plainte.*
> *Une éternelle nuit l'oblige à me quitter....*
>
> *Encor si je pouvais le suivre en ces lieux sombres!*
> *Que ne m'est-il permis d'errer parmi les ombres!*
>
> *Je ne demandais pas que la Parque cruelle*
> *Prît à filer leur trame une peine éternelle;*
> *Bien loin que mon pouvoir l'empêchât de finir,*
> *Je demande un moment, et ne puis l'obtenir....*

And so on. One might easily mistake the author's name.

Acante was nineteen at the time when these verses might have become known. Many people must have known them, if not through the famous manuscript—a masterpiece of the calligrapher Nicolas Jarry—which the poet dedicated to Fouquet, at least through the copies which must have passed from hand to hand and circulated from group to group and from salon to salon.

I would not wager that Racine did not know our *Adonis* by heart.

Perhaps these accents of Venus gave to that pure voice, of whose quality I was speaking just now, its original tone and first awareness of itself. Little enough is needed to bring to birth the great man within a young man ignorant of his gifts. The greatest, and even the holiest, men have needed forerunners.

* * *

It is natural, and absurd, to regret the fine things which have not been done and which still seem to us to have been possible, even after events have shown that there was no place in the world for them. This odd feeling is almost inseparable from the contemplation of history: we look on the passage of time as a road of which each point is a crossroads. . . .

With *Adonis* before me, I regret all the hours spent by La Fontaine on the mass of *Tales* he left us whose falsely rustic tone I cannot bear, or the disgustingly facile verse,

> *Nos deux époux, à ce que dit l'histoire,*
> *Sans disputer n'étaient pas un moment. . .etc.,*

or their general vulgarity, and all the boredom of lewdness, so contrary to voluptuousness and so fatal to poetry. And I miss even more the several *Adonis*es he could have written instead of those deadly *Tales*. What idylls and eclogues he was born to write! Chénier, who undertook them with such felicity and who to a certain extent is La Fontaine's successor, does not entirely console us for this imaginary loss. His art seems thinner, less pure, and less mysterious than that of our author. One can see its workings more clearly.

* * *

The *Adonis* of La Fontaine was written about 260 years ago. Since that time the French language has not been without its changes. Moreover, the reader of today is very remote from the reader of 1660. He has other memories, and quite a different "sensibility"; he has not the same culture, always supposing he has any (sometimes he has several, and it may happen that he has none at all); he has lost and he has won; he is almost a different species. But the consideration of *the most probable reader* is the most important ingredient of literary composition; the author's mind, whether he wills it, or knows it, or not, is as it were *tuned* to the idea that he has necessarily formed of his reader; and so the change of period, which is a change of reader, is like a change in the text itself, a change always unexpected and incalculable.

Let us be glad that we can still read *Adonis*, and nearly all of it with delight; but let us not imagine that we are reading the very same poem as the author's contemporaries. What they most valued perhaps escapes us; what they hardly noticed sometimes touches us strangely. Some charming passages have become profound, others quite insipid. Think of the attraction and repulsion this text can inspire in a man of our day, nourished on the modern poets; all these contemporary works have attuned him to themselves; and his mind and ear have become sensitive to impressions that the author had never thought of producing, and insensitive to effects that he had carefully studied. For example, when Racine wrote his famous line

Dans l'Orient désert quel devint mon ennui!

he never thought of depicting anything but a lover's despair. But the magnificent harmony of those three words, when it has been carried by time across the nineteenth century, acquires an unexpected reinforcement and an extraordinary resonance in romantic poetry; for a mind of our time it mingles wonderfully with some of Baudelaire's finest lines. It is detached from Antiochus and acquires a pure and nostalgic universality. Its finished elegance is transformed into infinite beauty: that *Orient*, that *désert*, that *ennui*, brought together in the time of Louis XIV, have acquired an unlimited meaning and the power of a spell through the intervention of another century, which could perceive them only in its own colors.

It is the same with *Adonis*. What pleasure can be derived nowadays from this gallant tale? It is revived, perhaps, by the contrast of such a sweet form and such clear melodies with our system of discords and the tradition of excess that we have so docilely accepted. Our burning eyes seek rest in those melting graces and those translucent shades; our exacerbated palate finds novelty in pure water. Something well said may even charm us of itself.

La Graulet, 1920

Funeral Oration for a Fable

DAPHNIS loves Alcimadura. Alcimadura loves neither Daphnis nor Love.

Daphnis very soon dies of the rejection of his great love, bequeathing all he has to the callous one, of whom, so as to waste no words, it is not said whether she accepts the legacy.

In the evening of the very day of the lover's death, Alcimadura, freed from a nuisance and all overjoyed at having gained a fortune, gives a dance for her young friends. These maidens, who seem to be happy only among themselves, do not fail to go leaping and twirling, doubtless lightly clad, around the statue of that essentially blind God of whom it has never been known whether one should desire his favors or fear them.

The pure idol falls, it strikes down and crushes the fair one under its weight. Alcimadura, fallen into Hades, there becomes a gracious and unhappy Shade; and this new Shade at once flies toward the Shade of Daphnis. But now the roles are altered, the shepherd's desires have changed into disdain, and here below, her erstwhile disdain gnaws the soul of Alcimadura, who was so disdainful when on earth. One would think that death had transferred from one to the other the feelings of these two beings. On both of them the suddenness of their passing has the same effect as a long period of reflection, and the change from life into death changes their hearts so much that Daphnis's heart regrets having died of love, just as Alcimadura's deplores not having known tenderness. This is not the place to try to go deeply into the metaphysics of regret. Hope or regret has never caused philosophers of any age to say much that is clear or substantial.

How explain that we nearly always live before and after the actual moment? "Nothing any longer exists for me," said a widowed princess. "I never live but two years hence," wrote the indomitable emperor. . . .

We hardly ever are; but we were and we shall be. Our very body subsists and sustains itself, prevents itself from perishing only so as to be somewhat more than an event.

However that may be, once Daphnis and Alcimadura are in Hades, the ineffectual phantom of the boy flees the regrets and vague excuses of the ineffectual phantom of the girl.

This pale and perfect work, this fine but feeble piece, a delicate child among the last of La Fontaine's offspring—is not this fable itself a literary Shade, a wandering apparition of a poem, all but invisible to the eyes of a posterity that rejects it without knowing it? It is still printed and reprinted, but to no purpose; does it find any way of living again in anyone's mind? Nobody needs it and nobody cares about it.

As dead as Alcimadura, as Madame de La Mésangère, as King Louis XIV, and as all the wishes, tastes, and ideals of an era many of whose works, although admirable, gradually become astonishingly insipid, it is indeed in the same indefinable state as the sad inhabitants of Hades. They are and are not.

The inevitable fate of the majority of our works is to become unnoticeable or odd. Successive generations are either less and less moved by them or consider them more and more as being the artless or inconceivable or bizarre products of another species of man. Between the fullness of life and the final death of materially preserved works there is a lapse of time which assures their imperceptible degradation and alters them by degrees. They weaken irremediably, but not at first in their actual substance, for this is formed from a language which is still intelligible and still used. But as is proper with things of the mind, they see one after another all their chances of pleasing vanish, and all the props of their existence crumble. Little by little those who loved them, those who appreciated them, those who could understand them, disappear. Those who loathed them, those who tore them to pieces, those who mocked them, are dead too. The passions they stirred are cool. Other human beings desire or reject other books. Very soon an instrument of pleasure or of emotion becomes a school accessory; what was true, what was beautiful changes into a means of discipline, or an object of curiosity, but of a curiosity that forces itself to be curious. The unwilling amateur who, moved by his duties and unvoluptuous desires, visits these works in their tombs of leather or parchment is only too conscious that he is troubling and tormenting rather than reviving them, and that, without hope and as though regretfully, he is giving them an empty and artificial meaning and worth. Sometimes fashion, which is constantly seeking everywhere the wherewithal to nourish her future, discovers a few novelties in the sepulchers. For a little while she props them open, delves within, and passes on. But this deceptive longing only defaces a little more the sad object of its restlessness. She barely disturbs its absence. She can never offer the dead beauties more than a mistaken notion in exchange for her whim.

Finally the very matter of works of the mind, a matter

not properly corruptible, a singular matter made of the most immaterial relations one can imagine, the matter of speech, is changed without changing. It loses touch with man. The word ages, becomes very rare, becomes opaque, changes its form or its function. Syntax and turns of phrase grow old, astonish, and end by repelling. Everything ends in the Sorbonne.

A Foreword

ABOUT forty years ago a doubt was lifted from our minds. Conclusive proof dismissed as an illusion the ancient ambition of squaring the circle. How fortunate are the geometricians, who can from time to time resolve this kind of nebula in their system; but the poets are less fortunate; they are not yet assured of the impossibility of *squaring* every thought in a poetic form.

As the operations by which desire is led to build language into a harmonious and unforgettable shape are extremely secret and complex, it is still permissible—and will always be so—to doubt whether speculation, history, science, politics, ethics, and apologetics (and all prose subjects generally) can assume as their semblance the musical and personal semblance of a poem. It would be only a question of talent: there is no absolute prohibition. The anecdote and its moral, description and generalization, teaching, controversy—I see no intellectual matter that, in the course of the ages, has not been put under the constraints of rhythm and subjected by art to strange—even divine—exactions.

As neither the true object of poetry nor the means for attaining it have been made clear (those who know them remaining silent and those who do not holding forth about them), any clarity about these questions remains an individual matter, the greatest clash of opinions is permissible, and for each opinion there are famous examples and experiments not easily denied.

Thanks to this uncertainty, the production of poems upon the most diverse subjects has continued up to the present day; indeed, the greatest, and perhaps the most admirable, works in verse that have been handed down to us belong to the didactic or historical order. The *De rerum natura*, the *Georgics*, the *Aeneid*, the *Divine Comedy*, the *Légende des siècles*. . . derive a part of their substance and interest from notions that could have been treated in the most indifferent prose. They can be translated without being rendered entirely insignificant. It was to be expected, therefore, that a time would come when vast systems of this kind would yield to differentiation. Since one can read them in several unrelated ways, or break them up into separate moments of our attention, these many kinds of reading were bound to lead one day to a sort of division of labor. (In the same way the consideration of some single element eventually demanded the whole variety of sciences.)

Finally, toward the middle of the nineteenth century, we see asserting itself in our literature a remarkable will to isolate Poetry once for all from every other essence than itself. Such a preparation of poetry in its pure state had been very accurately predicted and advocated by Edgar Poe. It is therefore not surprising to see in Baudelaire the beginnings of this striving toward a perfection that is concerned only with itself.

To Baudelaire, too, can be attributed another innovation. He is the first of our poets to be influenced by, to invoke, and to explore Music. Through Berlioz and Wagner, Romantic music had sought after literary effects. It achieved them to a superlative degree; this is easily understood, since the violence, even frenzy, and the exaggerated profundity, grief, radiance, or purity which were to the taste of that period can hardly be translated into language without entailing many insipidities and absurdities inassimilable to time; these elements of ruin are less obvious in musicians than in poets. This is perhaps because music bears in itself a kind of life that it imposes on us physically, whereas, on the other hand, the monuments of speech require us to provide it for them....

However that may be, there came an epoch when poetry felt itself fade and weaken before the energy and resources of the orchestra. The richest and most resounding poem of Hugo is very far from communicating to its hearer those extreme illusions, those thrills, those raptures and, in the more or less intellectual sphere, those feigned lucidities, those models of thought, those images of strange mathematics made real, which the symphony releases, hints at, or thunders forth, and which it draws out into silence or annihilates at one blow, leaving in the mind the extraordinary impression of omnipotence and deception.... Never before, perhaps, have the trust that poets place in their particular genius, those promises of eternity which they have received since the childhood of the world and of language, their immemorial possession of the lyre, and the leading rank they imagine they occupy in the hierarchy of servants of the universe, appeared so directly menaced. They came away from concerts overwhelmed. Overwhelmed—dazzled; as though, transported to the seventh heaven by a cruel favor, they had been caught up to that height only that they might experience a luminous contemplation of forbidden possibilities and inimitable marvels. The sharper and more incontestable their sense of these imperious delights, the more real and despairing was the suffering of their pride.

Pride was their counselor. Among men of intellect it is a vital necessity.

Into each man according to his nature it breathed the spirit of combat—a strange intellectual combat; every means of the art of verse, every known artifice of rhetoric and prosody were called upon, and many novelties summoned to present themselves to the overexcited consciousness.

What was baptized *Symbolism* can be very simply described as the common intention of several groups of poets (otherwise mutually inimical) to "reclaim their own from Music." The secret of that movement is nothing else. The obscurities and peculiarities with which it was so often reproached; the apparently overintimate relations with English, Slavic, or Germanic literature; the syntactical disorders, the irregular rhythms, the curiosities of vocabulary, the continual images ...this is all easily deduced, once the principle is acknowledged. In vain did those who watched these experiments, and even those who put them into practice, attack the poor word *Symbol*. It means only what one wants it to; if someone fastens his own hopes upon it, he will find them there!—But we were nourished on music, and our literary minds dreamed only of extracting from language the same effects, almost, as were produced on our nervous systems by sound alone. Some cherished Wagner, others Schumann. I could as well say that they hated them. In the heat of passionate interest these two states are indistinguishable.

A description of the endeavors of that epoch would require a systematic work. Rarely have more fervor, more audacity, more theoretical research, more knowledge, more reverent attention, more disputes, been devoted in the space of so few years to the problem of pure beauty. One might say that it was approached from all sides. Language is a complex thing; its many-sided nature allowed investigators a diversity of attempts. Some, who preserved the traditional forms of French verse, studied how to eliminate descriptions, maxims, moralizing, and arbitrary details; they purged their poetry of nearly all those intellectual elements which music cannot express. Others gave to every object endless meanings that presupposed a hidden metaphysics. They made use of delightfully ambiguous matter. They peopled their enchanted parks and evanescent groves with an entirely ideal Fauna. Everything was an allusion; nothing was confined merely to being; in those kingdoms adorned with mirrors, everything thought; or at least everything seemed to think.... Elsewhere, a few more determined and argumentative magicians grappled with ancient prosody. For some of them color in sound and the combinative art of alliteration seemed to hold no further secrets; they deliberately transposed the tones of the orchestra to their verse: they were not always wrong. Others skillfully recovered the simplicity and spontaneous grace of old popular poetry. Philology and phonetics were quoted in the unending debates of those exacting lovers of the Muse.

It was a time of theories, curiosities, commentaries, and passionate explanations. A young and somewhat stern generation rejected the scientific dogma which was beginning to be unfashionable, without adopting the religious dogma which was not yet so. In the profound and scrupulous worship of the arts as a whole, it thought it had found an unequivocal discipline or even a truth. A sort of religion was very nearly established.... But the works of that period did not themselves positively disclose these preoccupations. Quite to the contrary, one must note carefully what they prohibit and what ceased to appear in poems during the time of which I am speaking. It would seem that abstract thought, formerly admitted even into verse, having now become almost impossible to combine with the immediate emotions that it was desired continually to arouse, being banished from a poetry that was endeavoring to reduce itself to its own essence, and dismayed by the multiple effects of surprise and of music demanded by modern taste, had betaken itself to the preparatory phase and to the theory of poetry. Philosophy, and even ethics, tended to shun the actual works and take their place among the reflections preceding them. This was a very real *progress*. If we discount vague and refuted matters, philosophy now comes down to five or six problems, precise in appearance, indeterminate in essence, deniable at will, and always reducible to linguistic quarrels, their solution depending on the way in which they are *written*. But the interest of these meticulous labors is not so restricted as one might imagine; it lies in their fragility and in those very quarrels, that is, in the delicate balance of the more and more subtle apparatus of logic and psychology that they force one to use; it no longer lies in their conclusions. To state opinions, however admirable, on nature and its creator, on life, death, duration, and justice is no longer to philosophize. . . . Our philosophy is determined by its apparatus, and not by its object. It cannot be separated from its own difficulties, which constitute its *form;* and it will not take the *form* of verse without losing its own being, or corrupting the verse. To speak nowadays of philosophic poetry (even invoking the names of Alfred de Vigny, Leconte de Lisle, and a few others) is naïvely to confuse incompatible conditions and uses of the mind. Is not this to forget that the aim of speculation is to fix or create an idea—that is, a *power* and an *instrument of power*—whereas the modern poet tries to produce in us a *state* and to raise this exceptional state to the level of perfect enjoyment?. . .

*　*　*

On the whole this is how, at the distance of a quarter of a century and across the intervening abyss of events, the great scheme of the Symbolists appears to me. I do not know what the future will preserve of their multiform efforts; it is not necessarily a clear-headed and equitable judge. Such experiments do not take place without audacity, risks, exaggerated cruelties, and childishness.... Tradition, intelligibility, and psychic equilibrium, which are the usual victims of the mind's progress toward its object, suffered sometimes from our devotion to the purest beauty. We were sometimes obscure and sometimes puerile. Our language was not always so worthy of praise and of survival as our ambition hoped; and our innumerable themes are now the melancholy occupants of the quiet underworld of our memory.... I grant you the works, the opinions, and the technical preferences! But our Idea itself and our Sovereign Good, are they now no more than pale elements of oblivion? Must all perish so completely? How can it perish, O comrades?—What is it that has so secretly deformed our certainties, diminished our truth, destroyed our courage? Has the discovery been made that light can grow old? And how is it (here is the mystery) that those who came after us and who in their turn will vanish, grown sterile and disillusioned through a similar change, could have had other desires than ours, and other gods? It was so clear to us that there was no fault in our ideal! Was it not deduced from the experience of all preceding literatures? Was it not the supreme and miraculously retarded flower of the whole accumulation of culture?

Two explanations of this kind of ruin suggest themselves. First, it may be thought that we were merely the victims of a spiritual illusion. Once it was dissipated, there remained to us only the memory of absurd acts and of an inexplicable passion. . . . But a desire cannot be illusory. Nothing is more specifically real than a desire, *qua* desire: like the God of St. Anselm, its idea and its reality are indissoluble. Another reason must be sought, a more ingenious argument found for our ruin. It must, in fact, be assumed that our way was indeed the only one, that by our desire we reached the very essence of our art, and that we really had deciphered the whole significance of the labors of our ancestors, salvaged from their works what seemed most delightful, built our path from these fragments, and followed to infinity this precious track blessed with palms and wells of sweet water; ever on the horizon was pure poetry. . . . There was the danger; there, precisely, our downfall; and there, too, our goal.

For a truth of this kind is a frontier of the world; one may not settle there. Nothing so pure can coexist with the circumstances of life. We only traverse the idea of perfection as a hand passes with impunity through a flame; but the flame is uninhabitable, and dwelling places on the serene heights are necessarily deserted. I mean that our leaning toward the extreme rigors of art—toward the logical result of premises suggested to us by earlier successes—toward a beauty ever more conscious of its origins, ever more independent of all *subjects*, and of the vulgar attractions of sentiment as well as the blatant effects of eloquence—all this overenlightened zeal resulted perhaps in an almost inhuman state. That is a general truth: metaphysics, ethics, and even the sciences have experienced it.

Absolute poetry can only proceed by way of exceptional marvels; works composed entirely of it constitute the rarest and most improbable portion of the imponderable treasures of a literature. But, as the perfect vacuum and the absolute zero of temperature, neither of which can be reached, can only be approached at the cost of an exhausting series of efforts, so the final purity of our art demands from those who conceive it such prolonged and such harsh restraints as absorb all the natural joy of being a poet, leaving at the end nothing but the pride of never being satisfied. This severity is unbearable for the majority of young men gifted with the poetic instinct. Our successors did not envy our torment; they did not adopt our scruples; they sometimes mistook for liberties what we had attempted as new problems; and sometimes they tore apart what we meant only to dissect. They opened again upon the accidents of being, eyes we had closed to make ourselves more like its substance. . . . All this was to be expected. But it was also not impossible to guess the sequel. Was it not likely that one day someone would try to link our former past with the past which had followed it, borrowing from each those of their teachings which were compatible? Here and there I see this natural work going on in a few minds. Life itself works in this way; and the same process we observe in the succession of lives, a process in which continuity and atavism combine, reappears in the sequences of the life of literature. . . .

* * *

That is what I said one day to M. Fabre, when he came to talk to me about his researches and his poems. I do not know what spirit of rashness and error had aroused in his wise, clear mind the wish to consult another mind not particularly so. We tried to explain our points of view on poetry, and although this kind of conversation time and again passes beyond infinity, we managed not to lose each other. This was because our separate thoughts, each moving and changing within its impassable domain, managed to keep a wonderful correspondence. A common vocabulary—the most precise in existence—constantly enabled us not to misunderstand each other. Algebra and geometry, on which I am convinced the future will model a language for the intellect, enabled us, from time to time, to exchange precise signals. I found in my visitor one of those minds for which my own has a weakness. I like those lovers of poetry who venerate the goddess with too much lucidity to dedicate to her the slackness of their thought and the relaxation of their reason. They know well that she does not exact the *sacrifizio dell' Intelletto*. Neither Minerva nor Pallas nor luminous Apollo approves the abominable mutilations that some of their misguided worshipers inflict on the organism of thought; and they reject with horror these bearers of a bleeding logic they have torn from themselves and intend to sacrifice on the altar. True divinities have no taste for any but whole victims. Naturally they demand sacrificial food; this exaction is common to all supreme powers, for they must live; but they want it intact.

M. Lucien Fabre is well aware of this. It is not for nothing that he has provided himself with a singularly close-knit and thorough culture. The art of the engineer, to which he devotes not the best but perhaps the greatest part of his time, in itself requires prolonged study and involves any man who distinguishes himself at it in a complex activity: he must handle men, give form to matter, and find satisfactory solutions to unforeseen problems to which technology, economics, civil laws, and natural laws bring contradictory requirements. This kind of reasoning on complex systems hardly lends itself to generalization. There are no formulas for such special cases, no equations between such heterogeneous data; nothing happens infallibly, and even gropings are here only a waste of time if they are not guided by a very subtle instinct.

In the eyes of an observer who knows how to ignore appearances, this activity, these reflective hesitations, this way of expecting under constraint, and these discoveries are very like the inner moments of a poet. But I fear there are few engineers who realize that they are as near as I have suggested to the inventors of figures and the arrangers of words. . . . There are not many who, like M. Fabre, have penetrated deeply into the metaphysics of being. He is familiar with philosophy. Theology itself is no stranger to him. He has never believed that the world of the intellect is as young and as restricted as is commonly imagined nowadays. Could it be that his positive mind simply assessed the smallness of a probability? How can one believe, without being strangely credulous, that the best brains have for ten centuries exhausted themselves without result in empty and austere speculations? I sometimes think (though with shame and only in the secret depths of my heart) that a more or less remote future will look on the vast work accomplished in our day on the *continuous*, the *transfinite*, and a few other Cantorian concepts, with that air of pity which we bestow on scholastic libraries. . . . But the substance of theology is in certain texts; M. Fabre did not recoil from Hebrew ! . . .

This general culture and yet these habits of discipline, this practical and decisive judgment and yet this gloriously useless knowledge, all together bear witness to a will that organizes and directs them. It so happens that it directs them to poetry. This case is quite remarkable; one must expect a mind with this preparation and precision to take up in its own way those eternal problems of which I said a few words a few pages back. If it were nothing but a purely technical intelligence we should doubtless see it make abrupt innovations, and bring to an ancient art an energy naïve in its inventions.

Examples are not wanting: paper accepts everything; the desire to astonish is the most natural and most easily understandable of desires; it allows the meanest reader to decipher with no effort the very simple secret of many surprising works.

But on a slightly higher level of consciousness and knowledge one can see that language is not so easily perfectible, and that prosody has not been unsolicited in many ways over the course of the centuries; one can see that all the care and labor we can expend in confuting the results of so much acquired experience must necessarily fail us on other points. One must pay an unknown price for the pleasure of not using what is known. An architect can despise statics or try to transgress the formulas for the resistance of materials. This is flouting probability; only once in a hundred thousand times will the penalty be far behind. In literature the penalty is less terrifying; it is also much less prompt; but, in any case, time quickly undertakes to counter by the neglect of a work the neglect of the simplest rules of applied psychology. It is therefore to our interest to calculate our audacities and our cautions as exactly as possible.

M. Fabre, the calculator, has not ignored Lucien Fabre, the poet. The latter having decided to perform the most difficult and most enviable task in our art—I mean a sequence of poems forming a spiritual drama, a finished drama that is played out between the very powers of our being—the accuracy and standards of the former found their natural employment in this composition. The reader must judge this curiously daring attempt to endow with the most passionate life and movement entities brought directly into play. Eros, a beautiful and violent Eros, but an Eros secretly in thrall to a certain Reason which knows how to unleash and to restrain his frenzy, is the true coryphaeus of these poems. I would not say that Reason does not sometimes show a bit too clearly through the language. I felt I had to challenge some of the words that M. Fabre has used, and which seem to me not easily absorbed into the language of poetry. I was not on very firm ground with this criticism, since poetic language changes like any other; and the geometrical terms that here and there aroused my opposition will perhaps eventually be amalgamated, as so many other technical words have been, with the abstract and homogeneous metal of the language of the gods.

But any judgment one wishes to make on a work should take into account primarily the difficulties that its author has set himself. One may say that a survey of these deliberate restrictions immediately reveals, once one has managed to reconstruct them, the intellectual level of the poet, the quality of his pride, the fastidiousness and despotism of his nature. M. Fabre has assigned himself noble and rigorous conditions. He wanted his emotions, however intense they might appear in his verse, to be closely co-ordinated and subject to the invisible command of knowledge. Perhaps, in places, this mysterious and prophetic sovereign suffers a few shocks and diminutions of her empire—for, as the author says so magnificently:

> *L'ardente chair ronge sans cesse*
> *Les durs serments qu'elle a jurés.*

But what poet would complain at this?

Poetry and Abstract Thought

THE IDEA of Poetry is often contrasted with that of Thought, and particularly "Abstract Thought." People say "Poetry and Abstract Thought" as they say Good and Evil, Vice and Virtue, Hot and Cold. Most people, without thinking any further, believe that the analytical work of the intellect, the efforts of will and precision in which it implicates the mind, are incompatible with that freshness of inspiration, that flow of expression, that grace and fancy which are the signs of poetry and which reveal it at its very first words. If a poet's work is judged profound, its profundity seems to be of a quite different order from that of a philosopher or a scientist. Some people go so far as to think that even meditation on his art, the kind of exact reasoning applied to the cultivation of roses, can only harm a poet, since the principal and most charming object of his desire must be to communicate the impression of a newly and happily born state of creative emotion which, through surprise and pleasure, has the power to remove the poem once and for all from any further criticism.

This opinion may possibly contain a grain of truth, though its simplicity makes me suspect it to be of scholarly origin. I feel we have learned and adopted this antithesis without reflection, and that we now find it firmly fixed in our mind, as a verbal contrast, as though it represented a clear and real relationship between two well-defined notions. It must be admitted that that character always in a hurry to have done, whom we call *our mind*, has a weakness for this kind of simplification, which freely enables him to form all kinds of combinations and judgments, to display his logic, and to develop his rhetorical resources—in short, to carry out as brilliantly as possible his business of being a mind.

At all events, this classic contrast, crystallized, as it were, by language, has always seemed to me too abrupt, and at the same time too facile, not to provoke me to examine the things themselves more closely.

Poetry, *Abstract Thought*. That is soon said, and we immediately assume that we have said something sufficiently clear and sufficiently precise for us to proceed, without having to go back over our experiences; and to build a theory or begin a discussion using this contrast (so attractive in its simplicity) as pretext, argument, and substance. One could even fashion a whole metaphysics—or at the least a "psychology"—on this basis, and evolve for oneself a system of mental life, of knowledge, and of the invention and production of works of the mind, whose consequence would inevitably be the same terminological dissonance that had served as its starting point. . . .

For my part I have the strange and dangerous habit, in every subject, of wanting to begin at the beginning (that is, at my *own* beginning), which entails beginning again, going back over the whole road, just as though many others had not already mapped and traveled it. . . .

This is the road offered to us, or imposed on us, by *language*.

With every question, before making any deep examination of the content, I take a look at the language; I generally proceed like a surgeon who sterilizes his hands and prepares the area to be operated on. This is what I call *cleaning up the verbal situation*. You must excuse this expression equating the words and forms of speech with the hands and instruments of a surgeon.

I maintain that we must be careful of a problem's first contact with our minds. We should be careful of the first words a question utters in our mind. A new question arising in us is in a state of infancy; it stammers; it finds only strange terms, loaded with adventitious values and associations; it is forced to borrow these. But it thereby insensibly deflects our true need. Without realizing it we desert our original problem, and in the end we shall come to believe that we have chosen an opinion wholly our own, forgetting that our choice was exercised only on a mass of opinions that are the more or less blind work of other men and of chance. This is what happens with the programs of political parties, no one of which is (or can be) the one that would exactly match our temperament and our interests. If we choose one among them, we gradually become the man suited to that party and to that program.

Philosophical and aesthetic questions are so richly obscured by the quantity, diversity, and antiquity of researches, arguments, and solutions, all produced within the orbit of a very restricted vocabulary, of which each author uses the words according to his own inclinations; that taken as a whole such works give me the impression of a district in the classical Underworld especially reserved for deep thinkers. Here, are the Danaïdes, Ixions, and Sisyphuses, eternally laboring to fill bottomless casks and to push back the falling rock, that is, to redefine the same dozen words whose combinations form the treasure of Speculative Knowledge.

Allow me to add to these preliminary considerations one last remark and one illustration. Here is the remark: you have surely noticed the curious fact that a certain *word*, which is perfectly clear when you hear or use it in *everyday* speech, and which presents no difficulty when caught up in the rapidity of an ordinary sentence, becomes mysteriously cumbersome, offers a strange resistance, defeats all efforts at definition, the moment you withdraw it from circulation for separate study and try to find its meaning after taking away its temporary function. It is almost comic to inquire the exact meaning of a term that one uses constantly with complete satisfaction. For example: I stop the word *Time* in its flight. This word was utterly limpid, precise, honest, and faithful in its service as long as it was part of a remark and was uttered by someone who wished to say something. But here it is, isolated, caught on the wing. It takes its revenge. It makes us believe that it has more meanings than uses. It was only a *means*, and it has become an *end*, the object of a terrible philosophical desire. It turns into an enigma, an abyss, a torment of thought. . . .

It is the same with the word *Life* and all the rest.

This readily observed phenomenon has taken on great critical value for me. Moreover, I have drawn from it an illustration that, for me, nicely conveys this strange property of our verbal material.

Each and every word that enables us to leap so rapidly across the chasm of thought, and to follow the prompting of an idea that constructs its own expression, appears to me like one of those light planks which one throws across a ditch or a mountain crevasse and which will bear a man crossing it rapidly. But he must pass without weighing on it, without stopping—above all, he must not take it into his head to dance on the slender plank to test its resistance! . . . Otherwise the fragile bridge tips or breaks immediately, and all is hurled into the depths. Consult your own experience; and you will find that we understand each other, and ourselves, only thanks to our *rapid passage over words*. We must not lay stress upon them, or we shall see the clearest discourse dissolve into enigmas and more or less learned illusions.

But how are we to think—I should say *rethink*, study deeply whatever seems to merit deep study—if we hold language to be something essentially provisional, as a banknote or a check is provisional, what we call its "value" requiring us to forget its true nature, which is that of a piece of paper, generally dirty? The paper has passed through so many hands. . . . But words have passed through so many mouths, so many phrases, so many uses and abuses, that the most delicate precautions must be taken to avoid too much confusion in our minds between what we think and are trying to think, and what dictionaries, authors, and, for that matter, the whole human race since the beginning of language, want us to think. . . .

I shall therefore take care not to accept what the words *Poetry* and *Abstract Thought* suggest to me the moment they are pronounced. But I shall look into myself. There I shall seek my real difficulties and my actual observations of my real states; there I shall find my own sense of the rational and the irrational; I shall see whether the alleged antithesis exists and how it exists in a living condition. I confess that it is my habit, when dealing with problems of the mind, to distinguish between those which I might have invented and which represent a need truly felt by my mind, and the rest, which are other people's problems. Of the latter, more than one (say forty per cent) seem to me to be nonexistent, to be no more than apparent problems: *I do not feel them*. And as for the rest, more than one seem to me to be badly stated. . . . I do not say I am right. I say that I observe what occurs within myself when I attempt to replace the verbal formulas by values and meanings that are nonverbal, that are independent of the language used. I discover naïve impulses and images, raw products of my needs and of my personal experiences. *It is my life itself that is surprised,* and my life must, if it can, provide my answers, for it is only in the reactions of our life that the full force, and as it were the necessity, of our truth can reside. The thought proceeding from that life never uses for its own account certain words which seem to it fit only for external consumption; nor certain others whose depths are obscure and which may only deceive thought as to its real strength and value.

I have, then, noticed in myself certain states which I may well call *poetic,* since some of them were finally realized in poems. They came about from no apparent cause, arising from some accident or other; they developed according to their own nature, and consequently I found myself for a time jolted out of my habitual state of mind. Then, the cycle completed, I returned to the rule of ordinary exchanges between my life and my thought. But meanwhile *a poem had been made,* and in completing itself the cycle left something behind. This closed cycle is the cycle of an act which has, as it were, aroused and given external form to a poetic power. . . .

On other occasions I have noticed that some no less insignificant incident caused—or seemed to cause—a quite different excursion, a digression of another nature and with another result. For example, a sudden concatenation of ideas, an analogy, would strike me in much the way the sound of a horn in the heart of a forest makes one prick up one's ears, and virtually directs the co-ordinated attention of all one's muscles toward some point in the distance, among the leafy depths. But this time, instead of a poem, it was an analysis of the sudden intellectual sensation that was taking hold of me. It was not verses that were being formed more or less easily during this phase, but some proposition or other that was destined to be incorporated among my habits of thought, some formula that would henceforward serve as an instrument for further researches. . . .

I apologize for thus revealing myself to you; but in my opinion it is more useful to speak of what one has experienced than to pretend to a knowledge that is entirely impersonal, an observation with no observer. In fact there is no theory that is not a fragment, carefully prepared, of some autobiography.

I do not pretend to be teaching you anything at all. I will say nothing you do not already know; but I will, perhaps, say it in a different order. You do not need to be told that a poet is not always incapable of solving a *rule of three;* or that a logician is not always incapable of seeing in words something other than concepts, categories, and mere pretexts for syllogisms.

On this point I would add this paradoxical remark: if the logician could never be other than a logician, he would not, and could not, be a logician; and if the poet were never anything but a poet, without the slightest hope of being able to reason abstractly, he would leave no poetic traces behind him. I believe in all sincerity that if each man were not able to live a number of other lives besides his own, he would not be able to live his own life.

My experience has thus shown me that the same *self* can take very different forms, can become an abstract thinker or a poet, by successive specializations, each of which is a deviation from that entirely unattached state which is superficially in accord with exterior surroundings and which is the average state of our existence, the state of undifferentiated exchanges.

Let us first see in what may consist that initial and *invariably accidental* shock which will construct the poetic instrument within us, and above all, what are its effects. The problem can be put in this way: Poetry is an art of Language; certain combinations of words can produce an emotion that others do not produce, and which we shall call *poetic*. What kind of emotion is this?

I recognize it in myself by this: that all possible objects of the ordinary world, external or internal, beings, events, feelings, and actions, while keeping their usual appearance, are suddenly placed in an indefinable but wonderfully fitting relationship with the modes of our general sensibility. That is to say that these well-known things and beings—or rather the ideas that represent them—somehow change in value. They attract one another, they are connected in ways quite different from the ordinary; they become (if you will permit the expression) *musicalized*, resonant, and, as it were, harmonically related. The poetic universe, thus defined, offers extensive analogies with what we can postulate of the dream world.

Since the word *dream* has found its way into this talk, I shall say in passing that in modern times, beginning with Romanticism, there has arisen a fairly understandable confusion between the notion of the dream and that of poetry. Neither the dream nor the daydream is necessarily poetic; it may be so: but figures formed *by chance* are only *by chance* harmonious figures.

In any case, our memories of dreams teach us, by frequent and common experience, that our consciousness can be invaded, filled, entirely absorbed by the production of an *existence* in which objects and beings seem the same as those in the waking state; but their meanings, relationships, modes of variation and of substitution are quite different and doubtless represent, like symbols or allegories, the immediate fluctuations of our *general* sensibility uncontrolled by the sensitivities of our *specialized* senses. In very much the same way the *poetic state* takes hold of us, develops, and finally disintegrates.

This is to say that the *state of poetry* is completely irregular, inconstant, involuntary, and fragile, and that we lose it, as we find it, *by accident*. But this state is not enough to make a poet, any more than it is enough to see a treasure in a dream to find it, on waking, sparkling at the foot of one's bed.

A poet's function—do not be startled by this remark—is not to experience the poetic state: that is a private affair. His function is to create it in others. The poet is recognized—or at least everyone recognizes his own poet—by the simple fact that he causes his reader to become "inspired." Positively speaking, inspiration is a graceful attribute with which the reader endows his poet: the reader sees in us the transcendent merits of virtues and graces that develop in him. He seeks and finds in us the wondrous cause of his own wonder.

But poetic feeling and the artificial synthesis of this state in some work are two quite distinct things, as different as sensation and action. A sustained action is much more complex than any spontaneous production, particularly when it has to be carried out in a sphere as conventional as that of language. Here you see emerging through my explanations the famous ABSTRACT THOUGHT which custom opposes to POETRY. We shall come back to that in a moment. Meanwhile I should like to tell you a true story, so that you may feel as

I felt, and in a curiously clear way, the whole difference that exists between the poetic state or emotion, even creative and original, and the production of a work. It is a rather remarkable observation of myself that I made about a year ago.

I had left my house to relax from some tedious piece of work by walking and by a consequent change of scene. As I went along the street where I live, I was suddenly *gripped* by a rhythm which took possession of me and soon gave me the impression of some force outside myself. It was as though someone else were making use of my *living-machine*. Then another rhythm overtook and combined with the first, and certain strange *transverse* relations were set up between these two principles (I am explaining myself as best I can). They combined the movement of my walking legs and some kind of song I was murmuring, or rather which was being murmured *through me*. This composition became more and more complicated and soon in its complexity went far beyond anything I could reasonably produce with my ordinary, usable rhythmic faculties. The sense of strangeness that I mentioned became almost painful, almost disquieting. I am no musician; I am completely ignorant of musical technique; yet here I was, prey to a development in several parts more complicated than any poet could dream. I argued that there had been an error of person, that this grace had descended on the wrong head, since I could make no use of a gift which for a musician would doubtless have assumed value, form, and duration, while these parts that mingled and separated offered me in vain a composition whose cunningly organized sequence amazed my ignorance and reduced it to despair.

After about twenty minutes the magic suddenly vanished, leaving me on the bank of the Seine, as perplexed as the duck in the fable, that saw a swan emerge from the egg she had hatched. As the swan flew away, my surprise changed to reflection. I knew that walking often induces in me a quickened flow of ideas and that there is a certain reciprocity between my pace and my thoughts—my thoughts modify my pace; my pace provokes my thoughts—which after all is remarkable enough, but is fairly understandable. Our various "reaction periods" are doubtless synchronized, and it is interesting to have to admit that a reciprocal modification is possible between a form of action which is purely muscular and a varied production of images, judgments, and reasonings.

But in the case I am speaking of, my movement in walking became in my consciousness a very subtle system of rhythms, instead of instigating those images, interior words, and potential actions which one calls *ideas*. As for ideas, they are things of a species familiar to me; they are things that I can note, provoke, and handle. . . . *But I cannot say the same of my unexpected rhythms.*

What was I to think? I supposed that mental activity while walking must correspond with a general excitement exerting itself in the region of my brain; this excitement satisfied and relieved itself as best it could, and so long as its energy was expended, it mattered little whether this was on ideas, memories, or rhythms unconsciously hummed. On that day, the energy was expended in a rhythmical intuition that developed before the awakening in my consciousness of *the person who knows that he does not know music.* I imagine it is the same as when *the person who knows he cannot fly* has not yet become active in the man who dreams he is flying.

I apologize for this long and true story—as true, that is, as a story of this kind can be. Notice that everything I have said, or tried to say, happened in relation to what we call the *External World*, what we call *Our Body*, and what we call *Our*

Mind, and requires a kind of vague collaboration between these three great powers.

Why have I told you this? In order to bring out the profound difference existing between spontaneous production by the mind—or rather by our *sensibility as a whole*—and the fabrication of works. In my story, the substance of a musical composition was freely given to me, but the organization which would have seized, fixed, and reshaped it was lacking. The great painter Degas often repeated to me a very true and simple remark by Mallarmé. Degas occasionally wrote verses, and some of those he left were delightful. But he often found great difficulty in this work accessory to his painting. (He was, by the way, the kind of man who would bring all possible difficulty to any art whatever.) One day he said to Mallarmé: "Yours is a hellish craft. I can't manage to say what I want, and yet I'm full of ideas. . . ." And Mallarmé answered: "My dear Degas, one does not make poetry with ideas, but with *words.*"

Mallarmé was right. But when Degas spoke of ideas, he was, after all, thinking of inner speech or of images, which might have been expressed in *words.* But these words, these secret phrases which he called ideas, all these intentions and perceptions of the mind, do not make verses. There is something else, then, a modification, or a transformation, sudden or not, spontaneous or not, laborious or not, which must necessarily intervene between the thought that produces ideas—that activity and multiplicity of inner questions and solutions—and, on the other hand, that discourse, so different from ordinary speech, which is verse, which is so curiously ordered, which answers no need *unless it be the need it must itself create,* which never speaks but of absent things or of things profoundly and secretly felt: strange discourse, as though made by someone *other* than the speaker and addressed to someone *other* than the listener. In short, it is a *language within a language*.

Let us look into these mysteries.

Poetry is an art of language. But language is a practical creation. It may be observed that in all communication between men, certainty comes only from practical acts and from the verification which practical acts give us. *I ask you for a light. You give me a light:* you have understood me.

But in asking me for a light, you were able to speak those few unimportant words with a certain intonation, a certain tone of voice, a certain inflection, a certain languor or briskness perceptible to me. I have understood your words, since without even thinking I handed you what you asked for—a light. But the matter does not end there. The strange thing: the sound and as it were the features of your little sentence come back to me, echo within me, as though they were pleased to be there; I, too, like to hear myself repeat this little phrase, which has almost lost its meaning, which has stopped being of use, and which can yet go on living, though with quite another life. It has acquired a value; and has acquired it *at the expense of its finite significance*. It has created the need to be heard again. . . . Here we are on the very threshold of the poetic state. This tiny experience will help us to the discovery of more than one truth.

It has shown us that language' can produce effects of two quite different kinds. One of them tends to bring about the complete negation of language itself. I speak to you, and if you have understood my words, those very words are abolished. If you have understood, it means that the words have vanished from your minds and are replaced by their counterpart, by images, relationships, impulses; so that you have within you the means to retransmit these ideas and images in a language that may be very different from the one you received. *Understanding* consists in the more or less rapid replacement of a system of sounds, intervals, and signs by something quite different, which is, in short, a modification or interior reorganization of the person to whom one is speaking. And here is the counterproof of this proposition: the person who does not understand *repeats* the words, or *has them repeated* to him.

Consequently, the perfection of a discourse whose sole aim is comprehension obviously consists in the ease with which the words forming it are transformed into something quite different: the *language* is transformed first into *non-language* and then, if we wish, into a form of language differing from the original form.

In other terms, in practical or abstract uses of language, the form—that is the physical, the concrete part, the very act of speech—does not last; it does not outlive understanding; it dissolves in the light; it has acted; it has done its work; it has brought about understanding; it has lived.

But on the other hand, the moment this concrete form takes on, by an effect of its own, such importance that it asserts itself and makes itself, as it were, respected; and not only remarked and respected, but desired and therefore repeated—then something new happens: we are insensibly transformed and ready to live, breathe, and think in accordance with a rule and under laws which are no longer of the practical order—that is, nothing that may occur in this state will be resolved, finished, or abolished by a specific act. We are entering the poetic universe.

Permit me to support this notion of a *poetic universe* by referring to a similar notion that, being much simpler, is easier to explain: the notion of a *musical universe*. I would ask you to make a small sacrifice: limit yourselves for a moment to your faculty of hearing. One simple sense, like that of hearing, will offer us all we need for our definition and will absolve us from entering into all the difficulties and subtleties to which the conventional structure and historical complexities of ordinary language would lead us. We live by ear in the world of noises. Taken as a whole, it is generally incoherent and irregularly supplied by all the mechanical incidents which the ear may interpret as it can. But the same ear isolates from this chaos a group of noises particularly remarkable and simple—that is, easily recognizable by our sense of hearing and furnishing it with points of reference. These elements have relations with one another which we sense as we do the elements themselves. The interval between two of these privileged noises is as clear to us as each of them. These are the *sounds*, and these units of sonority tend to form clear combinations, successive or simultaneous implications, series, and intersections which one may term *intelligible:* this is why abstract possibilities exist in music. But I must return to my subject.

I will confine myself to saying that the contrast between noise and sound is the contrast between pure and impure, order and disorder; that this differentiation between pure sensations and others has permitted the constitution of music; that it has been possible to control, unify, and codify this constitution, thanks to the intervention of physical science, which knows how to adjust measure to sensation so as to obtain the important result of teaching us to produce this sonorous sensation consistently, and in a continuous and identical fashion, by instruments that are, in reality, *measuring instruments*.

The musician is thus in possession of a perfect system of

well-defined means which exactly match sensations with acts. From this it results that music has formed a domain absolutely its own. The world of the art of music, a world of sounds, is distinct from the world of noises. Whereas a *noise* merely rouses in us some isolated event—a dog, a door, a motor car —*a sound evokes, of itself, the musical universe.* If, in this hall where I am speaking to you and where you hear the noise of my voice, a tuning fork or a well-tempered instrument began to vibrate, you would at once, as soon as you were affected by this pure and exceptional noise that cannot be confused with others, have the feeling of a beginning, the beginning of a world; a quite different atmosphere would immediately be created, a new order would arise, and you yourselves would unconsciously *organize* yourselves to receive it. The musical universe, therefore, was within you, with all its associations and proportions—as in a saturated salt solution a crystalline universe awaits the molecular shock of a minute crystal in order *to declare itself.* I dare not say: the crystalline idea of such a system awaits. . . .

And here is the counter proof of our little experiment: if, in a concert hall dominated by a resounding symphony, a chair happens to fall, someone coughs, or a door shuts, we immediately have the impression of a kind of rupture. Something indefinable, something like a spell or a Venetian glass, has been broken or cracked. . . .

The poetic universe is not created so powerfully or so easily. It exists, but the poet is deprived of the immense advantages possessed by the musician. He does not have before him, ready for the uses of beauty, a body of resources expressly made for his art. He has to borrow *language*—the voice of the public, that collection of traditional and irrational terms and rules, oddly created and transformed, oddly codified, and very variedly understood and pronounced. Here there is no physicist who has determined the relations between these elements; no tuning forks, no metronomes, no inventors of scales or theoreticians of harmony. Rather, on the contrary, the phonetic and semantic fluctuations of vocabulary. Nothing pure; but a mixture of completely incoherent auditive and psychic stimuli. Each word is an instantaneous coupling of a *sound* and a *sense* that have no connection with each other. Each sentence is an act so complex that I doubt whether anyone has yet been able to provide a tolerable definition of it. As for the use of the resources of language and the modes of this action, you know what diversity there is, and what confusion sometimes results. A discourse can be logical, packed with sense, but devoid of rhythm and measure. It can be pleasing to the ear, yet completely absurd or insignificant; it can be clear, yet useless; vague, yet delightful. But to grasp its strange multiplicity, which is no more than the multiplicity of life itself, it suffices to name all the sciences which have been created to deal with this diversity, each to study one of its aspects. One can analyze a text in many different ways, for it falls successively under the jurisdiction of phonetics, semantics, syntax, logic, rhetoric, philology, not to mention metrics, prosody, and etymology. . . .

So the poet is at grips with this verbal matter, obliged to speculate on sound and sense at once, and to satisfy not only harmony and musical timing but all the various intellectual and aesthetic conditions, not to mention the conventional rules. . . .

You can see what an effort the poet's undertaking would require if he had *consciously* to solve all these problems. . . .

It is always interesting to try to reconstruct one of our complex activities, one of those complete actions which demand a specialization at once mental, sensuous, and motor, supposing that in order to accomplish this act we were obliged to understand and organize all the functions that we know play their part in it. Even if this attempt, at once imaginative and analytical, is clumsy, it will always teach us something. As for myself, who am, I admit, much more attentive to the formation or fabrication of works than to the works themselves, I have a habit, or obsession, of appreciating works only as actions. In my eyes a poet is a man who, as a result of a certain incident, undergoes a hidden transformation. He leaves his ordinary condition of general disposability, and I see taking shape in him an agent, a living system for producing verses. As among animals one suddenly sees emerging a capable hunter, a nest maker, a bridge builder, a digger of tunnels and galleries, so in a man one sees a composite organization declare itself, bending its functions to a specific piece of work. Think of a very small child: the child we have all been bore many possibilities within him. After a few months of life he has learned, at the same or almost the same time, to speak and to walk. He has acquired two types of action. That is to say that he now possesses two kinds of potentiality from which the accidental circumstances of each moment will draw what they can, in answer to his varying needs and imaginings.

Having learned to use his legs, he will discover that he can not only walk, but run; and not only walk and run, but dance. This is a great event. He has at that moment both invented and discovered a kind of *secondary use* for his limbs, a generalization of his formula of movement. In fact, whereas walking is after all a rather dull and not easily perfectible action, this new form of action, the Dance, admits of an infinite number of creations and variations or *figures*.

But will he not find an analogous development in speech?

He will explore the possibilities of his faculty of speech; he will discover that more can be done with it than to ask for jam and deny his little sins. He will grasp the power of reasoning; he will invent stories to amuse himself when he is alone; he will repeat to himself words that he loves for their strangeness and mystery.

So, parallel with *Walking* and *Dancing*, he will acquire and distinguish the divergent types, *Prose and Poetry*.

This parallel has long struck and attracted me; but someone saw it before I did. According to Racan, Malherbe made use of it. In my opinion it is more than a simple comparison. I see in it an analogy as substantial and pregnant as those found in physics when one observes the identity of formulas that represent the measurement of seemingly very different phenomena. Here is how our comparison develops.

Walking, like prose, has a definite aim. It is an act directed at something we wish to reach. Actual circumstances, such as the need for some object, the impulse of my desire, the state of my body, my sight, the terrain, etc., which order the manner of walking, prescribe its direction and its speed, and give it a *definite end*. All the characteristics of walking derive from these instantaneous conditions, which combine *in a novel way* each time. There are no movements in walking that are not special adaptations, but, each time, they are abolished and, as it were, absorbed by the accomplishment of the act, by the attainment of the goal.

The dance is quite another matter. It is, of course, a system of actions; but of actions whose end is in themselves. It goes nowhere. If it pursues an object, it is only an ideal object, a state, an enchantment, the phantom of a flower, an extreme of life, a smile—which forms at last on the face of the one who summoned it from empty space.

It is therefore not a question of carrying out a limited

operation whose end is situated somewhere in our surroundings, but rather of creating, maintaining, and exalting a certain *state*, by a periodic movement that can be executed on the spot; a movement which is almost entirely dissociated from sight, but which is stimulated and regulated by auditive rhythms.

But please note this very simple observation, that however different the dance may be from walking and utilitarian movements, it uses the same organs, the same bones, the same muscles, only differently co-ordinated and aroused.

Here we come again to the contrast between prose and poetry. Prose and poetry use the same words, the same syntax, the same forms, and the same sounds or tones, but differently co-ordinated and differently aroused. Prose and poetry are therefore distinguished by the difference between certain links and associations which form and dissolve in our psychic and nervous organism, whereas the components of these modes of functioning are identical. This is why one should guard against reasoning about poetry as one does about prose. What is true of one very often has no meaning when it is sought in the other. But here is the great and decisive difference. When the man who is walking has reached his goal—as I said—when he has reached the place, book, fruit, the object of his desire (which desire drew him from his repose), this possession at once entirely annuls his whole act; the effect swallows up the cause, the end absorbs the means; and, whatever the act, only the result remains. It is the same with utilitarian language: the language I use to express my design, my desire, my command, my opinion; this language, when it has served its purpose, evaporates almost as it is heard. I have given it forth to perish, to be radically transformed into something else in your mind; and I shall know that I was *understood* by the remarkable fact that my speech no longer exists: it has been completely replaced by its *meaning*—that is, by images, impulses, reactions, or acts that belong to you: in short, by an interior modification in you.

As a result the perfection of this kind of language, whose sole end is to be understood, obviously consists in the ease with which it is transformed into something altogether different.

The poem, on the other hand, does not die for having lived: it is expressly designed to be born again from its ashes and to become endlessly what it has just been. Poetry can be recognized by this property, that it tends to get itself reproduced in its own form: it stimulates us to reconstruct it identically.

That is an admirable and uniquely characteristic property.

I should like to give you a simple illustration. Think of a pendulum oscillating between two symmetrical points. Suppose that one of these extremes represents *form:* the concrete characteristics of the language, sound, rhythm, accent, tone, movement—in a word, the *Voice* in action. Then associate with the other point, the acnode of the first, all significant values, images and ideas, stimuli of feeling and memory, virtual impulses and structures of understanding—in short, everything that makes the *content*, the meaning of a discourse. Now observe the effect of poetry on yourselves. You will find that at each line the meaning produced within you, far from destroying the musical form communicated to you, recalls it. The living pendulum that has swung from *sound* to *sense* swings back to its felt point of departure, as though the very sense which is present to your mind can find no other outlet or expression, no other answer, than the very music which gave it birth.

So between the form and the content, between the sound

and the sense, between the poem and the state of poetry, a symmetry is revealed, an equality between importance, value, and power, which does not exist in prose; which is contrary to the law of prose—the law which ordains the inequality of the two constituents of language. The essential principle of the mechanics of poetry—that is, of the conditions for producing the poetic state by words—seems to me to be this harmonious exchange between expression and impression.

I introduce here a slight observation which I shall call "philosophical," meaning simply that we could do without it.

Our poetic pendulum travels from our sensation toward some idea or some sentiment, and returns toward some memory of the sensation and toward the potential act which could reproduce the sensation. Now, whatever is sensation is essentially *present*. There is no other definition of the present except sensation itself, which includes, perhaps, the impulse to action that would modify that sensation. On the other hand, whatever is properly thought, image, sentiment, is always, in some way, *a production of absent things*. Memory is the substance of all thought. Anticipation and its gropings, desire, planning, the projection of our hopes, of our fears, are the main interior activity of our being.

Thought is, in short, the activity which causes what does not exist to come alive in us, lending to it, whether we will or no, our present powers, making us take the part for the whole, the image for reality, and giving us the illusion of seeing, acting, suffering, and possessing independently of our dear old body, which we leave with its cigarette in an armchair until we suddenly retrieve it when the telephone rings or, no less strangely, when our stomach demands provender....

Between Voice and Thought, between Thought and

Voice, between Presence and Absence, oscillates the poetic pendulum.

The result of this analysis is to show that the value of a poem resides in the indissolubility of sound and sense. Now this is a condition that seems to demand the impossible. There is no relation between the sound and the meaning of a word. The same thing is called HORSE in English, HIPPOS in Greek, EQUUS in Latin, and CHEVAL in French; but no manipulation of any of these terms will give me an idea of the animal in question; and no manipulation of the idea will yield me any of these words—otherwise, we should easily know all languages, beginning with our own.

Yet it is the poet's business to give us the feeling of an intimate union between the word and the mind.

This must be considered, strictly speaking, a marvelous result. I say *marvelous*, although it is not exceptionally rare. I use *marvelous* in the sense we give that word when we think of the miracles and prodigies of ancient magic. It must not be forgotten that for centuries poetry was used for purposes of enchantment. Those who took part in these strange operations had to believe in the power of the word, and far more in the efficacy of its sound than in its significance. Magic formulas are often without meaning; but it was never thought that their power depended on their intellectual content.

Let us listen to lines like these:

Mère des souvenirs, maîtresse des maîtresses...

or

Sois sage, ô ma Douleur, et tiens-toi plus tranquille. . . .

These words work on us (or at least on some of us) without telling us very much. They tell us, perhaps, that they have nothing to tell us; that, by the very means which usually tell us something, they are exercising a quite different function. They act on us like a chord of music. The impression produced depends largely on resonance, rhythm, and the number of syllables; but it is also the result of the simple bringing together of meanings. In the second of these lines the accord between the vague ideas of Wisdom and Grief, and the tender solemnity of the tone produce the inestimable value of a spell: the *momentary being* who made that line could not have done so had he been in a state where the form and the content occurred separately to his mind. On the contrary, he was in a special phase in the domain of his psychic existence, a phase in which the sound and the meaning of the word acquire or keep an equal importance—which is excluded from the habits of practical language, as from the needs of abstract language. The state in which the inseparability of sound and sense, in which the desire, the expectation, the possibility of their intimate and indissoluble fusion are required and sought or given, and sometimes anxiously awaited, is a comparatively rare state. It is rare, firstly because all the exigencies of life are against it; secondly because it is opposed to the crude simplifying and specializing of verbal notations.

But this state of inner modification, in which all the properties of our language are indistinctly but harmoniously summoned, is not enough to produce that complete object, that compound of beauties, that collection of happy chances for the mind which a noble poem offers us.

From this state we obtain only fragments. All the precious things that are found in the earth, gold, diamonds, uncut stones, are there scattered, strewn, grudgingly hidden in a quantity of rock or sand, where chance may sometimes uncover them. These riches would be nothing without the human labor that draws them from the massive night where they were sleeping, assembles them, alters and organizes them into ornaments. These fragments of metal embedded in formless matter, these oddly shaped crystals, must owe all their luster to intelligent labor. It is a labor of this kind that the true poet accomplishes. Faced with a beautiful poem, one can indeed feel that it is most unlikely that any man, however gifted, could have improvised without a backward glance, with no other effort than that of writing or dictating, such a simultaneous and complete system of lucky finds. Since the traces of effort, the second thoughts, the changes, the amount of time, the bad days, and the distaste have now vanished, effaced by the supreme return of a mind over its work, some people, seeing only the perfection of the result, will look on it as due to a sort of magic that they call INSPIRATION. They thus make of the poet a kind of temporary *medium*. If one were strictly to develop this doctrine of pure inspiration, one would arrive at some very strange results. For example, one would conclude that the poet, since he merely transmits what he receives, merely delivers to unknown people what he has taken from the unknown, has no need to understand what he writes, which is dictated by a mysterious voice. He could write poems in a language he did not know. . . .

In fact, the poet has indeed a kind of spiritual energy of a special nature: it is manifested in him and reveals him to himself in certain moments of infinite worth. Infinite for him. . . . I say, *infinite for him*, for, alas, experience shows us that these moments which seem to us to have a universal value are sometimes without a future, and in the end make us ponder on this maxim: *what is of value for one person only has no value*. This is the iron law of Literature.

But every true poet is necessarily a first-rate critic. If one doubts this, one can have no idea of what the work of the mind is: that struggle with the inequality of moments, with chance associations, lapses of attention, external distractions. The mind is terribly variable, deceptive and self-deceiving, fertile in insoluble problems and illusory solutions. How could a remarkable work emerge from this chaos if this chaos that contains everything did not also contain some serious chances to know oneself and to choose within oneself whatever is worth taking from each moment and using carefully?

That is not all. Every true poet is much more capable than is generally known of right reasoning and abstract thought.

But one must not look for his real philosophy in his more or less philosophical utterances. In my opinion, the most authentic philosophy lies not so much in the objects of our reflection as in the very act of thought and in its handling. Take from metaphysics all its pet or special terms, all its traditional vocabulary, and you may realize that you have not impoverished the thought. Indeed, you may perhaps have eased and freshened it, and you will have got rid of other people's problems, so as to deal only with your own difficulties, your surprises that owe nothing to anyone, and whose intellectual spur you feel actually and directly.

It has often happened, however, as literary history tells us, that poetry has been made to enunciate theses or hypotheses and that the *complete* language which is its own—the language whose *form*, that is to say the action and sensation of the *Voice*, is of the same power as the *content*, that is to say the eventual modification of a *mind*—has been used to communicate "abstract" ideas, which are on the contrary independent of their form, or so we believe. Some very great poets have occasionally attempted this. But whatever may be the talent which exerts itself in this very noble undertaking, it cannot prevent the attention given to following the ideas from competing with the attention that follows the song. The DE RERUM NATURA is here in conflict with the nature of things. The state of mind of the reader of poems is not the state of mind of the reader of pure thought. The state of mind of a man dancing is not that of a man advancing through difficult country of which he is making a topographical survey or a geological prospectus.

I have said, nevertheless, that the poet has his abstract thought and, if you like, his philosophy; and I have said that it is at work in his very activity as a poet. I said this because I have observed it, in myself and in several others. Here, as elsewhere, I have no other reference, no other claim or excuse, than recourse to my own experience or to the most common observation.

Well, every time I have worked as a poet, I have noticed that my work exacted of me not only that presence of the poetic universe I have spoken of, but many reflections, decisions, choices, and combinations, without which all possible gifts of the Muses, or of Chance, would have remained like precious materials in a workshop without an architect. Now an architect is not himself necessarily built of precious materials. In so far as he is an architect of poems, a poet is quite different from what he is as a producer of those precious elements of which all poetry should be composed, but whose composition is separate and requires an entirely different mental effort.

One day someone told me that lyricism is enthusiasm, and that the odes of the great lyricists were written at a single stroke, at the speed of the voice of delirium, and with the wind of inspiration blowing a gale. . . .

I replied that he was quite right; but that this was not a

privilege of poetry alone, and that everyone knew that in building a locomotive it is indispensable for the builder to work at eighty miles an hour in order to do his job.

A poem is really a kind of machine for producing the poetic state of mind by means of words. The effect of this machine is uncertain, for nothing is certain about action on other minds. But whatever may be the result, in its uncertainty, the construction of the machine demands the solution of many problems. If the term *machine* shocks you, if my mechanical comparison seems crude, please notice that while the composition of even a very short poem may absorb years, the action of the poem on the reader will take only a few minutes. In a few minutes the reader will receive his shock from discoveries, connections, glimmers of expression that have been accumulated during months of research, waiting, patience, and impatience. He may attribute much more to inspiration than it can give. He will imagine the kind of person it would take to create, without pause, hesitation, or revision, this powerful and perfect work which transports him into a world where things and people, passions and thoughts, sonorities and meanings proceed from the same energy, are transformed one into another, and correspond according to exceptional laws of harmony, for it can only be an exceptional form of stimulus that simultaneously produces the exaltation of our sensibility, our intellect, our memory, and our powers of verbal action, so rarely granted to us in the ordinary course of life.

Perhaps I should remark here that the execution of a poetic work—if one considers it as the engineer just mentioned would consider the conception and construction of his locomotive, that is, making explicit the problems to be solved—would appear impossible. In no other art is the number of conditions and independent functions to be co-ordinated so large. I will not inflict on you a detailed demonstration of this proposition. It is enough for me to remind you of what I said regarding sound and sense, which are linked only by pure convention, but which must be made to collaborate as effectively as possible. From their double nature words often make me think of those complex quantities which geometricians take such pleasure in manipulating.

Fortunately, some strange virtue resides in certain moments in certain people's lives which simplifies things and reduces the insurmountable difficulties I spoke of to the scale of human energies.

The poet awakes within man at an unexpected event, an outward or inward incident: a tree, a face, a "subject," an emotion, a word. Sometimes it is the will to expression that starts the game, a need to translate what one feels; another time, on the contrary, it is an element of form, the outline of an expression which seeks its origin, seeks a meaning within the space of my mind. . . . Note this possible duality in ways of getting started: either something wants to express itself, or some means of expression wants to be used.

My poem *Le Cimetière marin* began in me by a rhythm, that of a French line . . . of ten syllables, divided into four and six. I had as yet no idea with which to fill out this form. Gradually a few hovering words settled in it, little by little determining the subject, and my labor (a very long labor) was before me. Another poem, *La Pythie*, first appeared as an eight-syllable line whose sound came of its own accord. But this line implied a sentence, of which it was part, and this sentence, if it existed, implied many other sentences. A problem of this kind has an infinite number of solutions. But with poetry the musical and metrical conditions greatly restrict the indefiniteness. Here is what happened: my fragment acted like a living fragment, since, plunged in the (no doubt nourishing) surroundings of my desire and waiting thought, it proliferated, and engendered all that was lacking: several lines before and a great many lines after.

I apologize for having chosen my examples from my own little story: but I could hardly have taken them elsewhere.

Perhaps you think my conception of the poet and the poem rather singular. Try to imagine, however, what the least of our acts implies. Think of everything that must go on inside a man who utters the smallest intelligible sentence, and then calculate all that is needed for a poem by Keats or Baudelaire to be formed on an empty page in front of the poet.

Think, too, that of all the arts, ours is perhaps that which co-ordinates the greatest number of independent parts or factors: sound, sense, the real and the imaginary, logic, syntax, and the double invention of content and form ... and all this by means of a medium essentially practical, perpetually changing, soiled, a maid of all work, *everyday language*, from which we must draw a pure, ideal Voice, capable of communicating without weakness, without apparent effort, without offense to the ear, and without breaking the ephemeral sphere of the poetic universe, an idea of some *self* miraculously superior to Myself.

Problems of Poetry

IN THE course of some forty-five years I have seen Poetry subjected to many enterprises and very diverse experiments, seen it venture down entirely unknown paths, return at times to certain traditions; share, in fact, in the sudden fluctuations and in the regime of frequent change which seem characteristic of the world at present. Variety and fragility of combinations, instability of taste and rapid alteration of values, and, lastly, belief in extremes and the disappearance of what is enduring are features of this epoch, and they would be even more noticeable if they did not satisfy very exactly our own sensibility, which is becoming progressively more obtuse.

During this past half century a succession of poetic formulas or methods has been enunciated, from those of the "Parnassus," rigid and easily definable, to the loosest possible productions, and to experiments that are, in the truest sense, free. It is useful, indeed necessary, to add to this sum of inventions certain revivals, often very felicitous: borrowings, from the sixteenth, seventeenth, and eighteenth centuries, of pure or learned forms, whose elegance is perhaps imprescriptible.

* * *

All these experiments were initiated in France, which is somewhat remarkable, as this country is considered to be not very poetic, although it has produced more than one famous poet.

It is true that for about three hundred years the French have been taught to misunderstand the true nature of poetry and to follow, mistakenly, roads leading in a quite opposite direction from its home. I shall easily demonstrate this in a moment. It explains why the outbursts of poetry which have occurred among us from time to time have had to occur in the form of revolt or rebellion; or else, on the contrary, have been confined to a small number of ardent minds, jealous of their own secret certainties.

But, in this very nation which sings so little, an amazing richness of lyric invention appeared during the last quarter of the past century. Around 1875, when Victor Hugo was still living, and Leconte de Lisle and his followers were reaching fame, the names of Verlaine, Stéphane Mallarmé, and Arthur Rimbaud arose, those three Magi of modern poetics, bearers of such costly gifts and such rare spices that even the time that has elapsed since then has altered neither the glory nor the power of these extraordinary gifts.

The extreme diversity of their works, added to the variety of models offered by the poets of the preceding generation, has conduced, and conduces, to the conception, understanding, and practice of poetry in an admirable number of very different ways. There are some today, no doubt, who still follow Lamartine; others continue the work of Rimbaud. The same man may change his tastes and his style, burn at twenty what he adored at sixteen; some kind of inner transmutation shifts the power of seduction from one master to another. The lover of Musset becomes more *mature* and leaves him for Verlaine. Another, after being first nourished by Hugo, devotes himself completely to Mallarmé.

These spiritual changes generally operate in one particular *direction* rather than in the other, which is much less probable: it must be extremely rare for *Le Bateau ivre* to lead eventually to *Le Lac*. On the other hand, by loving the pure and hard *Hérodiade* one does not lose one's taste for the *Prière d'Esther*.

These defections, these sudden accesses of love or of grace, these conversions and substitutions, this possibility of being successively *sensitized* to the work of incompatible poets, are literary phenomena of the first importance. Therefore no one ever mentions them.

But—what are we talking about when we talk about "Poetry"?

It amazes me that in no other sphere of our curiosity is the observation of the *things themselves* more neglected.

I know that it is always the same when one has reason to fear that a truly searching look may dissolve its object or strip it of illusion. I was interested to notice the displeasure aroused by what I once wrote about History, and which consisted merely of simple observations that everyone can make. This little uproar was quite natural and easily foreseen, since it is less trouble to react than to reflect, and since in the majority of minds this minimum is bound to triumph. For myself, I always refrain from following that flight of ideas which shuns the observable *object* and, from sign to sign, hastens to stir up subjective impressions. . . . I believe that one should give up the practice of considering only what habit and the strongest of all habits, language, present for our consideration. One should try pondering other points than those suggested by *words*, that is to say, *by other people*.

I shall therefore try to show how Poetry is commonly treated, and turned into what it is not, at the expense of what it is.

*　*　*

One can scarcely say anything about "Poetry" which will not be exactly useless for *those in whose inner life* the strange power that causes Poetry to be sought after, or produced, is re-vealed as an inexplicable demand of their being, or as its purest answer.

These persons feel the need of something which in the ordinary way serves no purpose, and sometimes they perceive a kind of rightness in certain arrangements of *words*, which to other eyes appear quite arbitrary.

These people do not easily allow themselves to be taught to love what they do not love, nor not to love what they love—which used to be the chief aim of criticism.

* * *

For those who are not strongly aware either of the presence or the absence of Poetry, it is doubtless only an abstract and mysteriously acknowledged thing: something as empty as you please—though a tradition which it is proper to respect attaches to this entity some indeterminate value, of a kind that has a vague place in the public mind. The respect accorded to a title of nobility in a democratic country may be given as an example.

I consider that the essence of Poetry is, according to different types of minds, either quite worthless or of infinite importance: in which it is like God Himself.

* * *

Fate has arranged that among those men with no great appe-tite for Poetry, who feel no need for it and would not have invented it, there should be many whose task or destiny it is to judge it, to comment on it, to provoke and cultivate a taste for it: in short, to dispense something they do not possess. They often employ all their intelligence and zeal in this: which is why the results are to be feared.

Under the magnificent and discreet name of "Poetry," they are inevitably either led or forced to consider everything except the object with which they think they are occupied. Without realizing it, they make everything serve their turn for escaping or eluding what is essential. Everything serves their turn except that one thing.

For instance, they list what seem to be the methods used by poets: they note the frequency or absence of certain words in their vocabulary; remark their favorite images; point out borrowings, and resemblances between this one and that. Some try to reconstruct the poets' secret designs and, with deceptive clarity, read intentions and allusions into their works. With a complacency that shows where they go wrong, they like to study what is known (or thought to be known) about an author's life; as though one could ever know its true inner development, and moreover, as though the beauties of expression and the delightful harmony—always . . . *providential*—of terms and sounds were the more or less natural results of the charming or pathetic incidents of an existence. But everyone has been happy and unhappy; and the extremes of joy, like those of grief, have not been denied to the coarsest and least lyrical souls. *To perceive* does not imply *to make perceptible*—still less: *beautifully perceptible*. . . .

*   *   *

Is it not extraordinary that one should seek and find so many ways of treating a subject without ever touching on its principle, and that, by the methods one uses, the kind of attention one brings to it, and even the trouble one inflicts on oneself, one should reveal a complete and perfect misapprehension of the true *problem?*

Further: among the many scholarly works which, for

centuries, have been devoted to Poetry, one finds amazingly
few (and I say "few" to keep from saying "none") which do
not imply a negation of its existence. The most perceptible
characteristics and the very real problems of this most complex art are, as it were, perfectly obscured by the very type
of glance turned on it.

*   *   *

What happens? The poem is treated as though it were (*and as
though it ought to be*) divisible into a *discourse in prose* which is
self-sufficient and self-contained and, on the other hand, a
piece of special music, more or less allied to music proper, and
such as the human voice can produce; but ours does not rise to
song, which, in any case, scarcely preserves the *words*, being
concerned only with the *syllables*.

As for the *discourse in prose*—that is, a discourse which if
put into other words would answer the same purpose—this
again is divided. It is thought that it can be broken up, on the
one hand, into a short text (which can sometimes be reduced
to one word, or to the title of the work) and, on the other, a
certain amount of *accessory speech*: ornaments, images, figures,
epithets, and "fine details," whose common characteristic is
their capacity for being inserted, augmented, or deleted
ad libitum. . . .

And as for the *music of poetry*, that *special music* I mentioned,
it is imperceptible to some; unimportant for most; for others
it is the object of abstract research, sometimes scientific and
nearly always sterile. I know that honest efforts have been
made to deal with the difficulties of this subject, but I fear that
this energy has been misplaced. Nothing is more misleading
than those so-called "scientific" methods (in particular, measurements and recordings) which always permit a "fact" to be

given in answer to a question, even if it is absurd or badly put. Their value (like that of logic) lies in the way they are used. The statistics, the marks on wax, the chronometric observations which are used to solve entirely "subjective" problems of origin or trend, do indeed say *something;* but here, instead of resolving our difficulties and ending all controversy, the oracles merely introduce a naïvely disguised metaphysics under the forms and apparatus of the material of physics.

Even if we measure the footsteps of the goddess, note their frequency and *average* length, we are still far from the secret of her instantaneous grace. So far, we have not seen that the laudable curiosity which exerts itself in sifting the mysteries of the music of "articulated" language has produced anything of new and capital importance. There is the whole point. The only gauge of real knowledge is power: power to do or power to predict. "All the rest is Literature...."

I must recognize, however, that these researches which I find not very fruitful have at least the merit of seeking precision. The intention is excellent.... Our epoch is easily satisfied by the *approximate*, wherever *material* things are not concerned. For this reason our epoch is at once more precise and more superficial than any other: in spite of itself, more precise; and of itself, more superficial. It values chance more than substance. It is amused by people and bored by man; and above all it dreads that happy borèdom which, in more peaceful and so to speak emptier times, provided us with profound, critical, and desirable readers. Who would nowadays weigh his own lightest words, and for whom? And what Racine would ask his friend Boileau for permission to substitute the word *misérable* for the word *infortuné* in a certain line—a permission which was not granted?

* * *

Since I am undertaking to disengage Poetry a little from the prose and the prosaic mentality that overwhelm it, veiling it with kinds of knowledge quite unnecessary for a knowledge and possession of its nature, I may well observe the effect these labors produce on more than one mind of our time. It sometimes happens that the habit of extreme exactness developed in certain fields (and familiar to many, from its applications in practical life) tends to make useless, if not unbearable, many traditional speculations, many theses or theories which could doubtless still occupy us, spur our intellects a bit, and cause many an excellent book to be written—and even glanced through—but which, on the other hand, make us feel that a somewhat keener glance, or a few unexpected questions, would be enough to make these abstract mirages, arbitrary systems, and vague perspectives dissolve into mere verbal possibilities. Henceforward all *the sciences whose only assets are what they say* are "virtually" depreciated by the development of those sciences whose results are continually felt and used.

Imagine the judgments that can be formed by an intellect accustomed to some discipline, when confronted with certain "definitions" and "developments" purporting to initiate it into an understanding of Letters, and particularly of Poetry. What value can we attach to the arguments about "Classicism," "Romanticism," "Symbolism," etc., when we should have the greatest difficulty in linking the peculiar characteristics and qualities of execution which constitute the worth of a particular work, and have assured its preservation, *kept it alive*, with the so-called general ideas and "aesthetic" tendencies which these fine names are supposed to indicate? They are abstract and conventional terms: but conventions that are anything but "convenient," since the lack of agreement among authors about their meaning is somehow the rule; and since they appear to have been made in order to provoke this disagreement and to form a pretext for endless differences of opinion.

*   *   *

It is only too clear that all these classifications and cavalier judgments add nothing to the delight of a reader who is capable of love, nor do they increase a craftsman's understanding of the methods that the masters have used: they teach neither reading nor writing. Moreover, they sidetrack the mind and release it from the consideration of the real problems of art, while allowing many blind men to discourse admirably on color. How many facile things have been written thanks to the word "Humanism," and how many stupidities in order to make people believe that Rousseau invented "Nature"! ... It is true that once they have been adopted and absorbed by the public, with a thousand other useless phantasms that occupy its mind, these simulacra of thoughts take on a kind of existence and provide reason and substance for a mass of combinations of a certain scholarly *originality*. A *Boileau* is thus ingeniously discovered in *Victor Hugo*, a romantic in *Corneille*, a "psychologist" or a realist in *Racine*. . . . All these things are neither true nor false—in fact they could not possibly be either.

*   *   *

I agree that literature in general and poetry in particular may be held of no account. Beauty is a private affair; the impression one has of recognizing and experiencing it at a given moment is an accident that may be more or less frequent during one's existence, like that of sorrow and pleasure; but even more fortuitous. It is never certain that a particular object will delight us, nor that having once pleased (or displeased) us, it will please (or displease) us the next time. This uncertainty, which baffles all calculations and all forethought, and which permits combining all sorts of works with all sorts of individuals, permits every rejection and every idolatry, involves the fate of writings with the caprices, passions, and moods of anyone at all. If someone really savors a particular poem, the fact can be known by this: he speaks of it as of a personal affection—if he speaks of it at all. I have known men so jealous of what they passionately admired that they could hardly endure that others should be taken by it, or even acquainted with it, feeling their love spoilt by sharing. They preferred to hide rather than disseminate their favorite books, and treated them (to the detriment of the authors' general fame, but to the advancement of their worship) as the wise husbands of the East treat their wives, surrounding them with secrecy.

* * *

But if one wishes, as is customary, to make of Letters a kind of public utility, to associate with a nation's renown—which is, in fact, a *State security*—the titles of "masterpieces," which must needs be inscribed after the names of its victories; and if, by turning instruments of intellectual pleasure into means of education, one assigns to these creations an important place in the formation and classifying of young people—then one should take care not to corrupt thereby the true and proper sense of art. This corruption consists in substituting meaningless and external kinds of precision or agreed opinions, for the *absolute* precision of pleasure or direct interest aroused by a work, and in turning this work into a *reagent* for pedagogical control, a ground for parasitic developments, a pretext for absurd problems....

All these aims lead to the same result: to avoiding the real problems and to forming a misconception....

When I look at what is done to Poetry, at the questions asked and the answers given about it, the idea of it got in the classroom (and almost everywhere), my mind, which (no doubt because of the intimate nature of the mind) thinks itself the most simple of minds, is astonished "to the very limits of astonishment."

It says to itself: I see nothing in all this which helps me either to read this poem better—to *perform* it better for my own pleasure—or to understand its structure more clearly. I am being urged toward something quite different, and nothing is omitted that will lead me away from the *divine*. I am taught dates and biography, I am told of quarrels and doctrines I care nothing about, when what is in question is the song and the subtle art of the voice transmitting ideas.... Where then is the essential matter of these remarks and theses? What has happened to the immediately perceptible part of a text, to the sensations that it was written to produce? It will be time enough to deal with the poet's life, loves, and opinions, his friends and enemies, his birth and death, when we shall have advanced sufficiently in the *poetic knowledge* of his poem, that is, when we shall have made ourselves the instrument of what is written, so that our voice, our intelligence, and all the fibers of our sensibility are banded together to give life and powerful actuality to the author's act of creation.

The superficial and fruitless character of the studies and teaching at which I have just been marveling appears at the slightest precise question. While I listen to these disquisitions which lack neither "documentation" nor subtlety, I cannot help thinking that I do not even know what a *Phrase* is. . . . I vary about what is meant by a *Verse*. I have read or invented twenty definitions of *Rhythm* and have adopted none of them. . . . Nay more! . . . If I merely stop to ask what a *Consonant* is, I begin to wonder; I search; and I find only the semblance of precise knowledge divided between twenty differing opinions. . . .

If I now decide to find out about those uses, or rather those abuses, of language which are grouped under the vague and general heading of "figures," I can discover no more than abandoned traces of the extremely imperfect analysis of these "rhetorical phenomena" which was attempted by the ancients. Now these figures, which are so neglected by modern criticism, play a role of the first importance not only in explicit and organized poetry, but also in that perpetually active poetry which harasses the rigid vocabulary, expands or contracts the meaning of words, works on them by symmetries or conversions, constantly altering the values of this legal tender—a poetry that, sometimes through the mouths of the people, sometimes from the unforeseen needs of technical expression, sometimes through the writer's hesitant pen, engenders that variation in the language which insensibly changes it completely. No one seems even to have attempted to resume this analysis. No one tries, by a profound examination of these substitutions, these abbreviated signs, these deliberate misconceptions, and these expedients (which until now have been so vaguely defined by the grammarians), to discover the particular qualities they imply, which cannot be very different from those that are sometimes shown by the genius of geometry, with its art of creating for itself instruments of thought progressively more flexible and penetrating. Without knowing it, the Poet moves within an order of *possible* relationships and transformations, perceiving or pursuing only those passing and special effects which are of use to him in a particular phase of his inner activity.

I agree that researches of this kind are terribly difficult and that their usefulness can be apparent to only a limited number of minds; and I grant that it is less abstract, more simple, more "human," more "living" to develop observations on poetic "sources," "influences," "psychology," "milieus," and "inspirations" than to devote oneself to the organic problems of expression and its effects. I neither deny the value nor contest the interest of a literature that has Literature itself as a décor, and authors for its characters; but I must observe that I have never found much there of any positive use to myself. It is suitable for conversations, discussions, lectures, examinations, or theses, and all external matters of that kind—the demands of which are very different from those of the merciless confrontation of someone's *purpose* with his *ability*. Poetry is formed or communicated in the purest abandon or in a state of profound attention: if one makes it an object of study, it is in this direction that one must look: into the living being and hardly at all at his surroundings.

How surprising it is (my simple mind runs on) that an age which, in the factory, the workshop, the arena, the laboratory, or the office, carries to incredible lengths the division of labor, the economy and efficacy of action, the purity and suitability of procedures, should reject in the arts the advantages of acquired experience and refuse to invoke anything but improvisation, the bolt from the blue, or dependence on chance under various flattering names! . . . At no other time has contempt been more strongly marked, expressed, affirmed, and even proclaimed for what ensures the true perfection of works of art, and what, by linking their different parts, gives them unity and consistency of form and all those qualities which the happiest inspirations cannot confer on them. But we are hasty. Too many metamorphoses and revolutions of every kind, too many rapid transmutations of likes into dislikes and of things mocked into things beyond price, too many and too differing values presented simultaneously, have accustomed us to be content with the first version of our impressions. And how, nowadays, are we to think of permanence, speculate on the future, and desire to *bequeath?* It seems useless to us to try to resist "time," and offer to unknown people who will live two hundred years hence models capable of moving them. We find it almost inexplicable that so many great men should have thought of us, and perhaps have become great men for having so thought. In fact, everything appears so precarious and so unstable in every way, so necessarily accidental, that we have ended by turning the accidents of sensation and unsustained consciousness into the substance of many works.

To sum up, the superstition of posterity having been abolished; concern for the day after tomorrow dissipated; composition, economy of means, elegance, and perfection having become imperceptible to a public less sensitive and more naïve than formerly, it is natural enough that the art of poetry and the understanding of that art should have declined (like so many other things) to the point of doing away with any forethought, and even any notion, of their immediate future. The fate of an art is linked, on the one hand, with that of its material means and, on the other, with that of the minds who are capable of being interested in it and who find in it the satisfaction of a real need. From the remotest antiquity to the present time, reading and writing have been the sole means of exchange and the only methods of developing and preserving expression through language. One can no longer answer for their future. As for minds, one already sees that they are wooed and captured by so much immediate magic, so many direct stimuli, which with no effort provide the most intense sensations and show them life itself and the whole of nature, that one may doubt whether our grandchildren will find the slightest savor in the outdated graces of our most extraordinary poets and of poetry in general.

* * *

My purpose being to show, by the way Poetry is generally considered, how it is generally unrecognized—the lamentable victim of intellects which are sometimes very powerful but which have no feeling for Poetry—I must go on with it and give some details.

I shall first quote the great d'Alembert: "Here, in my opinion," he wrote, "is the strict but just rule that our century imposes on poets: it now recognizes as good in verse only what it would find excellent in prose."

This pronouncement is one of those the reverse of which is exactly what we think should be thought. It would have sufficed for a reader in 1760 to state the contrary to discover what was going to be sought after and appreciated in the not too remote future. I do not say that either d'Alembert or his century was wrong. I say that he thought he was talking about Poetry, while he was thinking of something quite different under the same name.

Heaven knows that since the postulation of the "d'Alembert Theorem" poets have striven to contradict it! . . .

Some, moved by instinct, have fled in their works as far as possible from prose. They have even happily divested themselves of eloquence, ethics, history, philosophy, and everything in the intellect that can be developed only by expending *verbal currency*.

Others, a little more exacting, have tried, by a more and more subtle and precise analysis of poetic desire and delight, and of their workings, to construct a poetry that could never be reduced to the expression of a thought nor, consequently, be translated into other terms without perishing. They knew that the communication of a poetic state that involves the whole feeling organism is a different thing from the communication of an idea. They understood that the literal sense of a poem is not, and does not fulfill, its whole end; that the literal sense is therefore not necessarily *unique*.

* * *

However, in spite of some admirable researches and creations, our acquired habit of judging verse by the standard of prose and its function, of evaluating it, to a certain extent, *by the amount of prose it contains;* our national temperament, which has become more and more *prosaic* since the sixteenth century; the astonishing errors in the teaching of literature; the influence of the theater and of dramatic poetry (that is, of *action*, which is essentially *prose*): all these perpetuate many an absurdity and many a practice which show the most flagrant ignorance of the conditions of poetry.

It would be easy to draw up a table of "criteria" for the antipoetic mind. It would be a list of the ways of treating a poem, of judging and speaking of it, which constitute maneuvers directly contrary to the poet's efforts. Transferred to teaching, where they are the rule, these useless and barbarous operations tend to ruin the sense of poetry from childhood, together with any notion of the pleasure it could give.

To distinguish between form and content in poetry; between a subject and its treatment; between sound and sense; to consider rhythm, meter, and prosody as naturally and easily separable from the *verbal expression* itself, from the *words* themselves, and from the *syntax;* these are so many symptoms of noncomprehension or insensibility in poetic matters. *To turn a poem or to have it turned into prose, to make of a poem a matter for instruction or examinations:* these are no slight acts of heresy. It is a real perversion to insist on misconstruing the principles of an art in this way when, on the contrary, one should initiate other minds into a universe of language that is not the common system of exchanging signs for acts or ideas. The poet's use of words is quite different from that of custom or need. The words are without doubt the same, but their values are not at all the same. It is indeed nonusage—the *not saying* "it is raining"— which is his business; and everything which shows that he is not speaking prose serves his turn. Rhymes, inversion, elaborated figures, symmetries, and images, all these, whether inventions or conventions, are so many means of setting himself in opposition to the prosaic leanings of the reader (just as the famous "rules" of the art of poetry have the effect of constantly reminding the poet of the *complex universe* of that art). The impossibility of reducing his work to prose, of *saying* it, or of *understanding it as prose* are imperious conditions of its existence, without which that work is *poetically* meaningless.

* * *

After so many negative propositions, I should now go on to the positive side of the subject; but I should think it hardly proper to preface a collection of poems, in which the most diverse tendencies and styles of execution appear, by an exposé of ideas that remain highly personal in spite of my efforts to preserve and produce only those observations and reasons which everyone can make for himself. Nothing is more difficult than not being oneself, or than being oneself only so far and no farther.

Memoirs of a Poem

I WAS LIVING remote from all literature, innocent of any intention of writing to be read, and therefore at peace with all who read, when, about 1912, Gide and Gallimard asked me to collect and print some verses I had written twenty years before, which had appeared in various reviews at the time.

I was completely taken aback. For no more than a moment could I even consider this proposal, which made no appeal to anything still active in my mind and aroused no feeling that could tempt it. My indistinct recollection of these little pieces gave me no pleasure: I felt no affection for them. Some of them may have pleased a small circle at the time they were produced, but that favorable time and environment had vanished, as had my own attitude of mind. Besides, though I had not followed the fortunes of poetry during all those years, I was not unaware that taste was no longer the same: the fashion had changed. But even had it remained as I had known it, I should scarcely have cared, for I had made myself, as it were, insensitive to fashion of any kind.

I had, in fact, given up the game, which I had engaged in carelessly and for only a moment, as a man whom such hopes do not dazzle and who sees primarily in the amusement of aiming at others' minds the certainty of losing his own "soul," by which I mean the liberty, purity, uniqueness, and universality of the intellect. I do not say "I was right." . . . I know nothing more stupid and indeed vulgar than wanting *to be right*.

* * *

I had always felt a certain uneasiness of mind when I thought of Letters. A most beguiling and zealous friendship encouraged me to venture on this strange career, in which one must be oneself to others.

It seemed to me that to live for the sake of being published would be to condemn oneself to a perpetual equivocation. "How can one please others and yet please oneself?" I wondered ingenuously.

No sooner had the pleasure given me by certain books aroused the demon of wishing to write, than considerations of equal force tending the other way opposed the temptation.

I admit that I took the affairs of my mind very seriously, and that I was occupied with its salvation as others are with that of their soul. I did not care for, and had no wish to preserve, anything it could produce without effort, for I believed that effort alone changes us and transmutes our original facility, born of the occasion and dying with it, into another facility that is able to create and dominate the occasion. In the same way, from the enchanting movements of infancy to the pure and graceful precision of the athlete or the dancer, the living body advances to self-possession by conscious analysis and exercise.

But as for Letters, this meant putting them to an extraordinary use and curiously defining them. According to my theory, a man's works were a means of modifying, by reaction, their author's inner being; whereas in the opinion of most people they are an end in themselves—either because they result from a need for self-expression or because they are aimed at some exterior benefit: money, women, or fame.

*　　*　　*

Literature exists first of all as a way of developing our powers of invention and self-stimulation in the utmost freedom, since its matter and tool is the *word*, freed from the burden of immediate use and suborned to every conceivable fiction and delight. But this fine prospect is at once clouded by the necessity of influencing an ill-defined public. The aim of art can only be to produce the happiest effect on strangers, either the most numerous or the most sensitive possible. . . . However the enterprise may end, it involves us in dependence on others, and the state of mind and the tastes we attribute to them thus insinuate themselves into our own mind. Even the most disinterested and seemingly most independent scheme insensibly draws us away from the great design of leading our *self* to the very limits of its desire for self-possession, and puts consideration for hypothetical readers in the place of our first idea of an immediate witness or incorruptible judge of our efforts. Without realizing it, we abandon all extremes of severity or perfection, all depth of thought that is not easily communicable, we pursue only what can be brought down, we conceive only what may be printed; for it is impossible to journey in company to the limits of one's thought: one gets there only by a kind of abuse of one's inner sovereignty.

*　　*　　*

All these observations, which were specious, probably signified only an unusual repugnance in my nature toward a form of activity that could almost be defined as a perpetual confusion between life, thought, and profession in the man who

undertakes it. Palissy threw only his furniture into the fire
of his kiln. The writer consumes everything he is and everything around him. His pleasures and griefs, his business,
his God, his childhood, his wife, his friends and enemies, his
knowledge and ignorance—all are tossed onto the fateful
paper. Some there are who bring on a crisis, irritate a wound,
or cherish their sufferings so as to write of them, and since the
invention of "sincerity" as valid literary currency (which is
rather surprising, where all is fiction), there is no fault, anomaly, or reserve which has not acquired its value: a confession
is as good as an idea.

I shall now make my own confession and reveal my own
anomaly. If this system of exposing one's private affairs to
the public is called *human*, I must declare myself essentially
inhuman.

This is by no means to say that I get no pleasure from
literary effects obtained by the somewhat easy method of
contrasting average manners with rather special ones, the
accepted with the just possible, as long as they are given for
what they are: in this genre I prefer Restif to Jean-Jacques
and, generally, M. de Seingalt to M. de Stendhal. Shameless-
ness does not require any general considerations. I prefer it
plain.

As for history and novels, my interest is sometimes held,
and I can admire them as stimulants, pastimes, and works of
art; but if they lay claim to "truth" and hope to be taken
seriously, their arbitrary quality and unconscious conventions
at once become apparent, and I am seized with a perverse
mania for trying possible substitutions.

In this respect, my own life does not escape. I feel curiously
isolated from its circumstances. My memory retains almost
nothing but ideas and a few sensations. Events rapidly dis-

appear. Whatever I have done soon ceases to be part of me. Those recollections which lead me to relive the past are painful: and the best of them are unbearable. I certainly would not busy myself by trying to recover time past! In short, situations, groupings of characters, and the subjects of stories and dramas find nothing in me in which to take root and develop in a single direction. Perhaps it would be interesting, *just once*, to write a work which at each juncture would show the diversity of solutions that can present themselves to the mind and from which it *chooses* the unique sequel to be found in the text. To do this would be to substitute for the illusion of a unique scheme which imitates reality that of the *possible-at-each-moment*, which I think more truthful. It has sometimes happened that I have published different versions of the same poem: some of them have even been contradictory, and there has been no lack of criticism on this score. But no one has told me why I should refrain from such variations.

* * *

I do not know whence I derive this very lively sense of the arbitrary. Have I always had it, or have I acquired it?... Without meaning to, I try in thought to modify or vary everything I meet that seems susceptible of alteration, and my mind enjoys these virtual acts; it is somewhat like turning an object over and over, becoming familiar with it by touch. This is an inveterate habit, or a method, or both at once: there is no contradiction. It sometimes happens when I am faced with a landscape that the shape of the ground, the lines of the horizon, the placing and contours of woods and fields seem purely accidental, doubtless defining a certain site; but I contemplate them as if I could as freely transform them as one would on paper by pencil or brush. I am not interested for any length of time in the prospects before me. In any case, I have only to move to alter them. On the other hand, the *substance* of the objects under my eye—the rock, the water, the stuff of the bark or the leaf, and the faces of living things —holds my attention. I can be interested only in things I cannot invent.

This same inclination in me affects the works of man. I find it almost impossible to read a novel without beginning, the moment my active attention is aroused, to substitute for its sentences other sentences which the author might equally have written without much detriment to his effect. Unfortunately, the whole appearance of reality that the modern novel wishes to produce lies entirely in such fragile decisions and insignificant particulars. It cannot be otherwise: the life we see, even our own, is woven of details that *must be* in order to fill a particular square on the chessboard of understanding, but which *may be this or that*. There is never anything in observable reality that is visibly necessary; and necessity never appears without the accompaniment of some action on the part of the will and the mind. But in that case—no more illusion! I must admit that my feeling for and instinctive practice of substitution are detestable: *they spoil so much pleasure*. I marvel at, and envy, those novelists who assure us that they believe in the "existence" of their characters, whose slaves they claim to be, blindly following their destinies, ignorant of their plans, suffering for their misfortunes, and experiencing their feelings—all astonishing cases of *possession* that recall the wonders of occultism and the working of those "mediums" who hold the pen for "spirits," or allow their sensitivity to be transferred into a glass of water so that they cry out in pain if a knife is plunged into the water.

I need not add that history itself, even more than the novel, provokes me to indulge in this game of possible alterations, which blend extremely well with the real falsifications to be found from time to time in the most respectable documents. All this is very useful in emphasizing the naïve and curious structure of our belief in the "past."

Even in the exact sciences there is so much that could be stated otherwise, described or arranged in a different way, without harming the unalterable part of these disciplines, which consists only of verifiable formulas and results.

When my mind, untrammeled in its freedom, alights of its own accord on some object that fascinates it, it seems to see it in a kind of *space* where, no longer present and completely defined, the object is removed into the possible. . . .

And I am almost at once aware that what comes into my thoughts is a "specimen," a special case, one element from a variety of other and equally conceivable combinations. My opinions soon evoke opposing or complementary opinions. I should be wretched if I did not see any actual event or any particular impulse I experience, simply as a part of some whole —a *facet* of one system among all those I am capable of.

*   *   *

I was therefore rather ill equipped to venture, for life, on an occupation which interested me only in its least "human" aspects. I saw it merely as a refuge, a recourse, and in fact much more as a method of separating or organizing thought in itself than as a means of communicating with or influencing unknown persons. I considered it an *exercise* and in that way justified it.

Writing was, for me, an operation quite distinct from the instantaneous expression of some "idea" in immediately evoked language. Ideas cost nothing, no more than events or sensations. Those which seem most valuable, the images, analogies, themes, and rhythms that are born within us, are accidents of greater or less frequency in our inventive life. Man does little else but invent. But he who becomes aware of the facility, fragility, and incoherence of this production will oppose to it the effort of his mind. As a wonderful result, the most powerful "creations," the most splendid monuments of thought, have been derived from the considered use of voluntary *resistance* to our immediate and continuous "creation" of observations, narratives, and impulses, which without more ado are interchangeable. For example, a purely spontaneous work may comfortably contain contradictions and "vicious circles"; logic raises a barrier to them. Logic is the best known and most important of all the explicit, formal conventions that the mind sets up against itself. Well-defined poetic rules, methods, canons and proportions, rules of harmony, laws of composition, fixed forms—all these are not (as is generally supposed) formulas of restricted creation. Their fundamental aim is to lead the complete and organized man— *the being made for action, whom, in return, his action perfects*—to bring his whole self to bear upon the production of works of the mind. These restrictions may be entirely arbitrary: it is enough that they hamper the natural and inconsequent flow of digression or gradual creation. As our impulses, when translated into action, must be subordinated to the demands of our motor apparatus, and clash with the material conditions around us, and as by this experience we acquire an even more exact knowledge of our form and powers, so invention, when it is checked and disciplined. . . .

So, *writing* seemed to me a labor very different from immediate expression, just as the treatment by analysis of a problem in physics differs from the recording of observations: the treatment demands that one should rethink the phenomena and define those notions that do not occur in everyday language; and one may find oneself obliged to create new methods of calculation. In the same way I found that studies in form, to which this conception of *writing* must lead, demanded an outlook and a certain idea of language which were subtler, more precise, and more conscious than those which suffice for normal use.

Moreover, the refinements and painstaking embellishments which, since around 1850, poets had introduced into the art of verse, the necessity of separating, more than ever before, the original stimulus and intent from the execution of a work, predisposed me to consider Letters in the light I have mentioned. They seemed to me no more than a combination of asceticism and play. Their effect on others was no doubt one of the conditions to be, more or less strictly, fulfilled; but nothing more.

* * *

I had, too, to recognize in my nature certain peculiarities that I shall call *insular*. By these I mean curious gaps in my system of intellectual instincts, faults that seem to me to have counted for a great deal in the development of my opinions and prejudices, and even in the subjects and form of my few works.

For example, I have never felt the need to make others share my feelings on any subject. I tend to the opposite direction. A strong predilection for "being right," for convincing others, for conquering or subjecting other minds, for provoking them for or against somebody or something is essentially foreign, if not repellent, to me. As I cannot bear anyone's wishing to change my ideas by emotional means, I assume the same intolerance in others. Nothing offends me more than proselytism and its methods, which are always tainted. I am sure that in the long run apologetics do more harm than service to religions—at least if one judges by the quality of the converted. From this I have drawn the advice: *Hide your*

God, for as He is your strength, in that He is your greatest secret, He is your weakness as soon as others know Him.

If you wish to utter your thought, I would have you speak it without heat, quite clearly, so that it appears less as the product of an individual than as the result of circumstances agreeing and blending in a moment, or as a phenomenon from another world than this one of people and their moods. I dislike picturing, while I read a page, a flushed or derisive face disclosing the resolve to make me like what I hate or hate what I like. The whole business of politics of every kind is to act on people's nerves: where would politics be without epithets? Politicians would be hard put to it if they were expected to organize their thought from beginning to end. True strength, however, makes itself felt by its structure and asks nothing. It compels men without seeing them.

In short, I regard methods with much more affection than results, and for me the end does not justify the means, since —*there is no end.*

Then, as I am not interested in influencing other people's sentiments, I am myself quite unstirred by their schemes for moving me. I feel no need of my neighbor's passions, and the idea has never occurred to me to work for those who ask that a writer should teach them or restore to them what can be discerned or learned simply by living. Besides, the majority of authors undertake this, and the greatest poets have miraculously performed the task of reproducing for us the immediate emotions of life. This is a traditional task. Masterpieces of this kind abound. I was wondering whether something else could be done.

* * *

That is why I would give my favor not to Letters but rather to the nonrepresentational arts; they do not pretend, they play only upon our actual capacities, without recourse to our ability to imagine lives, with all the spurious detail we so easily give them. Their "pure" methods are not encumbered with personalities and events drawn from everything arbitrary and superficial in observable reality, for only such things are imitable. On the contrary, they exploit, they compose and organize the values of each power of our sensibility, free of all reference, of all function as a *sign*. Thus reduced to itself, the sequence of our feelings has no longer a chronological order, but a kind of intrinsic, instantaneous order, which is revealed step by step. . . . I cannot at this point explain the details, arguments, and consequences of my theory: to understand me one has only to consider the productions that are bracketed together under the general heading of *Ornament*, or, better still, *pure music*. The musician, for instance, finds himself as it were *faced with* a number of possibilities upon which he can work without any reference to the world of things and people. By his management of the elements of the world of hearing, "human" affections and emotions can be stimulated without one's ceasing to perceive that the musical formulas arousing them form part of the general system of sounds, are born of it and dissolve into it again, so that their separate units may regroup in new combinations. Thus, *it is never possible to confuse the effect of the work with the semblance of some unknown life: but what is possible is communion with the deep springs of all life.*

However, I had neither the talent nor the technical knowledge needed to follow this formal instinct for those productions of the sensibility developed apart from all representation, whose structure resembles nothing that exists, and which tend to group themselves into self-sufficient compositions. This gives rise to a curiously antihistorical frame of mind—that is, to a lively apprehension of the present and immediate substance of our images of the "past," and of our inalienable freedom to modify them as easily as we conceive them, without any consequence. . . .

* * *

Certain of the poems I have written had as a starting point merely one of these impulses of the "formative" sensibility which are anterior to any "subject" or to any finite, expressible idea. *La Jeune Parque* was, literally speaking, an endless research into the possibility of attempting in poetry something analogous to what in music is called "modulation." The "transitions" gave me a lot of trouble, but these difficulties led me to discover and take note of many of the precise problems of the workings of my mind, and that, fundamentally, was what mattered to me. Besides, nothing in the arts interests me more than these transitions, which I perceived to be so delicate and subtle to accomplish, although the moderns ignore or despise them. I never tire of admiring the nuances of form by which the shape of a living body, or of a plant, imperceptibly and in accordance with its nature, draws to its fulfillment; or how the spiral of a shell, after several turns, opens out at last, bordered with a layer of its inner mother-of-pearl. The architect in one of the great periods made use of the most exquisitely calculated cornices to unite the successive planes of his work. . . .

Another poem began merely with the hint of a rhythm, *which gradually acquired a meaning.* This production, which developed, as it were, from "form" to "content," and which from being an empty structure ended as stimulus to the most conscious work, was no doubt related to the preoccupation I had had for several years with research into the general conditions of all thought, regardless of its content.

I shall mention here something rather remarkable that I observed about myself a short time ago.

I had left my house to find, in walking and looking about me, relaxation from some tedious work. As I went along my street, which mounts steeply, I was *gripped* by a rhythm which took possession of me and soon gave me the impression of some force outside myself. Another rhythm overtook and combined with the first, and certain strange *transverse relations* were set up between them. This combination, which went far beyond anything I could have expected from my rhythmic faculties, made the sense of strangeness, which I have mentioned, almost unbearable. I argued that there had been an error of person, that this grace had descended on the wrong head, since I could make no use of a gift which, in a musician, would doubtless have assumed a lasting shape, and it was in vain that these two themes offered me a composition whose sequence and complexity amazed my ignorance and reduced it to despair. The magic suddenly vanished after about twenty minutes, leaving me on the bank of the Seine, as perplexed as the duck in the fable, which saw a swan emerge from the egg she had hatched. As the swan flew away and my astonishment lessened, I observed that in my case walking is often conducive to a quickened flow of ideas and that this action is sometimes reciprocal: speed provokes thought, thought modifies speed; one brings the walker to a halt, the other spurs him on. But this time my movements assailed my consciousness through a subtle arrangement of rhythms, instead of provoking that amalgam of images, inner words, and virtual acts that one calls an Idea. But however new and unexpected an "idea" may be, it is still no more than an idea: it belongs to an order of things familiar to me, which I know how to note, handle, and adapt to my use. Diderot said: *My ideas are my whores.* That is a good formula. But I cannot say the same of my unexpected rhythms. What was I to think? I fancied that the mental activity produced by walking was probably related to a general stimulus that found its outlet as best it could in the brain; and that this kind of quantitative function could be as well fulfilled by the emission of some rhythm as by verbal images or some sort of symbols; and, further, that, at a certain point in my mental processes, all ideas, rhythms, images, and memories or inventions were merely *equivalents.* It must be that at that point we are *still* not entirely ourselves. *The person who knows that he does not know music* had not yet become operative in me when my rhythm seized me, just as the person who knows he cannot fly is not operative in the man who dreams he is flying. . . .

Moreover I believe (for other reasons) that all thought would be impossible if at every moment we were entirely present. Thought requires a certain liberty, which is acquired by the abstention of some of our own powers.

However that may be, I thought this incident worth recording, for use in a study of invention. As for the *equivalence* I mentioned, it is certainly one of the principal resources of the mind, offering it the most valuable substitutions.

* * *

This quirk of appreciating in the art of writing whatever leaves the majority of readers unmoved, indifferent, or bored, and of being repelled by precisely those qualities in a book that they enjoy, drew me further and further from the desire to rely in any way on the uncertain pleasure of others. I knew, moreover, from a chance early experience, that the magic of literature necessarily derives from "some misunderstanding," owing to the very nature of language, which often enables one to give more than one possesses; and sometimes to give a good deal less.

I was so afraid of being caught in this trap myself that for several years I placed a ban on the use in my notes, which were for myself alone, of a number of *words* . . . I shall not say which. If they came into my head, I tried to substitute an expression which said no more than I wanted to say. If I could not find one, I gave the words a symbol, to show that they were only temporary. To me they were *for external use only*. . . . By doing this I put bounds to literature, in some measure, by contrasting its means with those of thought working for itself. Generally speaking, literature requires that this work should be limited, halted at a certain point, and even, in the end, camouflaged. An author should try to make people believe that he could not treat his work in any other way. Flaubert was convinced that each idea can have but one form, which must be discovered or invented, and which one must struggle to attain. This fine theory is unfortunately quite meaningless. But it does no harm to follow it. An effort is never lost. Sisyphus was developing his muscles.

* * *

How delightful it is to live and work with no outward expectation or plan, without thinking of a goal set outside oneself, of a finished work, or an aim that can be expressed in a few words; without having to worry about producing an effect on somebody or about someone else's judgment, a consideration that inevitably leads one to do what, of oneself, one would not have done, and to be reticent on other matters: in short, to behave like the next man. The next man becomes your character: *The Man of Fame*.

"Time" cost me nothing, it did not count; so none was lost.

My friends could not understand this indifference to the future. Nothing came out of an existence that yet did not seem idle or divorced from the things of the mind. Nothing would have come from it had not circumstances beyond my control (as the Code naïvely puts it) done their task, which is to do everything. In my particular case they had to solve a rather difficult problem: how to turn into a professional writer an amateur of intellectual exercises pursued in a vacuum. I gave them a certain opportunity, however, in that I had once and for all committed to chance the direction of my exterior life. Events are unmanageable; moreover, the most triumphant success is only superficial; planning is illusory: what one thinks of as getting a good result requires the numberless conditions that constitute "reality." . . . My whole will tended outwards only in an attempt to preserve my inner freedom. What was I doing with it?

* * *

I think with regret of the time when I enjoyed that sovereign good—that liberty of the mind. My time was so easily divided between the hours devoted to a necessary occupation (one quite distinct, however, from my private undertakings) and those unrestricted hours whose worth was only whatever it was—the worth of an unending gambol in utter independence! The ideal aim of my thinking life seemed to me the attainment of such awareness of its own act and effort as to realize the invisible conditions and limits of its powers: hence I imagined myself as a swimmer, cut off from all that is solid, let loose in the fullness of the water, and surrounded by an absence of obstacles, who thus acquires a sense of the forms and limits of his strength, from the center of his defined powers to their farthest reach.

All I desired was the ability to act, not its exercise in the world.

*　*　*

I am afraid that metaphysics had little to do with my case. My early, and very short, practice of the art of verse had accustomed me to making use of words, and even "ideas," as means which have only passing values and are effective only by reason of their placing. I considered it idolatrous to isolate them from their everyday employment and to make difficulties about them when one was handling them familiarly. Metaphysics, however, compels one to linger on these footbridges of fortune. "What is Time?" it asks, as though everyone did not know perfectly well. The answers it provides are arrangements of words. I therefore thought it more . . . philosophical to be concerned, simply and immediately, with these arrangements. *Doing* then replaces a so-called *knowing*, and the *True* rises to the level of a well-applied rule.

It is terrible to say all this. But I could not bring myself to shoulder others' problems, and not to be surprised that they had not imagined mine. Am I, perhaps, too easily surprised? One day I was surprised that no one had ever thought of amusing himself by drawing up a conversion table of the various philosophic doctrines, thus permitting one to be translated into another. Again, I was once surprised at being unable to find another table: that of all the reflex actions ever observed. . . . I could write a whole treatise on my surprises, more than one of which would call into question myself and my actions.

To sum up, day by day a kind of "system" was taking shape in me, whose first principle was that it neither could nor should apply to anyone but myself. I do not know whether the word *Philosophy* can bear a sense exclusive of the individual and implying a structure of precepts and explanations that imposes itself and is independent of everyone. To my mind, on the contrary, a philosophy is a strictly personal matter, hence intransmissible, inalienable, *to which end it must be made independent of the sciences.* Science is of necessity transmissible, but I cannot conceive of a "system" of thought that is so, for thought is not confined to combining *common* elements or states.

* * *

I need hardly say that in those days I read very little. I began by taking a strong dislike to reading and even gave away my favorite books to various friends. Later on, when this crisis had passed, I had to buy some of the same books again. But I still read little, because what I look for in a book is only what in some way will aid or hinder my own activity. To remain passive, to believe in a story, etc. . . . costs very little; and great pleasure and relief from boredom can be obtained by this trifling expenditure. But the sort of awakening that follows absorbed reading is for me rather unpleasant. I am left with the impression of having been tricked, managed, treated like a sleeping man, the smallest incidents in whose dream cause him to live through absurdities, to suffer unbearable torments and raptures.

* * *

I lived like this for some years, as though the years were not passing, further and further removed from that state of mind in which the idea of having anything to do with the public can germinate. My thoughts came more and more to develop their own language, which I stripped as far as possible of all facile expressions, particularly of those which a solitary man, studying closely how to circumscribe and refine a problem, never uses.

If I occasionally pondered on the state of literature in an epoch that was changing rapidly around me, I concluded merely as an observer that in this new age whatever demanded even a moderate amount of application from the reader no longer existed, and that henceforward not one person in a million would be found to give a work the quantity and the quality of attention that would permit a hope of carrying him along very far with oneself, for whom it would be worth while to weigh one's words and to take that care and trouble with construction and arrangement by which alone a work becomes for its author an *instrument of the pleasure of perfecting*.

Now, rather serious anxieties came to disturb this apparently static existence, which neither took in nor gave out anything; moreover, a kind of weariness at its continuation on somewhat abstract lines became more marked; and, finally, the *unknowable* factor (age or some crucial moment of the body) coming into play, all the conditions were right for poetry to recover its power over me, should the occasion arise.

Those who had asked whether they might publish my old verses had had those scattered little poems copied and gathered together and had turned the collection over to me; I neither opened it nor had remembered their proposal. One day when I was tired and bored, chance (which does everything) arranged for this copy, which was lost among my papers, to rise to the disordered surface. I was in a black mood. No poems have ever come under a colder eye. They found in their author the one man who had made himself the least responsive to their effects. This hostile father turned the pages of the very slender volume of his complete poems and discovered nothing but grounds for rejoicing that he had retired from the game. If he did linger over a page, it was merely to think how weak most of the lines were: *he felt an indefinable desire to strengthen them, to remold their musical substance....* Here and there were some fairly well-turned lines which only threw the others into relief and spoiled the whole, for, *suddenly, unevenness in a work seemed to me the worst of evils....*

This observation was a seed. It did no more that day than pass into my mind—just long enough to deposit the imperceptible germ that, a little later, grew into a labor of several years.

Other observations induced me to ponder anew the old ideas I had formed of the poet's art; to clarify them; more often to sweep them away. I soon began to find pleasure in attempting to correct a few lines, without the shadow of a plan in this temporary little distraction, beyond that of affording myself a light, free task, consisting of an indefinite series of substitutions, to be taken up and laid down at will, into which one puts only a modest part of oneself. I must admit that it is not without precedent, while thus detachedly running over the keyboard of the mind, to light occasionally upon very felicitous harmonies.

* * *

I was playing with fire. My pastime was leading me in an unexpected direction. What is more common in love? A passing glance, congenial laughter—and the philosopher can already see the genius of the species aroused, and the liveliest consequences, leading from one act to another and from the first stirrings to the cradle.

But the paths of the mind are less well worn; no instinct

has mapped them. I was traveling toward poetry without knowing it, by the roundabout way of problems to be found in it or introduced into it (as into anything), the solution of which matters little in the practice of that art.

As I had not the least intention of taking up poetry again, I was completely free and could try the effect of a certain peculiar and private "method" I had evolved, or rather, which had evolved of itself from my observations, from my refusals, from niceties and analogies I had followed, from my real needs, from my strength and my weakness.

I shall mention only two points of this method, and I should certainly be hard put to it to explain it further. Here is the first: *As much consciousness as possible.* And here is the second: *Try by conscious will to achieve a few results similar to those interesting or usable ones which come to us (out of a hundred thousand random events) from mental chance.*

I scandalized several people a few years ago by saying that I would rather have composed a mediocre work in all lucidity than a brilliant masterpiece in a state of trance. . . . This is because brilliance leads me nowhere. All it provides is the opportunity for self-admiration. I am much more interested in producing a tiny spark of my own than in waiting for the random flashes of an uncertain thunderbolt.

At the time, however, there was no question of composing. If I held such strict opinions, it was not for the sake of establishing precepts and a discipline that I was not going to use; it was because I was mentally countering certain prejudices that had formerly offended me.

There was in those days an opinion, widely held, which is perhaps not entirely without substance. Many people—in fact, nearly everyone—thought rather vaguely that the analytical work of the intellect, the exercise of the will, and the precision to which thought is thereby committed were incompatible with a certain ingenuousness of source, a certain overflow of power, or graceful reverie, which are expected in poetry and which make it recognizable at its first words. It was said that abstract meditation on his art, a cultivation as rigorous as that of roses, could only harm a poet, since the chief and most alluring effect of his work should be to give an impression of a new and happily born condition which should, by surprise and pleasure, exempt the poem indefinitely from all ulterior criticism. Is it not a question of emitting a perfume so delicate or so strong that it would disarm and intoxicate the chemist, and force him perpetually to inhale with rapture the very substance he was about to analyze?

* * *

I did not care for this attitude. There are too many things on earth, still more in heaven, which require the sacrifice of our mind: life and death conspire to hinder or degrade all thought, for it seems to me that thought tends to act as though neither material needs nor passions nor fears nor anything human, anything sentimental, fleshly, or social could corrupt or alter its supreme function of differentiating itself from everything else—even from the man who thinks. All these are but means, pretexts, sources of mystery and proof, which stimulate and nourish *thought*, and answer or question it—for, in order that *there be light*, vibrating energy must strike upon bodies and be reflected from them.

From 1892 on, therefore, I could not bear to hear the state of poetry contrasted with the complete and sustained action of the intellect. This distinction is as crude as that said to exist between "sensibility" and "intelligence," two terms that are extremely difficult to define without retraction or contradiction, and which are distinctly divided only at school, where the famous contrast between the "mathematical" and the "intuitive" mind is developed *ad nauseam*, providing a theme for interminable dissertations and an inexhaustible source of didactic variations.

In fact, everything that concerns the mind is still expressed by very old words (such as "mind" itself) which through the ages have taken on a number of meanings none of which has a point of reference. These old words have grown up independently and unaware of each other, like English measurements, which have no common divisor. "Inspiration," "weight," "choice," "taking as a whole," etc. . . . these are our primal tools for analysis and notation. . . . The (hitherto) inevitable use of these confused terms, in research that aims at precision, often leads to astonishing conclusions, to purely verbal contrasts, etc. . . . But what are we to do?

I must apologize for having strayed toward another subject than my own. I was saying that I did not like any attempt to force me not to be my complete self, to divide myself against myself. My desire, on the contrary, was to work with my two hands. . . . Has anyone ever had the idea of persuading a musician that the long years he spends studying harmony and orchestration weaken his genius? Why subject the poet to the whim of a moment?

I must confess to an occasional twinge of envy when I think of a skilled musician grappling with a vast page of twenty staves, ordering his calculations of tempo and form on this ruled field, really able to *compose*, conceive, and handle both the whole and the detail of his undertaking, to move from one to the other and note their mutual dependence. To me his act seems sublime. Unfortunately, this kind of work is almost impossible in poetry, owing to the nature of language and to the habits of mind resulting from its permanent, practical function: we insist, for example, that a discourse should have only one meaning.

I remember being intoxicated by the mere idea of composition or construction; I could not imagine a work more admirable than the drama of a work's generation, as it stirs and brings into play all the higher powers at our command. I was only too keenly aware of the impotence of the greatest poets when faced with this problem of the organization of the whole, a problem that can by no means be reduced to a particular order of "ideas," or to a particular movement. . . . Neither passion, nor logic, nor the chronology of events or emotions suffices. I had reached the point of looking on their finest works as badly built monuments, easily disintegrating into wonders, divine fragments, single lines. The very admiration aroused by these priceless fragments worked on the remainder of the poem like acid on a mineral ore and destroyed the *wholeness* of the work: but for me that *wholeness* was everything.

* * *

It can be seen that preoccupation with outer effect was subordinated in my view to preoccupation with "inner work." What is called the "content" or "matter" of a work, which I prefer to call its "mythical" part or, rather, aspect, was of secondary importance to me. In the same way as, for purposes of demonstration, one takes a particular case "to fix one's ideas," so, according to my taste for speculation, should one do with "subjects." I meant to reduce *idolatry* to the minimum.

In short, I worked out a sort of definition of "great art" that defied all practice! This ideal imperiously demanded that the act of production be a complete act, which even in the most trivial work should give the sense of control over the abundance of the warring powers within us: on the one hand, those which might be termed "transcendent" or "irrational," such as "causeless" evaluations, unexpected interventions, raptures, sudden flashes of insight—everything by which we become for ourselves mines of astonishment, sources of spontaneous problems, of questions without answers, or answers without questions; everything that makes our hopes "creative," our fears, too, and peoples our sleep with the rarest combinations, which can be produced in us only in our absence. . . . On the other hand, our powers of "logic," our feeling for the preservation of conventions and relations, a feeling that proceeds in its working without skipping a single step, a single moment of the transformation that develops from one equilibrium to another, and finally our will to co-ordinate, to foresee by the processes of reason the properties of the system we intend to construct—everything that is "rational."

* * *

It is always very difficult, however, to combine considered and "conservative" work with the spontaneous forms that spring from the sensuous and affective life (like the shapes formed by sand shaken on a tightly stretched membrane) and that possess the faculty of propagating states and emotions but not that of communicating ideas.

While I gave myself up with considerable pleasure to reflections of this kind and found in poetry a subject for infinite inquiries, that very self-awareness which led me to do so made it clear to me that, however profoundly or ardently one may pursue it within oneself, speculation that does not produce works or acts to support it is too pleasant not to become a near temptation to facility under the guise of abstraction. I noticed that what interested me from now on in the art of poetry was how much of the mind it seemed capable of engaging, stimulating it all the more as one formed a deeper conception of that art. I saw no less clearly that all this expense of analysis could have a meaning and a value only if linked with practice and production. But the difficulties of execution grew with the precision and diversity of the requirements I liked to imagine, while the attainment of success would necessarily remain arbitrary.

Moreover, I had become too attached to much wider researches. Poetry, at least certain poetic works, had captivated me. Its aim seemed to me to be *enchantment*. I placed this feeling of generalized rapture at the opposite pole from everything intended and performed by prose. . . . It was the remoteness from man which ravished me. I did not know why an author should be praised for being human when everything that exalts man is inhuman, or superhuman, and when, furthermore, one cannot increase one's knowledge or acquire any power without first divesting oneself of the confusion of values, of the mediocre and muddled view of things, of expedient wisdom—in a word, of everything that results from our statistical relations with our fellows and from our necessary, and necessarily impure, commerce with the monotonous disorder of external life.

* * *

After some months of reflection, toward the end of my twenty-first year, I felt free of any desire to write verse, and I deliberately broke with poetry, which nevertheless had given me the feeling of a treasure of mysterious worth, and had instilled in me the worship of a few marvels very different from those the schools and the world taught one to admire. . . . I was glad that what I loved was not loved by those who delight in talking of what they love. I liked to hide what I loved. It did me good to have a secret, which I carried within me like a conviction and like a seed. But seeds of this kind nourish their carrier, instead of being nourished by him. And conviction protects its possessor from the opinions around him, from printed observations and communicable beliefs.

But, in fact, poetry is not a private cult: poetry is literature. In spite of all we can do, and whether we will or not, literature comprises a sort of politics and competitiveness, numerous idols, a devilish combination of priest and tradesman, of intimacy and publicity, indeed, of everything needed to frustrate its first-born aims, which are generally very remote from all this, being noble, delicate, and profound. The literary atmosphere is hardly favorable to the cultivation of the enchantment I was speaking of: it consists of vain contentions and is troubled by the same ambitions, lures, and impulses that fight for the surface of the public mind. This urgent thirst, these passions, are not conducive to the slow formation of works, nor to their meditation by desirable persons whose attention is the author's only reward, if he attaches no price to crude and impertinent admiration. I thought I had occasionally observed that art is the more skillful and subtle as man is socially more naïve, more careless of what happens and of what is said. It was undoubtedly only in the Far and Middle East and in some medieval cloisters that one could really dwell in the way of poetic perfection unalloyed.

On this point I shall conclude with two observations that may perhaps illustrate the difference to be seen, if one will, between Literature and Letters.

* * *

Literature is perpetually in the throes of an activity very like that of the stock exchange. The talk is of nothing but "values," which open, rise, or fall as though they could be compared with each other, as completely differing industries and businesses can be, on the stock exchange, once they are represented by symbols. As a result, it is the persons or the names, the speculations built on them, and the rank attributed to them which cause all the excitement on this market, not the works themselves, which to my mind should be considered in complete isolation from each other and without reference to their authors. Anonymity would be the paradoxical condition that a spiritual dictator would impose on Letters. "When all is said and done," he would say, "one has no name in oneself.... No one in himself is *So-and-so!*"

Another consequence of this state of literary affairs, which forces them into rivalry and into the absurdity of *comparing the incomparable* (which requires both products and producers to be expressed in simple, almost homogeneous terms) is this: each newcomer feels obliged to try to *do something else*, forgetting that if he himself is *someone*, he will necessarily do that *something else*. This demand for novelty leads to ruin, since, to begin with, it creates a kind of automatism. *Counter-imitation* has become a very real reflex. Works are made subject not to the state of mind of their author but to that of his surroundings. But, as with all effects of shock, reaction sets in very quickly; in fifty years I have seen the rise of innumerable novelties, the flash of creations *a contrario*, now swallowed up by others and claimed by oblivion. If anything from them survived, it was a result of qualities quite unconnected with the desire for novelty. The rapid succession of quests for the new at all costs leads to a real exhaustion of the resources of art. Boldness of ideas, of language, even of form, is valuable; it is indispensable to the solution of the problems an artist finds in himself. If he has it, he is an innovator without being aware of it. It is the *rule of being bold* that is detestable. It has a dangerous effect on the public, in whom it inculcates first the need for shock and then boredom with it, while giving birth to facile amateurs who admire everything put before them so long as they can be sure they are the first to admire.

Besides, the number of combinations is not infinite; if one were to amuse oneself by compiling a history of all the surprises invented in the course of a century and of the works produced to provoke amazement—either by oddities, systematic deviations, and *anamorphoses*, or by violences of language, or by the enormity of their confessions—one could easily draw up a table of complete or partial aberrations which would reveal a curiously symmetrical distribution of the means of being original.

* * *

To return invincibly, but by such small degrees and such varied details that one perceives it only after a long time, to a state of mind one thought had vanished forever, produces a strange impression.

One day I discovered that I had been insensibly led back, by the most fortuitous and disparate circumstances, into a region of the mind that I had abandoned, even fled from. It was as though, having fled from a place—the form of space being such that the farthest point from that place was the place itself—one were suddenly there again, and should find oneself, with great surprise, still the same and yet quite different.

I had fled from the innocent state of poetry, and I had

deliberately cultivated a side of myself which by general consent is looked on as the most antagonistic to the life and fruits of that state.

But perhaps the universe of the mind has its own curve, about which, if it exists, we know and can know nothing. I have observed, with regard to other matters of the mind, that if sometimes we can reach our antipodes, we can then do little else but come back from them. It is no longer a "question of time," for each new change can only lead us nearer to our beginning. I am inclined to think that, on condition that his mind remained fairly active, a man living to a great age would, toward the end of his periplus, have made the full circle of his feelings and, having at last adored and burnt, burnt and adored everything in his sphere of consciousness that deserved it, he could die fulfilled. I conclude that in general we see, and are, only fragments of existence, and that our actual life does not fulfill all its capacity of what it is possible for us to feel and conceive. Consequently when we impute tastes, opinions, beliefs, or negations to someone, we are accentuating only a certain aspect of him, the one hitherto revealed by circumstances, which, though it exists, is and cannot help but be liable to change—and even *must be so*, for the simple reason that it exists. This "sufficient reason" is essential: *the mind*, in what makes it most a mind, *absolutely can not repeat itself.* What is repeated in it is no longer itself: the same is true of its substance; it has gone where the first attempts of our hand went when we were learning to write. Whatever merges gradually into our functions and material powers ceases to be noticeable in ceasing to be *without a past.* For this reason every conscious recapture of an idea renews it, and modifies, enriches, simplifies, or destroys what is recaptured; and even if, on its recurrence, we find nothing to alter in what has once been thought, the very judgment approving and conserving a particular acquisition thereby makes up an event which has never before occurred, an original fact.

*   *   *

So there I was, once more toying with syllables and images, similes and contrasts. The forms and words proper to poetry became once more quickened and frequent in my mind; now and then I forgot to expect those remarkable groupings of terms which suddenly offer us a felicitous arrangement forming of itself in the troubled current of things of the mind. As a distinct compound is precipitated from a mixture, so an interesting *figure* detaches itself from the disorder, vagueness, or mediocrity of our interior flounderings.

It is a pure sound ringing out above mere noise. It is a perfectly executed fragment of a nonexistent building. It is a chip of diamond protruding from a mass of "blue earth": a moment infinitely more precious than any other, more precious even than the circumstances that engender it! It gives rise to an incomparable satisfaction and also to an immediate temptation: it leads one to hope that *in its neighborhood* one will find the treasure of which it is both the sign and the proof; and this hope sometimes leads a man into a labor that may be endless.

Many believe that at this moment a heaven opens, letting fall a special ray, which lights up simultaneously ideas hitherto unconnected and, as it were, ignorant of one another; all at once they are miraculously united and as though made for each other from all eternity; and all this happens without direct preparation, without labor, through the fortunate workings of illumination and certainty. . . .

But fate wills that it is often a naïveté, an error, a stupidity that is thus revealed to us. We must not count only the lucky chances: this miraculous method of production by no means ensures the worth of what is produced. The spirit blows where it will; one sees it blow on fools, and it whispers to them what they are able to hear.

*　*　*

As I pondered all this at leisure, wondering what particularly pleased me in imagining the poetic order of things, I thought of a certain purity of form and so came back to my feelings about inequalities in a work, which displease and even irritate me, perhaps more than they should. What is more impure than the very frequent mixture of the excellent and the mediocre?

Doubtless I find so few reasons for *writing* that even so much as to begin, and not to be content with the sensations and ideas one exchanges with oneself, one must look on *writing* as a problem, be seized with curiosity about form, and spur oneself on to some perfection. Everyone can define his own—some following a model, others following reasons of their own: the main thing is to oppose thought, to arouse resistance to it, and to prepare for freeing oneself from a confused arbitrariness by means of an explicit and well-defined arbitrariness. Thus one has the illusion of proceeding toward the formation of an "object" with its own consistency, very clearly separated from its author.

It is strange that one cannot obtain this continuity and equality or this completeness, which for me are the conditions of an unmixed pleasure and which should comprehend all other qualities of a work, without a necessarily *discontinuous* labor. Art is antagonistic to the mind. Our mind does not care what the matter is: it takes in everything; it gives out everything. It literally lives on incoherence; it moves only by leaps and is subject to, or makes, vast digressions which continually break any line that begins to form. It is only by repeated efforts that it can collect into a uniform substance, outside itself, the elements of its own activity, selected to adjust themselves gradually and conduce to a unity of composition. . . .

* * *

I was quite free to speculate thus and not to tolerate what attracts and holds the majority of those who love poetry. The time came for me to take it up again; I had to pass from theory to practice.

The Prince and *La Jeune Parque*

I KNOW not by what mysterious revival, by what return to my youth, I came back to being interested in poetry more than twenty years after I had broken with it.

Perhaps there is in us a slow, periodic memory, deeper than the memory of impressions and objects, a long-term memory or echo of ourselves which carries us back and unexpectedly restores to us our former inclinations, powers, and even hopes of long ago.

I perceived that I was again becoming sensitive to the ring of language. I lingered to catch the music of speech. The words I heard touched off in me some kind of harmonic relations and the hidden presence of imminent rhythms. Syllables took on color. Certain turns and forms of speech sometimes appeared of themselves on the frontiers of the mind and voice, and seemed to demand life.

These preludes to the state of song, these intimate springtimes of expressive invention are delightful, as is the preliminary stammering of an orchestra just before it forms and gathers itself for obedience, and when it is still giving out only a lively and confused variety of exploratory tones, which become bolder, interrupt and contradict each other, and, in their separate ways, prepare for their miraculous unity to come.

I gradually became trained and accustomed to reliving my adolescence. I caught myself versifying. I rediscovered in myself the anxieties and cares of the poet. I took pleasure in offering no resistance. I confess that I was tired of having debated certain very difficult problems for so long. My mind, occupied with certain subjects it had set itself, which were not easy to get rid of by exhausting them, found itself caught in a vicious circle; it traveled endlessly through the same complementary states of light and shadow, power and impotence.

But when I set myself once more to poetry, this state of mind did not leave me; and I was not slow to recognize many problems and enigmas of an abstract nature in the first flowers of my renewed season. One can find them anywhere, and poetry is not exempt; it is a question of demands. After the pleasure of the first few strokes and the promise of fine things as yet only glimpsed, after being charmed by those divine murmurings of an inner voice, and when a few pure fragments have already, of themselves, emerged from what does not yet exist, one must set to work, give these murmurs speech, join these fragments, query the whole intellect, search one's mind, and—wait. . . .

I began the work. My scheme was to compose a kind of discourse in which the sequence of lines would be so developed or deduced that the whole of the poem would give an impression like that of the *recitatives* of former times. Those which are to be found in Gluck, particularly in his *Alceste*, had given me much to think about. I coveted their pace.

I soon stumbled against perennial difficulties. After spending nearly a whole day in making, unmaking, and remaking a part of my poem, I was seized with that despairing disgust of it known to all artists. The artist would be nothing if he were not the plaything of what he does. I decided to give up the struggle; I convinced myself that it must be abandoned; and wishing to break by action the sad spell which bound me to my unfinished work, I forced myself to go out. I walked furiously through the streets, half dazzled by the confusion of lights, and I wandered, like a thought suddenly tossed into the tumult of the City, troubled by the movement of people and shadows, voluntarily mingling with the vague, general agitation of the evening crowd. I felt that I was still held and at moments obsessed, in the midst of all those human beings in movement, by the same attempts and rejections I had just fled and whose torment I was trying to annul among that multitude of strangers. I was like a bad mother who wanders far from home in order to lose a child she cannot stand.

After walking for a long time, I entered a deserted café. Newspapers lay about on the marble tables. I glanced idly over the whole world, the incoherence of its events under various skies replacing in my mind the chaotic crowd in the street. Leaving the crimes, the parliaments, the stock exchanges, and the news, all of them statistically always the same, my eyes lighted near the bottom of a page of *Le Temps*.

I am not very fond of premonitions; I am disinclined to believe in those mysterious attractions by which people are pleased to explain so many of the remarkable coincidences observable in all lives, and which modify or direct them with a kind of intelligence. But something made me linger over this copy of the paper and feel that I should find some precious material there. I glanced at Adolphe Brisson's column. . . . I read. I reread. I *saw* my way.

It was a summer article. The theatres being closed, the critic bereft of his prey had taken the tragedienne Rachel as the subject of his article for the day.

Here is how it began:

How did this artist compose and play her roles? What were her methods, her manner, her mime, the tone of her voice, her way of moving and of wearing her costumes? Rachel does not appear very alive when seen through the lyric prose of Gautier and the diffuse prose of Janin; their judgments give a general impression of her acting, but they are sometimes contradictory: they lack detail. What we should like is a vigorous and sincere analysis, with detailed, meticulous indications which would fix these fleeting things: the actress's physiognomy, the emotions aroused in those who heard her. Well, such a document exists. A rather strange circumstance put it into my hands. During a stay at Ems, not long ago, I had the honor of being presented to an important personage allied to the Prussian royal family, Prince George, a second cousin of the Emperor William I. He talked to me about Rachel, with whom—as I guessed from his confidences—he had obviously been in love. He retained incredibly faithful impressions and recollections of her, her intonations, attitudes, and gestures. Anxious that these should not be lost, he had applied himself to putting them down on paper. He gave me a copy of this anonymous pamphlet printed for his friends. This valuable little work contains a line-by-line commentary, a photographic description, a musical notation—the minutes, one might almost say, of the famous artist's interpretations. The first page is a hymn in her honor, and is also a portrait.

"Rachel! incomparable genius, sublime artist, you will remain in our memory like a flame in a dark night. Sobriety, energy, and grace of gesture, a magical glance, purity of diction, the deep metallic tone of an unequaled voice—all were hers, everything that charms, seduces, exalts. To see Rachel was one of the great emotions of life. She was pale and slender, she had every mark of being very delicate. Her hands were extremely distinguished; her brilliant brown eyes were of unexampled depth. Her contralto voice sank to F in this line from *Bajazet*:

"*N'aurais-je tout tenté que pour une rivale?*

"*Que* was uttered on F below middle C, then her voice rose. When she said, in *Andromaque*:

"*Va, cours, mais crains encor d'y trouver Hermione,*

cours was spoken on C above middle C with great force. The cry she uttered in the fifth act of *Adrienne Lecouvreur*, compared to the lines from *Andromaque*, was on F four notes higher. She thus had a range of two octaves.

"Usually, when speaking, she remained in the register between F sharp and E natural. In *Valéria*, a drama by Auguste Maquet and Jules Lacroix, she played the part of the Empress Messalina in a low voice, and that of Lycisca in a higher voice. Without being so, she appeared very tall on the stage. Her nervous tension was communicated to the audience; one shuddered in following these moving scenes; it often seemed as though the force of emotion would break her. Whoever saw her in *Marie Stuart* will certainly remember the terrible, savage energy with which she said:

"*Malheur, malheur à vous, quand, d'une vie austère*
Vous venant quelque jour arracher le manteau,
La Vérité sur vous fait luire son flambeau!

"The word *arracher* was pronounced with incredible fury. She was beside herself, trembling with rage. No other actress has knelt before Queen Elizabeth with the same proud inflexibility. I can still see her in the fifth act of *Marie Stuart*, with her beautiful black velvet costume, her historic white bonnet, whose point touched her forehead, her long white veil, and her old lace."

The prince mentions the most insignificant details of Rachel's diction; he appraises the length of her silence; he notes her "breathings."

"*Je voudrais assister à ta dernière aurore,*
Voir sombrer dans les flots ton sanglant météore,
(Deep breath)
Et seule
(Breath) *au bord des mers*
　　　　　　(Breath) *respirer la fraîcheur*
(Breath)
De l'éternelle nuit.

"She filled her lungs deeply before speaking, like a person at the edge of the sea giving herself up with joy to the freshness of the element. It was admirable."

Etc.

* * *

I cannot explain how much I was touched by reading this. The naïve, precise remarks of the German prince, the loving attention he had concentrated on the great artist's diction, the feeling for verse, the understanding of the relation between breathing, rhythm, syntax, and accentuation, all I found there interested me directly, enlightened me indirectly, and brought me the help I wanted at the very moment it was needed and by the most unexpected channel. . . . When I think of this, I think of an incident which took place in Rome in the sixteenth century, and which is related somewhere or other. In the presence of the Pope and his whole Court, the obelisk in St. Peter's Square was being erected. The machines were ill-adjusted, and the monolith came to a halt in its movement between the horizontal and the vertical. The cables, stretched to the uttermost, threatened to break and let the mass fall and be shattered on the ground. At that moment a voice arose from the great silence imposed on pain of death and cried, "Wet the ropes!" and an idea set the stone upright. . . .

Adolphe Brisson's article and Prince George of Hohenzollern's note so opportunely arriving to suggest a solution to my poetic difficulties might be thought, even by myself, to be no more than a *subjective event*—that is, practically independent of the quality of the writing and almost entirely dependent on my state of mind on a particular evening. But it happened that several years later, my work being finished or nearly so, I showed it to Pierre Louÿs, an excellent judge of poetry, and at the same time I told him this little story. Pierre gave an exclamation and, hastening to the files where he kept a mass of documents, pulled out a large cutting of the article in *Le Temps* of December 1, 1913, marked, bordered, and underlined with red pencil. . . .

Concerning *Le Cimetière marin*

I DO not know whether it is still the fashion to elaborate poems at length, to keep them between being and nonbeing, suspended for years in the presence of desire; to nourish doubts, scruples, and regrets—so that a work perpetually resumed and recast gradually takes on the secret importance of an exercise in self-reform.

This way of producing little was not uncommon among poets and some prose writers forty years ago. For them, time did not count; in that, they were rather like gods. Neither the Idol of Beauty nor the superstition of Literary Eternity had yet been destroyed; and belief in Posterity was not entirely abolished. There existed a kind of *Ethic of Form* that led to infinite labor. Those who devoted themselves to it well knew that the greater the labor, the fewer the people who understand and appreciate it; they toiled for very little—and, as it were, holily....

Thus one moves away from the "natural" or ingenuous conditions of literature and comes little by little to confuse the composition of a work of the mind, which is a *finished* thing, with the very life of the mind—which is a power of transformation always in action. One ends by working for work's sake. In the eyes of these lovers of anxiety and perfection, a work is never *complete*—a word which to them is meaningless—but *abandoned;* and this abandonment, which delivers the work to the flames or to the public (whether it be the result of weariness or the necessity of delivering), is for them a kind of *accident* comparable to the interruption of a thought annulled by fatigue, an importunate person, or some sensation.

* * *

I had contracted this sickness, this perverse taste for endless revision, and this indulgence in the reversible state of works at the critical age when the intellectual man is formed and fixed. I rediscovered them in their full force when, toward the age of fifty, circumstances led me to start composing once more. I have therefore lived a good deal with my poems. For nearly ten years they were for me an undertaking of indeterminate duration—an exercise rather than an act, a search rather than a deliverance, a maneuver of myself by myself rather than a preparation intended for the public. It seems to me that they have taught me several things.

However, I do not advise the adoption of this system: I am not qualified to give anyone the slightest advice, and besides I doubt whether it would suit the young men of an urgent, confused time with no outlook. We are in a fog bank....

If I have mentioned this long intimacy between a work and a "self," it is merely in order to give some idea of the strange sensation I experienced one morning at the Sorbonne on hearing M. Gustave Cohen develop *ex cathedra* an explication of *Le Cimetière marin.*

* * *

What I have published has never lacked commentaries, and I cannot complain of the least silence about my few writings.

I am used to being elucidated, dissected, impoverished, enriched, exalted, and cast down—to the point of no longer knowing myself *what* I am or *who* is in question: but reading what has been written about you is as nothing to the peculiar sensation of hearing yourself commented on at the University in front of the blackboard, just like a dead author.

In my day the living did not exist for the professorial chair; but I do not find it entirely a bad thing that this should no longer be so.

The teaching of literature takes from it what the teaching of History might take from the analysis of the present—that is, the suspicion or the awareness of the *forces* that engender acts and forms. The past is only the *place* of forms without force; it is for us to provide it with life and necessity and to credit it with our passions and values.

* * *

I felt as though I were my own *shadow*. . . . I felt like a shadow taken captive, and yet I sometimes identified myself with one of the students who listened, made notes, and from time to time looked smilingly at the shadow whose poem their teacher was reading and commenting on stanza by stanza. . . .

I confess that *as a student* I discovered in myself little reverence for the poet—isolated, exposed, and embarrassed on his bench. My presence was oddly divided among several ways of being there.

* * *

Among the variety of sensations and reflections that made up this hour at the Sorbonne, the dominant one was indeed the sensation of the contrast between the memory of my toil, which was revived, and the finished figure, the determinate, fixed work to which M. Gustave Cohen applied his exegesis and analysis. This made me aware how our *being* is in opposition to our *seeming*. On the one hand was my poem, studied as an accomplished fact, revealing to expert examination its composition, intentions, modes of action, its place in the system of literary history, its affiliations, and its author's probable state of mind. . . . On the other hand was the memory of my attempts, my gropings, inner decipherings, those imperious verbal illuminations which suddenly impose a particular combination of words—as though a certain group possessed some kind of intrinsic power. . . . I nearly said: some kind of *will* to live, quite the opposite of the "freedom" or chaos of the mind, a will that can sometimes force the mind to deviate from its plan and the poem to become quite other than what it was going to be and something one did not dream it could be.

(One can see by this that the notion of an *Author* is not simple: it is so only *in the eyes of a third person*.)

*   *   *

As I listened to M. Cohen reading the stanzas of my text and giving to each its finished meaning and its right place in the development, I was divided between satisfaction at seeing how the aims and expressions of a poem reputedly very obscure were here perfectly understood and set forth and the odd, almost painful feeling to which I have just referred. I shall try to explain this briefly so as to complete the commentary of a particular poem considered as a *fact*, by a glance at the circumstances that accompanied the generation of that poem, or of what it was when it was within me in a state of desire and seeking.

Incidentally, I intrude only to introduce, by means (or by

the digression) of a special case, a few remarks on the relationship between a poet and his poem.

* * *

It must first be said that the *Cimetière marin, as it stands*, is *for me* the result of the *intersection* of an inner labor and a fortuitous event. One afternoon in the year 1920, our much regretted friend Jacques Rivière, coming to call on me, found me at one "stage" of my *Cimetière marin*, thinking of revising, suppressing, substituting, altering here and there. . . .

He did not rest until he was allowed to read it and, having read it, until he could snatch it away. Nothing is more decisive than the mind of an editor of a review.

Thus it was *by accident* that the form of this work was fixed. It was none of my doing. Moreover, in general I cannot go back over anything I have written without thinking that I should now make something quite different of it, if some outside intervention or some circumstance had not broken the enchantment of never finishing with it. I enjoy work only as work: beginnings bore me, and I suspect everything that comes at the first attempt of being capable of improvement. Spontaneity, even when excellent or seductive, has never seemed to me sufficiently *mine*. I do not say that "I am right," but that that is how I am. . . . The notion of Myself is no simpler than that of Author: a further degree of consciousness opposes a new *Self* to a new *Other*.

* * *

Literature, then, interests me *profoundly* only to the extent to which it urges the mind to certain transformations—those in which the stimulating properties of language play the chief part. I can, indeed, take a liking for a book, read and reread it with delight; but it never possesses me wholly unless I find in it traces of a thought *whose power is equal to that of language itself*. The force to bend the common word to unexpected ends without violating the "time-honored forms," the capture and subjection of things that are difficult to say, and above all the simultaneous management of syntax, harmony, and ideas (which is the problem of the purest poetry) are in my eyes the supreme objects of our art.

* * *

This way of feeling is perhaps shocking. It makes of "creation" a means. It leads to excesses. Further, it tends to corrupt the innocent pleasure of *believing*, which engenders the innocent pleasure of producing and puts up with any kind of reading.

If the author knows himself rather too well, if the reader is active, what becomes of pleasure, what becomes of literature?

* * *

This glimpse of the difficulties that may arise between the "consciousness of self" and the habit of writing will no doubt explain certain *biases* with which I have sometimes been reproached. I have, for instance, been blamed for having published several, perhaps even contradictory, texts of the same poem. This reproach is barely intelligible to me, as might be expected after what I have just explained. On the contrary, I should be tempted (if I followed my inclinations) to engage poets to produce, like musicians, a diversity of variants or solutions of the same subject. Nothing would seem to me more consistent with the idea I like to hold of a poet and of poetry.

* * *

To my mind the poet is known by his idols and his liberties, which are not those of the majority. Poetry is distinguished from prose by having neither all the same restraints nor all the same licenses. The essence of prose is to perish—that is, to be "understood"—that is, to be dissolved, destroyed without return, entirely replaced by the image or the impulse that it conveys according to the convention of language. For prose always implies the universe of experiences and acts, a universe in which—or *thanks to which*—our perceptions and our acts or emotions have finally to correspond or answer each other in a single way—*uniformly*. The practical universe is reduced to a collection of *aims*. An aim being reached, the word expires. That universe excludes ambiguity, eliminates it; it demands that one should proceed by the shortest way, and it stifles as soon as possible the harmonics of each event that occurs in the mind.

* * *

But poetry requires or suggests a very different "Universe": a universe of reciprocal relations analogous to the universe of sounds within which musical thought is born and moves. In this poetic universe, resonance triumphs over causality, and "form," far from dissolving into its effects, is as it were *recalled* by them. The Idea claims its voice.

(The result is an *extreme* difference between the moments of constructing prose and the moments of creating poetry.)

In the same way, in the art of the Dance, the state of the dancer (or that of the lover of ballet) being the object of that art, the movements and displacements of the bodies have no limit in *space*—no visible aim, no *thing* which, being reached, annuls them; and it never occurs to anyone to impose on choreographic actions the law of *nonpoetic* but *useful* acts, which is: to be accomplished *with the greatest possible economy of effort* and *in the shortest possible way*.

* * *

This comparison may give the impression that neither simplicity nor clarity is an absolute in poetry, where it is perfectly *reasonable*—and even necessary—to maintain oneself in a condition as remote as possible from that of prose, at the cost of losing (without too many regrets) as many readers as one must.

* * *

Voltaire said most felicitously that "Poetry is made up of nothing but beautiful details." I am saying no more than precisely that. The poetic universe of which I was speaking arises from the number, or rather from the density, of images, figures, consonances, dissonances, from the linking of turns of speech and rhythms—the essential being constantly to avoid anything that would lead back to prose, either by making it regretted or by following the *idea* exclusively. . . .

In short, the more a poem conforms to Poetry, the less it can be thought in prose without perishing. To summarize a poem or put it into prose is quite simply to misunderstand the essence of an art. Poetic necessity is inseparable from material form, and the thoughts uttered or suggested by the text of a poem are by no means the unique and chief objects of its discourse—but *means* which combine *equally* with the sounds, cadences, meter, and ornaments to produce and sustain a particular tension or exaltation, to engender within us a *world*, or *mode of existence*, of complete harmony.

* * *

If I am questioned; if anyone wonders (as happens sometimes quite peremptorily) what I "wanted to say" in a certain poem,

I reply that I did not *want to say* but *wanted to make*, and that it was the intention of *making* which *wanted* what I *said....*

As for the *Cimetière marin*, this intention was at first no more than a rhythmic figure, empty, or filled with meaningless syllables, which obsessed me for some time. I noticed that this figure was decasyllabic, and I pondered on that model, which is very little used in modern French poetry; it struck me as poor and monotonous. It was of little worth compared with the alexandrine, which three or four generations of great artists had prodigiously elaborated. The demon of generalization prompted me to try raising this *Ten* to the power of *Twelve*. It suggested a certain stanza of six lines, and the idea of a *composition* founded on the number of these stanzas and strengthened by a diversity of tones and functions to be assigned to them. Between the stanzas, contrasts or correspondences would be set up. This last condition soon required the potential poem to be a monologue of "self," in which the simplest and most enduring themes of my affective and intellectual life, as they had imposed themselves upon my adolescence, associated with the sea and the light of a particular spot on the Mediterranean coast, were called up, woven together, opposed.... All this led to the theme of death and suggested the theme of pure thought. (The chosen line of ten syllables bears some relation to the Dantesque line.)

My line had to be solid and strongly rhythmical. I knew I was tending toward a monologue as personal, but also as universal, as I could make it. The type of line chosen, and the form adopted for the stanzas, set me conditions that favored certain "movements," permitted certain changes of tone, called up a certain style.... The *Cimetière marin* was *conceived.* A rather long period of gestation ensued.

* * *

Whenever I think of the art of writing (in verse or in prose), the same "ideal" presents itself to my mind. The myth of "creation" lures us into wanting to make something from nothing. So I imagine that I discover my work little by little, beginning with pure conditions of form, more and more considered, defined to the point where they propose, or almost impose, a *subject*—or at least kinds of subject.

Note that precise conditions of form are nothing but the expression of the knowledge and consciousness we have of the *means* at hand, their capabilities, their limitations, and their defects. This is why I sometimes define the *writer* by a relationship between a particular "mind" and Language. . . .

But I know the illusory character of my "Ideal." The nature of language hardly lends itself to sustained combinations; moreover, the formation and habits of the modern reader, to whom his accustomed pabulum of incoherence and immediate effects renders imperceptible all concern for structure, hardly encourage one to wander so far from him. . . .

Yet the sole thought of constructions of this kind remains for me the most *poetic* of ideas: the idea of composition.

* * *

I pause on this word. . . . It would lead me into all kinds of diffuseness. Nothing in poets has more amazed me, or caused me more regret, than the little study they have given to composition. In the most famous lyrics I find almost nothing but developments that are purely linear, or . . . delirious—that is, which proceed bit by bit with no more sustained organization than is shown by a flame following a trail of powder. (I am not speaking of poems dominated by a story, where the chronology of events intervenes: these are mixed works— operas, not sonatas or symphonies.)

But my astonishment lasts only until I remember my own experiences and the almost discouraging difficulties I have met in my attempts to *compose* in the lyric order. The fact is that detail is here essential at each moment, and the cleverest and most beautiful scheme must come to terms with the uncertainty of discoveries. In the lyric universe each moment must consummate an indefinable alliance between the perceptible and the significant. The result is that, in some way, composition is continuous and can hardly withdraw into another time than that of execution. There is not one time for the "content" and another for the "form"; and composition in this *genre* is not only opposed to disorder or disproportion but also to *decomposition*. If the meaning and the sound (or the content and the form) can easily be dissociated, the poem *decomposes*.

Important result: the "ideas" that figure in a poetic work do not play the same part, are not at all *currency of the same kind*, as the ideas in prose.

* * *

I said that the *Cimetière marin* first came into my head in the shape of a composition in stanzas of six lines of ten syllables. This decision enabled me fairly easily to distribute through my work the perceptible, affective, and abstract content it needed so as to suggest a meditation by a particular *self*, translated into the poetic universe.

The necessity of producing contrasts, and of maintaining a kind of balance between the different moments of this *self*, led me (for example) to introduce at one point a certain touch of philosophy. The lines in which the famous arguments of Zeno of Elea appear (though here animated, confused, carried away in a burst of dialectic, like a whole rigging by a sudden gust of wind) have the role of offsetting by a metaphysical tonality the sensual and "too human" part of the preceding stanzas; also, they define more precisely *the person who is speaking*, a lover of abstractions; finally, they oppose to what in him was speculative and far too searching, the actual reflex power whose jerk breaks and dispels a state of somber fixity which is, as it were, complementary to the prevailing splendor —at the same time upsetting a mass of judgments on all human, inhuman, and superhuman things. I have corrupted those few images from Zeno to express the rebellion against the length and painfulness of a meditation that makes too cruelly felt the gap between *being* and *knowing* that is developed by the consciousness of consciousness. Naïvely, the *soul* wishes to exhaust the Eleatic's infinity.

But I meant no more than to borrow a little of the *color* of philosophy.

* * *

The various foregoing remarks may give some idea of an author's reflections when he is faced by a commentary on his work. He sees in the work what it should have been and what it could have been, rather than what it is. What, then, is more interesting to him than the result of a scrupulous examination and the impression of another's eye? It is not within myself that the real unity of my work is found. I wrote a "score"— but I can hear it performed only by the soul and mind of others.

This is why M. Cohen's work (leaving aside the far too amiable things in it about me) is particularly precious to me. He has sought my aims with remarkable care and method and has applied to a contemporary text the same learning and the same precision that he is in the habit of showing in his scholarly studies in literary history. He has with equal skill retraced the poem's architecture and called attention to its detail—noticing, for example, those recurrent terms which reveal the tendencies and characteristic repetitions of a mind. (Certain words above all others sound within us, like overtones of our deepest nature. . . .) Finally, I am very grateful to him for having so lucidly explained me to the young people who are his students.

As for the interpretation of the *letter*, I have already made myself clear elsewhere on this point; but it can never be too much insisted upon: *there is no true meaning to a text*—no author's authority. Whatever he may have *wanted to say*, he has written what he has written. Once published, a text is like an apparatus that anyone may use as he will and according to his ability: it is not certain that the one who constructed it can use it better than another. Besides, if he knows well what he meant to do, this knowledge always disturbs his perception of what he has done.

Commentaries on *Charmes*

A CERTAIN Amateur of Letters had, one day, the imprudence (which was a happy one) to entrust Alain with a very beautiful copy of a particular collection of poems. This volume had rather wide margins and its text much freedom for interpretation. *Charmes*, which was the book in question, divides its readers. It is well known that some see nothing in it; and that it is only too lucid for others, who judge it insipid by reason of the simplicity they find in it, once the futile defenses of expression are breached. Still others become attached to it.

After a time Alain gave back the volume. But, being rich and more than honest, he did better than give it back; he could not help adding his compound interest to the capital. Alain's wealth is in thought. He bestows it everywhere. Yet, however generously he throws it away, his substance always produces for him more than he can spend. In the economy of the spirit, thrift is ruinous; the prodigals grow rich.

Here then are the wide margins of *Charmes* all filled with firm, close writing that encircles the block of print. It hugs the arrangement of stanzas, besieges the closed forms, molds and seems to press with living force and to penetrate with active sensitivity the finished, regular, and as it were, crystallized structure of the typography. To consider these annotated pages is to see, along the borders of the poems, a man living what he reads. As one deciphers, one hears, alongside the verses, the murmur of the discursive monologue responding to the reading, cutting across it, supporting it by a more or less restricted counterpoint, continually accompanying it by the speech of a second voice, which sometimes breaks out.

In a way this writing in the margins presents to the eyes the secret complement of the text, shows the reader's function, brings out the spiritual environs of a reading. These environs of a work that is being read reveal the reader's depths; these are aroused or moved in each person by the differences and agreements, the consonances or dissonances that are gradually revealed between what is being read and what was secretly expected.

The Amateur could not agree to keep this intellectual profusion all to himself. He suggested that a book for the public should be made out of his teeming copy. Here the author of the verses appeared. I had to intervene. I could not help being embarrassed. Was not my taking even the least part in the publication of this commentary to *authorize* all its contents, all its judgments? But there are some among them of an exhilarating kind. The gloss is sometimes full of praise. Alain is not very harsh toward my work; I think that he sees and creates in it what I should have wished to do, which is not what I have done, far from it. The experience of praise and criticism, of sweet and bitter, has the following results. Praise arouses and disturbs the sensibility more than criticism does. Criticism stirs to action of a kind; it burnishes weapons in the mind. The spirit can nearly always reply fairly decidedly to disparaging words. It returns raillery for raillery, dissects the objection, circumscribes the blasphemer. Rarely does it not find, in that *Other* who torments it, some vice, some weakness, or some mean scheme that enables it to recover itself; more rarely still does it not find within itself some hidden beauty, some profound excuse that saves it in its own eyes. But what can be done with praise? Discussion is impossible, inhuman, immodest. Praise is relaxing and makes everything pleasantly confused. It is like making love—in this case to the public.

One is, therefore, uncertain, powerless, in the state of least resistance, when faced with homage; with no clear answer, and as though with no freedom of truth toward oneself. One knows that nobody who protests against the delights of being honored is believed, and the heart, intimidated by common opinion, doubts its power to mistrust its enjoyment. This is only a private hesitation about the choice of the truest feeling from among several which divide us and suit us equally. But the embarrassment becomes extreme if, in addition, one must produce it and if, as in my case, one must appear before the world and shake hands with the man who is expressing himself so very graciously about oneself.

Another difficulty occurred to me.

The text here annotated may prompt the reader to a very natural question. It has the reputation of being rather difficult to understand. Several good judges, and a host of others, find in it a set of enigmas. I see that henceforth I shall be asked whether I agree with Alain on the meaning he finds in my verses. It will be said: "Does he understand you as you do yourself? Is his commentary really close to your thought? Has he unfolded your aims, does he dispel your obscurities as we hoped you could yourself?"

My verses have the meaning attributed to them. The one I give them suits only myself and does not contradict anyone else. It is an error contrary to the nature of poetry, and one which may even be fatal to it, to claim that for each poem there is a corresponding true meaning, unique and conformable to, or identical with, some thought of the author's. A result of this error is the invention of that absurd school exercise which consists in having verses put into prose. This inculcates an idea most fatal to poetry, for it teaches that it is possible to divide its essence into parts which can exist separately. It implies the belief that poetry is an *accident* of the *substance* prose. But poetry exists only for those in whose eyes this operation is impossible and who recognize poetry by this impossibility. As for the others, by understanding poetry they mean substituting for it another language, whose condition is not to be poetic.

Poetry's object is by no means to communicate to someone some definite notion—for which prose should suffice. One need only observe the fate of prose, how it perishes once it is understood, and because it is understood—that is, because it is replaced in the attentive mind by a completed idea or figure. Once this idea, for which prose has aroused the necessary and adequate conditions, is produced, the means are at once dissolved, the language fades before it. It is a constant phenomenon on which there is a double check; our memory repeats the speech we have not understood. Repetition answers incomprehension. *It signifies that the act of language has not been able to complete itself.* But on the other hand, and as it were symmetrically, if we have understood, we are in a position to express in another manner the idea formed in us by speech. The act of language once accomplished has made us masters of the central point that commands the multiplicity of possible expressions of an acquired idea. In fact, meaning, which is the tendency toward a uniform mental substitution, unique and resolutive, is the object, law, and limit of existence of pure prose.

The function of poetry is quite different. Whereas the content alone is to be exacted from prose, it is here the form alone which commands and survives. It is the sound, the rhythm, the physical proximity of words, their effects of induction or their mutual influences which dominate at the expense of their capacity for being consummated in a defined and particular meaning. In a poem, therefore, the sense must not triumph over the form and destroy it beyond recall; on the contrary, it is the recall, the conservation of form, or rather its exact reproduction as the sole and necessary expression of the state or the thought it has provoked in the reader, which is the mainspring of poetic power. *A beautiful line is constantly reborn from its own ashes,* it becomes again—as the effect of its effect—its own harmonic cause.

This essential condition could hardly ever be fulfilled if the content, the meaning of a poetic work, had to be subjected to the narrow requirements of prose.

There is no question in poetry of transmitting to one person something intelligible happening within another. It is a question of creating within the former a state whose expression is exactly and peculiarly what communicates it to him. Whatever image or emotion is formed in the lover of poetry has value and sufficiency if it produces in him this reciprocal relation between cause-word and effect-word. As a result, such a reader enjoys very great freedom as to ideas, a freedom analogous to that which music allows to the hearer, although less extensive.

Alain, as a philosopher, peoples my constructions with words, he animates them with wonderful meanings. It remains for me to show that, praise apart, I have no control over what he says.

Once a work is finished and presented, whether in verse or prose, its author can propose or affirm nothing about it that would have any more weight or would explain it more exactly than what anyone else might say. A work is an object or event of the senses, whereas the various values or inter-pretations it suggests are consequences (ideas or affections) which cannot alter it in its entirely material capacity to pro-duce quite different ones. If a painter does a portrait of *Socrates* and a passer-by recognizes *Plato*, all the creator's explanations, protests, and excuses will not change this immediate recog-nition. The dispute will amuse eternity. An author can, no doubt, inform us of his intentions; but it is not a question of these; it is a question of what subsists, what he has made independent of himself.

This point must be well understood if one does not want to be involved in the confusion of judgments and points of view which is the most noticeable vice of nearly every for-mulation of aesthetics. In their very premises one finds a confusion of considerations some of which have no meaning except in the author's being, others are valid for the work, and yet others for him who experiences the work. Any pro-position that brings together these three entities is illusory.

There exist certain rather mysterious bodies which are studied in physics and used in chemistry; I always think of them when considering works of art. The simple presence of these bodies in a particular mixture of other substances determines the latter to unite, the former remaining unaltered, identical with themselves, neither transformed in their nature, nor increased or diminished in their quantity. They are then, present and absent, acting and not acted upon. Such is the text of a work. The action of its presence modifies minds, each according to its nature and state, provoking combinations latent within a certain head, but whatever reaction is thus produced, the text is found to be unaltered and capable of indefinitely generating other phenomena in other circum-stances or in another person.

On Speaking Verse

I MIGHT have expected any number of riddles, but not to be asked anything about the theater. I do not think there is anyone in France who knows less about such matters and who is more inexperienced or more naïve when faced with the magic of the stage and, moreover, more easily dazzled by the slightest talent displayed there. I admire anything I am unable to do myself even when it is ill done. If I now had to give you a conception of how marvelous I find everything that happens in the theater, I should merely elaborate certain ideas I formerly had, when I happened to speculate for amusement on the art of the stage.

I did not invent a subject, and it was not characters or dramatic situations which then came to my mind; nor did the plot or the dialogue engross me at first; but I lost myself in the pleasure of considering matters from a much greater distance—so great that I banished the true theater to infinity! You will not be surprised, ladies and gentlemen, that for a long time I took pleasure in imagining a great many conditions of form, a system of very rigid restrictions, which I reasoned out from an analysis of my own and which I imposed upon imaginary comedies and upon tragedies that could not possibly have existed. How perverse one must be to like these constraints and, perhaps, to prefer the invention of them to other merits that might be more perceptible!

As you may imagine, it was not long before I rediscovered the famous law of the three unities, and I did not fail to take pleasure in exaggerating it! After all, I said to myself, is it so reasonable to oppose what is called *Life* to these three venerable conditions? Do we not see, alas! that, on the contrary, life, real life, is subjected, for its very existence, to an enormous number of compulsory restrictions and unavoidable *unities*, compared with which these three celebrated unities, which have been so blasphemed, are light chains of small importance?

The fact is that at times I am incorrigible. Sometimes I am the kind of man who, if he met the inventor of the sonnet in the underworld, would say to him with great respect (if there is any left, in the other world):

"My dear colleague, I salute you most humbly. I do not know the worth of your verses, which I have not read, but I would wager that they are worthless, for the odds always are that verses are bad; but however bad they are, however flat, insipid, shallow, stupid, and naïvely made they may be, I still hold you in my heart above all other poets on earth and in Hades! . . . You invented a *form*, and the greatest poets have adapted themselves to that form."

But this is leading us too far. Away with my formal theater, and let us return to yours, which has the merit of existing.

Fortunately, for you it was only a question of a very limited consultation about a matter which, after all, was not so foreign to me. It was hoped that I could give some useful advice on the manner of speaking verse, for a production of *Bajazet* had been planned for the end of a hard season.

Various things that I had said or written, or might have been thought to think, involved me quite naturally in the affair. For myself, in virtue of the redoubtable fiction of responsibility—which consists, in fact, of being held to have willed without reservation, fully willed, willed even to the scaffold, even to damnation, all the consequences and particularly those least foreseeable, of what one had innocently willed only for one's pleasure—I had to accede to the idea that had been formed of my competence. I did not plead what I really am, I did not dare stand aside, which is why, one January morning, I had to take the risk of playing a part in a kind of concert of voices.

How should verse be spoken?

This is a thorny problem. Everything relating to poetry is difficult. All who have anything to do with it are excessively touchy. The inextricable mingling of individual feelings and general requirements gives rise to unending dissensions. Nothing is more natural than mutual misunderstanding; the contrary is always surprising. I believe that one never agrees on anything except by mistake, and that all harmony among human beings is the happy fruit of an error.

To mention only the speaking of verse, it is easy to estimate the infinitely small number of chances there are of agreeing on the way to set about it. Consider, first of all, that necessarily there are almost as many ways of speaking as there exist or have existed poets, for each composes his work to suit his own ear. On the other hand, there are as many manners of reciting as there are kinds of poetry and different forms or meters. There is another source of variety: there are as many ways of speaking as there are speakers, each of whom has his methods, his tone of voice, his reflexes, his habits, his aptitudes, his physiological difficulties and dislikes.

The product of all these factors is an amazing number of possible decisions and misunderstandings—not to mention differences of *interpretation*.

You know well enough how easy it is, by a very plausible

use of the variations of speech, to change a line that seemed beautiful into a line that seems ugly; and, on the other hand, to rescue a disastrous line by a slight spacing or softening of the syllables as they are spoken.

In short, an interpreter can, according to his intelligence and intentions, and sometimes in spite of them, bring about astounding transmutations from euphony to cacophony, or from cacophony to euphony. A poem, like a piece of music, offers merely a text, which, strictly speaking, is only a kind of recipe; the cook who follows it plays an essential part. To speak of a poem in itself, to judge of a poem in itself, has no real or precise meaning. It is to speak of a potentiality. The poem is an abstraction, a piece of writing that stands waiting, a law that lives only in some human mouth, and that mouth is simply a mouth.

However, as each poet necessarily relies, in his work, on some ideal reader who is the best of help and who, moreover, resembles him rather more closely than a brother, I for my part, and for my own use, had formed a certain idea of the delivery I wanted, and if this wholly personal idea were to take the form of advice, it could be summed up thus: in studying a piece of poetry to be spoken aloud, one should never take as a beginning or point of departure ordinary discourse or current speech, and then rise from the level of prose to the desired poetic tone; on the contrary, I believed one should start from song, put oneself in the attitude of the singer, tune one's voice to the fullness of musical sound, and from that point descend to the slightly less vibrant state suitable to verse. It seemed to me that this was the only way to preserve the musical essence of poems. Above all, one should *place* the voice well, as far from prose as possible, study the text from the point of view of the attacks, modulations, and sustained notes that it contains, and gradually reduce this tendency, which will have been exaggerated at first, to the proportions of poetry.

These very delicate proportions whereby poetry is distinguished from true song result from the relative importance of sound and sense in each of these uses of the human voice.

The plan of relating poetry to song seems to me exact in principle and in accordance with both the origins and the essence of our art. It was with this in mind that two years ago I made the experiment of calling on a singer to study some poems of Ronsard with me and to recite them before an audience. I do not know whether my idea was justified in the event; but at least the occasion was a triumph for Madame Croiza, who took the risk.

The first condition for speaking verse well is an understanding of what it is not, and of how great a difference separates it from ordinary language.

Ordinary, current speech, serving some purpose, flies toward its meaning and toward its purely mental translation and is there abolished and dissolved, like a germ in the egg it fertilizes.

Its form, or auditive appearance, is only a stage that the mind skips. Although the tone and rhythm are present to help the sense, they intervene only for a moment as immediate necessities and as aids to the meaning which they are transmitting and which at once absorbs them without an echo, for it is their aim and end. But the aim of verse is a continuing pleasure, and it demands, under pain of becoming nothing but a discourse oddly and unnecessarily metrical, a certain very intimate union between the physical reality of the sound and the virtual excitations of sense. It requires a kind of equality between the two powers of speech. The poet is a politician who makes use of two "majorities."

In short, we note that in song the words tend to lose their importance as meaning, that they do most frequently lose it, whereas at the other extreme, in everyday prose, it is the musical value that tends to disappear; so much so that song on the one side and prose on the other are placed, as it were, symmetrically in relation to verse, which holds an admirable and very delicate balance between the sensual and intellectual forces of language.

All this is very easy to grasp—the only obstacles being bad habits and a kind of misunderstood tradition.

From this I easily evolved a certain way of speaking verse, and in particular of speaking Racine.

Of all poets, it is Racine who bears the most direct relationship to music proper—Racine, whose periods so often suggest recitatives only a little less singing than those of musical compositions—Racine, whose tragedies Lully went so studiously to hear, and of whose lines and movements the beautiful forms and the pure developments of Gluck seem to be the immediate translations.

I therefore explained to the future performers of *Bajazet* the sentiments I have just expressed on the declamation of verse, and I urged them to repudiate a tradition which I find detestable and which consists in sacrificing the entire musical side of the play to the direct effects of the stage. This unfortunate tradition destroys the continuity, the infinite melody that is so enchantingly heard in Racine. As a result, the actor appears to be wrestling with the verse, to endure it with difficulty, to regret its presence in a work that could do without it. The verse is broken up, or obscured; or, at other times, only its awkwardnesses seem to be retained: the actor stresses and exaggerates the frame and supports of the alexandrine, those conventional signs which to my mind are very useful but which are crude procedures if diction does not envelop and clothe them with its grace.

I said, therefore, to our Racinian young Turks: "First of all, get used to the melody of these lines; study closely the structure of these doubly organized *sentences* in which the syntax on one hand and the prosody on the other compose a sonorous, spiritual substance and cunningly engender a form full of life. Do not confine yourself to respecting the rhymes and caesuras. Naturally, the admirable Author observed them; but a musical creation cannot be reduced to a mere observance, as was formerly believed by far too many people, who thus tended to sterility, made the rules absurd, and consequently provoked a dreadful reaction. But take time to experience and hear the tones of Racine, even to their harmonics, and the nuances, the reciprocal echoes of his vowels, the clear, pure action and supple linking of his consonants, and their arrangement.

"Moreover, and above all, do not be in a hurry to reach the meaning. Approach it without forcing and, as it were, imperceptibly. Attain the tenderness and the violence only by the music and through it. Refrain for as long as possible from emphasizing words; so far there are no *words*, only syllables and rhythms. Remain in this purely musical state until the moment the meaning, having gradually supervened, can no longer mar the musical form. You will finally introduce it as the supreme nuance which will transfigure your piece without altering it. But first of all you must have learned your piece.

"At last that moment will come. You will finally discern your role, and you will occupy yourself with portraying a particular existence. With this music that you have learned and felt so deeply, you will mingle the necessary accents and accidentals to make it seem to spring from the affections and passions of some human being. Now you should differentiate between the lines. Put yourself a bit inside the author. Look at his aims, his difficulties, his ease, and his unease. You will soon see that you must differentiate between the lines. Some help the play itself, being indispensable parts of it; they announce, provoke, and resolve events; they answer logical questions; they make it possible to summarize the drama and are, to a certain extent, on a level with prose. The articulation of these necessary lines is a great art; but the art of making them is greater. But other lines, which are the whole poetry of the work, sing, and comprise all that the poet draws from his deepest being. I do not have to commend these divine passages to you."

Such, no doubt, was my little exhortation. *Et cetera.*

Letter to Madame C.

OTHERS, dear Croiza, will praise the singer.

But I—kept by circumstances from such a desirable dinner, which I so fully visualize—I will say something else. Allow the absent one to borrow from a friend enough presence and breath to pay you his compliments.

A long time ago the idea came to me to win a singer to poetry. How did it come, and from what reflections?

Poetry is not music; still less is it speech. It is perhaps this ambiguity that makes its delicacy. One might say that it is about to sing, rather than that it sings; and that it is about to speak, rather than that it speaks. It dare not sound too loud nor speak too clearly. It haunts neither the heights nor the depths of the voice. It is contented with the hills and with a very modest skyline. But doing what it can with rhythm, accents, and consonances, it tries to communicate an almost musical power to the expression of certain thoughts. Not of all thoughts.

Ordinary diction starts from prose and raises itself to verse. It happens rather often to confuse the tone of drama or the movement of eloquence with the intrinsic music of the language. Then the speaker gains in effects what the poem loses in harmony.

But I wanted to make trial of a voice which, on the contrary, would descend from the full and complete melody of musicians to our poets' melody, which is restrained and tempered. I had dreamed of inviting a voice assured in its whole register to make itself heard in this singular fashion — a voice with a greater range than the voice that suffices for poetry: a practiced, living voice, much more conscious, clearer in its attack, richer in its sonorities, more attentive to pauses and silences, more marked in its changes of tone than the voice usually given to works in verse.

This idea encountered you. Or rather, it encountered itself in you, dear Croiza.

So, when I said to you,

> "You are a singer, I am delighted!
> Well, now dare!...
> Dare set yourself to verse!"

you at once showed me a face in which fear and enthusiasm blended in a great longing. Your look seemed to say to poetry: You would not have found me if I had not already sought you!

Do you remember our first attempts?

Ronsard open before us: the works of that Ronsard who sang his verses while accompanying himself on the lute, were the subject of our experiments. . . . The studies did not last long. I have never seen a more prompt understanding of the musical system of poetry. Your soul, dear and noble artist, possessed it in all its power. I salute and admire you. The purest fire burns in you.

The Poet's Rights over Language

PLEASE forgive me. I am worn out by various tasks, the most futile of which are the most urgent. The proofs of the *Revue de Philologie* are at hand—or, to be exact, under a copy of the first edition of your *Dictionary*. This book never leaves me. I "used" and thumbed it to an amazing extent during the lengthy elaboration of the *Jeune Parque*, a labor that I pursued —although you will never believe it—with a constant care for linguistics. I did not imagine, however, that it would one day afford me the pleasure of discussing a point of detail with a specialist, and precisely with him to whom I so often turned *in petto* fifteen years ago.

Let us come to the peccant line. It would be pleasant to linger over it and exhaust all the subtleties that are instinct in a problem of this kind. But, as I have said, all my time is taken up with rubbish, and I must confine myself to the mere outline of a reply.

It is true that, on my own authority and contrary to custom, I have made use of the "dieresis" *ti-è-de*, with the aim of obtaining a certain effect, that of symmetry: *déli-ci-eux— ti-è-de*. I found a voluptuous nuance in it.

I think that if the reader—any reader—feels the effect of it, the poet *ipso facto* is *justified*.

I consider that it is therefore a question of fact—and, in short, of force.

Ingres sometimes lengthened the necks of his odalisques. The anatomist must protest, even if he enjoys the drawing. Each to his own job.

Besides, it seems there is a precedent. I did not know of it. Thérive points it out in Vigny. The same cause must have produced the same effect.

In short, if I insist on *ti-è-de*, if some people find *ti-è-de* more tepid than *tiè-de*, I need not be disqui-e-ted at having vi-o-lated the rule.

Incidentally, I may point out here that the actual pronunciation varies in different regions. You know this much better than I. As regards diphthongization, I have noticed how infrequently *duel* is one syllable. As for words ending in *-tion*, *-sion*, and *-ssion*, whose diphthongization—as you so justly remark—would ruin many fine lines (particularly in Racine) —it seems to me that this way of pronouncing them depends on the lengthening of the preceding syllable, a lengthening that decreases perceptibly on going from the South toward the North. At the two extremes one finds the Italian *na-zione* and the English *na-tion*. Here *-tion* is mute, or almost so.

However that may be, I am sensitive to the harmony of this line from *Esther*:

La nation chérie a violé sa foi,

and there is no reason why I should not be.

There remain the questions of usage and of the "general trend."

As for usage, I make a clear distinction between general, that is, *unconscious*, usage and *poetic* usage.

General usage is subject only to statistics—which reflect the average ease of pronunciation. Ordinary spoken language is a practical tool. It is constantly resolving immediate problems. *Its task is fulfilled when each sentence has been completely abolished, annulled, and replaced by the meaning.* Comprehension is its end. But on the other hand, poetic usage is dominated by *personal* conditions, by a conscious, continuous, and sustained musical feeling. . . .

Moreover, these conditions usually combine with a careful observance of various technical conventions whose effect is constantly to remind the versifier that he is not moving within the system of vulgar speech, but in another quite distinct system.

Here language is no longer a transitive act, an expedient. On the contrary, it has *its own value*, which must remain intact *in spite of the operations of the intellect on the given propositions*. Poetic language must preserve itself, through itself, and remain the same, *not to be altered by the act of intelligence that finds or gives it a meaning*.

All literature which has passed a certain age reveals a tendency to create a poetic language apart from ordinary speech, with a vocabulary, syntax, licenses, and prohibitions that differ more or less from those in ordinary use. An account of these discrepancies would be very instructive. This differentiation is inevitable, since the functions of words and of means of expression are not the same. One could imagine that the language of poetry might develop to the point of constituting a system of notation as different from practical speech as is the artificial language of algebra or chemistry. The slightest poem contains all the germs and indications of this potential development. I do not say whether it is desirable or not. Such a judgment would have no meaning.

But it follows from these remarks that there must be—and that there is—a necessary, or I should say "constitutional," contrast between the writer and the linguist. The latter is by definition an observer and an interpreter of statistics. The writer is quite the opposite: he is a *deviation*, a maker of *deviations*. This does not mean that all deviations are permitted to him; but it is precisely his business and his ambition to find the deviations that enrich, that give the illusion of the power or the purity or the depth of language. In order to work *through* language he works *on* language. On this material he exercises an artificial—that is, a deliberate, recognizable—effect, and he does so at his own risk. If the linguist be compared to a physicist, the writer can be compared to an engineer, which is why it is good for him to consult linguistics. *Naturae non imperatur nisi parendo*—he must have a precise idea of the prevailing laws of language so as to use them for his personal ends and to accomplish the work of man, which is always to oppose nature by means of nature.

As for the "general trend of the language," I do not at all believe that it can furnish a legitimate argument one way or the other. We see it move, but we do not know where it is going. It has somewhat sudden turns, returns, and mutations. Brantôme wrote and pronounced *Asture* what we write and pronounce *A cette heure*.

What a state and what a state! as Bossuet would say. . . . To speak of this trend in order to forecast the fate of any given *deviation* is to make a wager. I must observe in this connection that the science of language has, I know not why, taken up a very biased position in questions concerning literature. It tends to consider sacred the average results of the ill-regulated practices of all! . . . But I must end this letter, at once too long and too short; I have let myself be carried away by a subject that never leaves me indifferent.

A Poet's Notebook

POETRY. Is it impossible, given time, care, skill, and desire, to proceed in an orderly way to arrive at poetry?

To end by *hearing* exactly what one wished to hear by means of a skillful and patient management of that same desire?

You want to write a particular poem, with a certain effect, more or less, on a particular subject: first of all, you have images of various *orders*.

Some are people, landscapes, points of view, attitudes; others are undefined voices, notes. . . .

So far, words are only placards.

Other words or scraps of phrases have no particular use, but want to be used; meanwhile they drift.

I see everything and I see nothing.

Other images make me see quite different conditions. They seem to show the states of mind of an individual undergoing the poem, his attention, his suspense, his expectations, his presentiments, all of which must be created, played with, disarmed, or satisfied.

I have, therefore, several levels of ideas, some of resul , others of execution; and the idea of uncertainty dominates them all; and, finally, there is the idea of my own expectation, ready to seize on the already realized, writable elements that are or will be offered, even those not confined to the subject.

It can happen, then, that the germ is no more than a word or a fragment of a sentence, a line that seeks and toils to create its own justification and so gives rise to a context, a subject, a man, etc.

What does reflection draw from the subject or the germ?

Reflection is a restraint on chance, a chance to which one adapts a *convention*. And what is a play of chance if not that addition which creates an expectation, gives a *different* importance to the various faces of dice?

These faces are equal from one point of view, unequal from another. . . . Where one loses, another wins. This idea or that expression which came into the mind of Racine and was rejected by him as a loss was seized on by Hugo as a gain.

*　*　*

So the poet at work is an expectation. He is a transition within a man—which makes him sensitive to certain terms of his own development: those which reward this expectation by conforming with the convention. He reconstructs what he desired. He reconstructs *quasi-mechanisms capable of giving back to him the energy they cost him and more* (for here the principles are apparently violated). *His ear speaks to him.*

We wait for the unexpected word—which cannot be foreseen but must be awaited. We are the first to hear it.

To hear? but that means *to speak.* One understands what one hears only if one has said it oneself from another motive.

To speak is to hear.

What is concerned, then, is a *twofold* attention. The state of being able to produce what is perceived admits of more or of less by reason of the number of elementary functions involved.

And this is on account of memory. This demonstrates that memory and understanding—and imagining—are intimately linked.

If a difficult discourse is addressed to us, we can repeat the words rather than the sentences; we retain the propositions rather than their order, and understanding is therefore memory in action. It implies a maximum that can only be a maximum of memory.

Understanding is a *closed* thing. To understand A is to be able to reconstruct A.

And to imagine is only to understand oneself.

One gets the idea of a reversible apparatus, like a telephone or a dynamo.

It is as though the auditive current reached a point where the waves would be thrown back onto the interruption of, the broken end of, the transmitting line.

"Off" and "On" cannot coexist.

Silence and attention are incompatible. The circuit must be closed.

The aim, then, is to create the kind of silence to which the *beautiful* responds. Or the pure line of verse, or the luminous idea. . . . Then the line seems to be born of itself, born of necessity—which is precisely my state—and finds that it is memory. Or rather, is at once the uniting element of memory, act, and perception, a fixed novelty and yet an organized, repeatable function; an energy and a generator of energy. At once astonishment and function. . . . Exception, chance, *and* act.

*   *   *

The passage from prose to verse, from speech to song, from walking to dancing.—A moment that is at once action and dream.

The aim of the dance is not to transport me from one point to another; nor of pure verse, nor of song.

But they exist to make me more present to myself, more entirely given up to myself, expending my energy to no useful end, replacing myself—and all things and sensations have no other value. A particular movement sets them free; and infinitely mobile, infinitely present, they hasten to serve as fuel to a fire. Hence metaphors, those stationary movements!

Song is more real than level speech, for the latter is of value only by a substitution and a deciphering operation, whereas the former stirs and provokes imitation, arouses desire, causes a vibration as though its variation and substance were the law and matter of my being. It stands in my stead; but level speech is on the surface, it sets out external things, divides and labels them.

One can get a wonderful conception of this difference by observing the efforts and inventions of those who have tried to make music speak and language sing or dance.

* * *

If you want to write verse and you begin with thoughts, you begin with prose.

In prose one can draw up a plan and *follow* it!

* * *

POETRY. Those ideas which cannot be put into prose are put into verse. If one finds them in prose, they demand verse and have the air of verse that has not yet been able to take shape. What ideas are these?

... They are ideas that are possible only in very lively, rhythmic, or spontaneous movements of thought.

Metaphor, for example, marks in its naïve principle a *groping*, a hesitation between several different expressions of one thought, an explosive incapacity that surpasses the *necessary* and *sufficient* capacity. Once one has gone over and made the thought rigorously precise, restricted it to a single object, then the metaphor will be effaced, and prose will reappear.

These procedures, observed and cultivated for their own sake, have become the object of a study and an employment: poetry. The result of this analysis is that poetry's special aim and own true sphere is the expression of what cannot be expressed in the finite functions of words. The proper object of poetry is what has no single name, what in itself provokes and demands more than one expression. That which, for the expression of its unity, arouses a plurality of expressions.

* * *

The habit of long labor at poetry has accustomed me to consider all speech and all writing as work in progress that can nearly always be taken up again and altered; and I consider *work itself* as having its own value, generally much superior to that which the crowd attaches only to the *product*.

No doubt the product is the thing that lasts and has, or should have, a meaning of itself and an independent existence; but the acts from which it proceeds, in so far as they *react* on their author, form within him another *product*, which is a man more skillful and more in possession of his domain of memory.

A work is never necessarily *finished*, for he who made it is never complete, and the power and agility he has drawn from it confer on him just the power to improve it, and so on. . . . *He draws from it what is needed to efface and remake it*. This is how a *free* artist, at least, should regard things. And he ends by considering as satisfactory only those works which have taught him something more.

This point of view is not that of ordinary art lovers. It could never suit them.

But I have written all this by following, from the beginning, a different road from the one I thought to take from that beginning.

I meant to talk of philosophers—and to philosophers.

I wanted to show that it would be of the greatest profit to them to practice this labor of poetry which leads insensibly to the study of word combinations, not so much through the conformity of the meanings of these groups to an idea or thought that one thinks should be *expressed*, as, on the contrary, through their effects once they are formed, from which one chooses.

Generally one tries to "express one's thought," that is, to pass from an *impure* form, a mixture of all the resources of the mind, to a *pure* form, that is, one solely verbal and organized, amounting to a system of arranged acts or contrasts.

But the art of poetry is alone in leading one to envisage pure forms in themselves.

*   *   *

Any man might see "poetry" in what he does, feels, etc. . . . It does not reside in any particular objects. And many men feel poetically what they encounter in their life and their business.

But this does not make them poets. Those who think it does are merely confusing effects produced with producing effects, the unique or intense vision and the means of provoking or reproducing it.—The engineer is not strong like his machine. He is strong differently, quite differently.

From this point, it is easy to understand that if the poetic impression is not linked to any special object, at least poetic fabrication can be. Not in any absolute way, but each literary age and each *fabricator* relies upon certain ideas or forms poetically ready-made, whose use at once simplifies the poetic problem, allowing him combinations of greater complexity and of a higher order, like a language he knows well. Etc. . . .

* * *

STUPIDITY AND POETRY. There are subtle relations between these two categories. The category of stupidity and that of poetry.

* * *

Thought must be hidden in verse like the nutritive essence in fruit. It is nourishing but seems merely delicious. One perceives pleasure only, but one receives a substance. Enchantment, that is the nourishment it conveys. The passage is sweet.

* * *

OBSCURITY, A PRODUCT OF TWO FACTORS. If my mind is richer, more rapid, freer, more disciplined than yours, neither you nor I can do anything about it.

* * *

Not the least of the pleasures of rhyme is the rage it inspires in those poor people who think they know something more important than a *convention*. They hold the naïve belief that a thought *can* be more profound, more organic . . . than any mere convention.

* * *

Prose is the kind of work that permits of beginning with the thought of things, with their image or idea, and of ending with *words*. Every time the game begins with language, whenever the mind attacks with words or sentences, prose is born rhythmical, as in oratory. Prose is born without rhythm when it results from a deciphering; it then admits an indefinite series of inner interruptions. All writing that is *rhythmical* and *deliberate* is *artificial*, that is, the apparent spontaneity due to the rhythm has been constructed later, out of a substance incompatible with it during its generation. The words and the music are not by the same author. I mean not of the same moment.

* * *

"X . . . is more poet than artist."

Does this mean that X . . . has more *energy* at his disposal than operations or machines for using it?

* * *

X . . . would like one to believe that a metaphor is a communication from heaven.

A metaphor is *what happens* when one *looks in a certain way*, just as a sneeze is what happens when one looks at the sun.

In what way? — You can feel it. One day, perhaps one will be able to *say* it precisely.

Do this and do that — and behold all the metaphors in the world. . . .

* * *

A poem's worth is its content of *pure poetry*, that is, of extraordinary truth; of perfect adaptation in the sphere of perfect uselessness; of apparent and convincing probability in the production of the improbable.

* * *

The poet has essentially the "intuition" of a special order of combinations. A certain combination of objects (of thought) which has no value for a normal man, has for him an existence and *makes itself noticed*. It strikes him in the way that a relationship of sounds, separately perceived by an ordinary ear, strikes a musical ear as a relationship—like a contrast of colors, etc.

Sometimes it is a combination of *things*, and this must be *translated;* sometimes one of *words* that will possess the quality already mentioned, and this must be *justified*.

(1) Combination of things. He sees figures of a particular order where anyone else sees only what interests a man picked at random.

For this poet a "subject" is that set of relations which can receive or furnish the maximum of things of this kind.

(2) Combination of sounds. It must not be forgotten that the poet, unlike the musician, does not start from an existing and already pure collection, which is sound. His scale must be reconstructed each time.

*   *   *

In what would the artist's special position consist if he did not consider certain details inviolable? For example, the alternation of masculine and feminine rhymes. No inspiration must be allowed to ignore them. *This* is irritating, *this* is nonsense, but without *this*, everything falls apart, and the poet corrupts the artist, and the arbitrariness of the moment overcomes the arbitrariness of an order superior to the moment.

*   *   *

Eternal glory to the inventor of the sonnet. However, although so many beautiful sonnets have been written, the most beautiful is still to be done: it will be the one whose four parts will each fulfill a quite different function from the others, and this progression of differences in the strophes will be well justified by the structure of the discourse as a whole.

Sonnets must be written. It is astonishing how much one learns by writing sonnets and poems in set form.

The fruit of these labors is not in them alone. (But poets in general let the best of their efforts go to waste.)

I have always written my verses while observing myself write them, in which respect, perhaps, I have never been exclusively a poet.

—I learned very quickly to distinguish clearly between the reality of thought and the reality of effects.

But without this confusion, is one a poet?

*   *   *

Literature is the instrument neither of a whole thought nor of an organized thought.

*   *   *

The great interest of classic art is perhaps in the series of transformations it requires to express things while respecting the imposed conditions *sine qua non*.

Problems of putting into verse. This obliges one to consider from a great height what one wishes or is compelled to say.

*   *   *

One must not aim at originality, particularly in our time; for everything original is object of a concentrated aim and a very avid attention that is anxious to exploit the slightest means for distinguishing itself. The result is that what was original in the morning is copied the same evening; and the more conspicuous and new it was in the morning, the more conspicuous and intolerable in the evening is the repetition of the effect one had created.—Despise the old and the new.

SYNTHESIS AND NOVELTY. One of Virgil's Eclogues would be nothing new to present to the reader (although I am not so sure!); but if an eclogue were obtained by methods very different from those of the first century, that might be new. The scent of the rose has been known since there were roses, but to reconstruct it from the molecules COH—that is fairly novel.

I confess once again that work interests me far more than the product of that work.

*　*　*

An epic poem is a poem that can be told.

When one *tells* it, one has a bilingual text.

*　*　*

LITERATURE. What is "form" for anyone else is "content" for me.

*　*　*

POET. Your kind of verbal materialism.

You can *look down* on novelists, philosophers, and all who are enslaved to words by credulity—who *must* believe that their speech is *real* by its content and signifies some reality. But as for you, you know that the reality of a discourse is only the words and the forms.

Pure Poetry

Notes for a Lecture

THERE is a great stir in the world (I mean in the world of the most precious and useless things), there is a great stir in the world about these two words: *pure poetry*. I have some responsibility for this stir. A few years ago, in a preface I wrote for a volume of poetry by one of my friends, I happened to use these words without attaching very much importance to them and without foreseeing the consequences that various minds interested in poetry would draw from them. I knew very well what I meant by these words, but I did not know that they would give rise to such echoes and reactions in the world of lovers of literature. I merely wanted to draw attention to a fact, not to enunciate a theory, still less to define a doctrine and hold as heretics all who did not share it. In my eyes all written works, all works of language, contain certain fragments or recognizable elements, endowed with properties which we are about to examine and which I shall provisionally call *poetic*. Every time words show a *certain deviation* from the most direct, that is, the most *insensible* expression of thought, every time these deviations foreshadow, as it were, a world of relationships distinct from the purely practical world, we conceive more or less precisely the possibility of enlarging this exceptional domain, and we have the sensation of grasping a fragment of a noble and living substance, which is perhaps susceptible of development and cultivation, and which, when developed and used, constitutes poetry in so far as it is an effect of art.

Broadly speaking, the problem of pure poetry is this: whether one can make a whole work out of these elements, so recognizable, so distinct from those of the language I have called *insensible;* and consequently whether by means of a work, in verse or not, one can give the impression of a complete system of *reciprocal* relations between our ideas and images on the one hand and our means of expression on the other—a system which would correspond particularly to the creation of an emotive state in the mind. I use the word *pure* in the sense in which the physicist speaks of pure water. I mean that the question arises of knowing whether one can manage to construct one of those works which may be pure of all nonpoetic elements. I have always held, and I still hold, that this aim is impossible to reach and that poetry is always a striving after this purely ideal state. In fact, what we call a *poem* is in practice composed of fragments of pure poetry embedded in the substance of a discourse. A very beautiful line is a very pure element of poetry. The banal comparison of a beautiful line with a gem shows that the awareness of this quality of purity is in every mind.

The inconvenience of this term *pure poetry* is that it gives rise to the thought of moral purity, which is not in question here, the idea of pure poetry being for me, on the contrary, an essentially analytical idea. Pure poetry, is in fact, a fiction deduced from observation, which should help us to clarify our ideas about poems in general, and should guide us in the difficult and important study of the varied and multiform relations between language and the effects it produces on men. Instead of *pure poetry* it would perhaps be better to say *absolute poetry*, and it should then be understood in the sense of a search for the effects resulting from the relations between words, or rather the relations of the overtones of words among themselves, which suggests, in short, *an exploration of that whole domain of sensibility which is governed by language*. This exploration can be made gropingly. That is how it is generally done. But it is not impossible that it may one day be carried out systematically.

I have tried to formulate for myself, and I am now trying to express, a clear idea of the poetic problem, or at least what I believe to be a *clearer* idea of this problem. What is remarkable is that nowadays these questions arouse widespread curiosity. It seems that never has such a large public taken interest not only in poetry itself but also in poetic theory. We take part in discussions, we watch experiments being made which are not, as formerly, restricted to small, closed groups of amateurs and experimenters; but, what is wonderful in our day, we see even among the general public an interest, even a passionate interest, attaching to these almost theological discussions. (What is more theological than to discuss, for example, inspiration, work, or the value of intuition compared with that of the artifices of art? Are not these problems quite comparable to the celebrated theological problem of Grace and Works? Similarly, there are problems in poetry which, by setting in opposition the rules laid down and fixed by tradition and the immediate data of personal experience or intuition, are absolutely analogous to the problems one finds in the domain of theology between private judgment, the direct knowledge of divine things on the one hand, and on the other the teachings of various religions, the texts of Scripture, and the forms of dogma. . . .)

But I come to the subject with the firm intention of saying nothing that is not pure observation or that does not result from simple reasoning. Let us start again from this word *poetry* and note first that this lovely name gives birth to two orders of distinct ideas. We say "poetry" and we say "a piece of poetry." We say of a landscape, of a situation, and sometimes of a person that they are *poetic;* on the other hand, we also speak of the *art of poetry* and we say: "This poetry is beautiful." But in the first case it is obviously a question of a certain kind of emotion; everyone knows that special disturbance, comparable to our condition when, as a result of certain circumstances, we feel excited, enchanted. This state is completely independent of any specific work, and it results naturally and spontaneously from a certain harmony between our inner physical and psychic disposition and the circumstances (real or imaginary) that impress us. But, on the other hand, when we say the *art of poetry*, or when we speak of *a piece of poetry*, it is obviously a question of the means of provoking a state analogous to the preceding one, of artificially producing this kind of emotion. That is not all. The means we use to provoke this state must be those which belong to the properties and mechanism of articulate language. The emotion of which I spoke can be aroused by things; it can also be aroused by means quite other than language, such as architecture, music, etc., but poetry, properly so called, has as its essence the employment of the means of language. As for independent poetic emotion, we must note that it is distinguished from other human emotions by a unique characteristic, an admirable property: it tends to give us the feeling of an illusion or the illusion of a world (a *world* in which events, images, beings, and things, although resembling those which people the ordinary world, are in an inexplicable but intimate relationship with the whole of our sensibility). Known objects and beings are in a way—if I may be forgiven the expression —*musicalized;* they have become resonant to each other and as though tuned to our own sensibility. Thus defined, the poetic world has great affinities with the state of dreaming, at least with the state produced in certain dreams.

A dream makes us understand, when we return to it in memory, that our consciousness can be awakened, or filled and satisfied, by an assembly of productions notably different in their laws from the ordinary productions of perception. But it is not within the power of our will to enter and leave, at our pleasure, this world of emotion which we can sometimes know through dreams. *It is enclosed in us and we are enclosed in it*, which implies that we have no means of acting on it in order to modify it, and that, on the other hand, it cannot coexist with our greater power of action on the external world. It appears and disappears capriciously, but man has done for it what he has done or tried to do for all precious and perishable things: he has sought and found the means to reconstruct this state at will, to recover it when he wishes, and finally to develop artificially these natural products of his sensitive being. He has, in a way, been able to extract from nature and withdraw from the blind hurry of time these uncertain formations or constructions; to this end he has used several means I have already mentioned. Now among these means of producing a poetic world, of reproducing and enriching it, the most ancient, perhaps the most venerable, and yet the most complex and difficult to use, is language.

Here I must make felt or understood how delicate the poet's task is in modern times and how many difficulties (of which he is, fortunately, not always aware) the poet meets with in his task. Language is a common and practical element; it is therefore necessarily a crude instrument, since everyone handles and adapts it to his own needs and tends to deform it according to his personality. However intimate language is to us, however close the fact of thinking in words is to our mind, it is none the less of *statistical origin* and has *purely practical ends.* So the poet's problem must be to *draw from this practical instrument the means to realize an essentially nonpractical work.* As I have already said, his task is to create a world or an order of things, a system of relations unconnected with the practical order.

To give some idea of the difficulty of this task I shall compare the initial state, the given material and means offered to the poet, with those offered to an artist of another kind whose aims are yet not very different. I shall compare *what is given to the poet* and *what is given to the musician.* Happy musician! The evolution of his art has, for many centuries, given him a privileged place. How was music developed? The sense of hearing gives us the *universe of noises.* Our ear admits an infinity of sensations, which it receives in any order and of which it appreciates four distinct qualities. Now, age-old observations and certain quite ancient experiments made it possible to deduce from the *universe of noises* the system or *universe of sounds,* which are particularly simple and recognizable noises, particularly apt at combining and forming associations and whose structure, connections, differences, and resemblances the ear, or rather the hearing, perceives immediately they are produced. These elements are pure, or composed of pure, that is recognizable, elements; they are well defined and, a very important matter, the means have been found to produce them in a consistent and identical fashion by instruments that are, in fact, true instruments of measure. A musical instrument is an instrument that can be standardized and controlled so that certain actions may uniformly obtain from it a certain result. And here is the extraordinary consequence of this organization in the domain of hearing: the world of sounds being distinct from the world of noises, and our ear being, moreover, accustomed to distinguishing clearly between them, *if a pure sound*, that is, a relatively exceptional sound, *is heard, a particular atmosphere is immediately created, a particular state of expectation is produced in our senses, and this expectation tends*, in some way, *to provoke sensations of the same order, and of the same purity as the first*. If a pure sound is heard in a hall, *everything in us is changed;* we expect the production of music. If, on the other hand, the counter proof is made, if in a concert hall, while a piece is being played, a noise is heard (a falling chair, a nonsinging voice, or someone coughing), then we feel that something within us is broken, that there is a breach in some kind of substance or law of association; *a universe is shattered*, a spell is abolished.

So, before the musician begins work, everything lies ready in front of him so that the operations of his creative mind may, from the beginning, find the appropriate matter and means with no chance of error. He does not have to submit this matter and these means to any modification; he only has to assemble well-defined and well-prepared elements.

But what a different state of things the poet finds! Before him is spread this ordinary language, this collection of means not adapted to his plan, not made for him. For him there was no physicist to determine the relations between these means; there was no constructor of scales; no tuning fork, no metronome; no certainty in that direction; all he has is the clumsy instrument of the dictionary and the grammar. Besides, he must address himself not to a special and unique sense such

as *hearing*—which the musician forces to undergo whatever he
inflicts on it and which is moreover the supreme organ of expectation and attention—but to a general and diffused expectation, and he addresses it by means of language, which is an
extremely odd mixture of incoherent stimuli. Nothing is
more complex or more difficult to disentangle than the strange
combination of qualities found in language. Everyone knows
how rarely *sound* and *sense* are in accord; and moreover, everyone knows that a discourse may display very differing qualities: it may be logical and deprived of all harmony; it may be
harmonious and insignificant; it may be clear and lacking in
all beauty; it may be prose or poetry; and, to sum up all these
independent modes, it is enough to mention all the sciences
that have been created to exploit this diversity of language
and to study it in its various aspects. Language falls successively
under the jurisdiction of *phonetics*, *metrics*, and *rhythmics;* it has
a *logical* and a *semantic* aspect; it includes *rhetoric* and *syntax*.
One knows that all these different disciplines study the same
text in many independent ways. . . . Here, then, is the poet at
grips with this diverse and too rich collection of primal
qualities—too rich, in fact, not to be confused; it is from this
that he must draw his *objet d'art*, his machine for producing
the poetic emotion, which means that he must compel the
practical instrument, the clumsy instrument created by everyone, the everyday instrument used for immediate needs and
constantly modified by the living, to become—for the duration that his attention assigns to the poem—the substance of
a chosen emotive state, quite distinct from all the accidental
states of unforeseen duration which make up the ordinary
sensitive or psychic life. One may say without exaggeration
that common language is the fruit of the disorder of life
in common, since beings of every nature, subjected to an

innumerable quantity of conditions and needs, receive it and use it to further their desires and their interests, to set up communications among themselves; whereas the poet's language, although he necessarily uses the elements provided by this statistical disorder, constitutes, on the contrary, *an effort by one man* to create an artificial and ideal order by means of a material of vulgar origin.

If this paradoxical problem could be entirely resolved, that is, if the poet could manage to construct works in which nothing of prose ever appeared, poems in which the musical continuity was never broken, in which the relations between meanings were themselves perpetually similar to harmonic relations, *in which the transmutation of thoughts into each other appeared more important than any thought,* in which the play of figures contained the reality of the subject—then one could speak of *pure poetry* as of something that existed. It is not so: the practical or pragmatic part of language, the habits and logical forms, and, as I already indicated, the disorder and irrationality that are found in its vocabulary (on account of the infinitely varied origins, the different periods at which the elements of the language were introduced), make the existence of these creations of absolute poetry impossible; but it is easy to see that the notion of such an ideal or imaginary state is most valuable in the appreciation of all observable poetry.

The conception of pure poetry is that of an inaccessible type, an ideal boundary of the poet's desires, efforts, and powers....

Contemporary Poetry

THIS is the great problem of our art: in some measure to prolong the happiness of a moment. There are happy minutes for everyone; no work is without its beauties. But I know of nothing rarer than a composition of some length—say a hundred lines—in which there are no inconsistencies and irregularities.

For each of us, therefore, there is an extreme rigor of desire, a *standard difficulty*. A certain unattainable point is essential for the movements of an artist's mind.

But in practice it is enough for a poet to have touched or charmed or enlivened someone—even if only himself—for him to be justified and deserving of praise. Whatever his methods, they have brought about the *poetic event* in some person. If anyone contests them or finds fault with the process, it is because he will not or cannot distinguish the end from the means.

These are my only principles. They enable me to survey the state of our poetry without displeasure. I am glad to see the present coexistence of all forms, a universal and perfectly commendable freedom of every conceivable tendency. Both daring and prudence are allowed. If programs, denunciations, curses, and reproaches, and all the absurd measures of the literary police are still sometimes seen, they are soon recognized for what they really are.

Our poetry seems, in the last forty years, to have entered into an experimental period. There is so much varied activity that it destroys many prejudices and combines many systems one had thought incompatible. The old and the new intermingle; one begins to understand that imitation on the one hand and invention on the other are not of themselves either good or bad. The most regular alexandrines, free verse, stanzas and strophes of a more or less complicated symmetry, quasi poems, almost lyrical prose . . . all is lawful at present, all is received without protest by public opinion, and acrimony is to be found only among those who cannot help infusing it into everything—even into something whose object is pleasure. Nothing is true in the arts: everything is unique. The absolute judgments pronounced on works judge only the judges themselves, revealing their tastes, intentions, and above all their character.

How can one expect to reason with some generality when the first elements of solid reasoning are not there? We talk of style, form, rhythm, tradition, and originality, and we should be hard put to it to settle for ourselves the meaning of these very useful and mysterious words. It is child's play to upset all the theses containing them.

This is why all our disputes are necessarily tainted by personal feeling. This spirit always imparts to the words I mentioned the meaning most favorable to our secret humors.

I can, therefore, find good grounds for satisfaction in the present state of freedom. I can even see in it an indication of a kind of progress of the public's critical and logical sense—for the first step in logic is the discernment of what can be proved and what cannot.

Fortunately, in the realm of poetry there is *no recognized means of prescribing or forbidding anything to anyone.* In truth there exist—there must exist—certain purely statistical laws, but this kind of law is, by definition, inapplicable to the judgment of works of art.

As for *rules*—but it betrays an ignorance of their essence to call them rules—there are no rules for pleasures, but one may associate *conventions* with them. One can learn to make the most of a few well-observed conventions: this is the mainspring of all games.

Once they exist and one is used to expecting them, one can then enjoy breaking them.

I believe I have never written any but fairly regular verses. . . . Some people have even complained of this, instead of commiserating with me. Moreover, I have sometimes, for very personal reasons, set myself some extra trammels and conditions. But if tomorrow I were to be seized by a desire to throw away rhyme and everything else, no longer to count by syllables, and to abandon myself completely to the desires of my ear, I know quite well that I should find no truth essential to poetry standing in their way, and I should do as I pleased.

Remarks on Poetry

WE ARE here today to talk about poetry. This subject is now the vogue. It is wonderful that in an age which is able to be at once practical and careless and which, one might suppose, is quite remote from all matters of speculation, so much interest should be given not only to poetry itself but also to the theory of poetry.

I shall therefore take the liberty today of being somewhat abstract, but I shall thus be able to be brief.

I shall set before you a certain idea of poetry, with the firm intention of saying nothing that is not pure observation and nothing that everyone cannot notice in himself or by himself or at least discover by a simple process of reasoning.

I shall begin at the beginning. The beginning of this account of ideas about poetry will necessarily be the consideration of the name itself as it is used in common speech. We know that this word has two meanings, that is, two very distinct functions. First of all, it indicates a certain kind of emotion, a special emotive state, that can be aroused by very differing objects and circumstances. We say of a landscape that it is poetic; we say the same of an event in life; we sometimes say it of a person.

But there is a second meaning to this term, a much narrower second sense. *Poetry*, in this sense, makes us think of an art, a strange industry whose aim is to re-create the emotion defined by the first meaning of the word.

To reconstitute poetic emotion at will—independently of the natural conditions in which it is spontaneously produced —and by means of the artifices of language, this is the poet's aim, this is the idea attaching to the name of *poetry* in its second meaning.

The same relations and the same differences exist between these two ideas as between the scent of a flower and the work of the chemist who tries to make it synthetically.

But these two ideas are constantly confused, with the result that a great many judgments, theories, and even works are vitiated from the start by the use of a single word for two things that, although linked, are very different.

* * *

Let us speak first of poetic emotion, the essential emotive state.

You know what most men feel, more or less strongly and purely, when faced with an impressive natural spectacle. We are moved by sunsets, moonlight, forests, and the sea. Great events, critical moments of the affective life, the pains of love, and the evocation of death are so many occasions for, or immediate causes of, inner reverberations more or less intense and more or less conscious.

This type of emotion is distinguishable from all other human emotions. How is it so? This is what we must now discover. We must contrast as clearly as possible poetic emotion with ordinary emotion. This is a delicate separation to perform, for it is never accomplished in fact. One always finds tenderness, sadness, fury, fear, or hope intermingled with the essential poetic emotion; and the particular interests and affections of an individual never fail to combine with that *sense of a universe* which is characteristic of poetry.

I said: *sense of a universe*. I meant that the poetic state or emotion seems to me to consist in a dawning perception, a tendency toward perceiving a *world*, or complete system of relations, in which beings, things, events, and acts, although they may resemble, *each to each*, those which fill and form the tangible world—the immediate world from which they are borrowed—stand, however, in an indefinable, but wonderfully accurate, relationship to the modes and laws of our general sensibility. So, the value of these well-known objects and beings is in some way altered. They respond to each other and combine quite otherwise than in ordinary conditions. They become—if you will allow the expression—*musicalized*, somehow commensurable, echoing each other. The poetic universe defined in this way bears a strong analogy to the universe of dream.

Since this word *dream* has found its way into my talk, I shall add, by the way, that in modern times, since Romanticism, there has arisen an understandable but rather regrettable confusion between the notion of poetry and that of dream. Neither a dream nor a reverie is necessarily poetic. They can be so; but figures formed *by chance* are only *by chance* harmonious figures.

However, a dream makes us see by a common and frequent experience how our consciousness can be invaded, filled, made up by an assembly of productions remarkably different from the mind's ordinary reactions and perceptions. It gives us the familiar example of a *closed world* where all *real* things can be represented, but where everything appears and is modified solely by the fluctuations of our deepest sensibility.

In very much the same way the poetic state begins, develops, and dissolves within us. That is, it is wholly *irregular, inconstant, involuntary, fragile*, and we lose it, as we acquire it, *by accident*. There are times in our life when this emotion and these precious formations do not appear. We do not even think them possible. Chance gives them and chance takes them away.

* * *

But man is man only through his will and power to preserve or to re-establish what it is important for him to salvage from the natural decay of things. Man has thus done for this higher emotion what he has done or tried to do for all things that perish and are regretted. He has sought and found means of fixing and reviving at will his finest or purest states, of reproducing, communicating, and preserving for centuries the formulas of his enthusiasm, his ecstasy, and his own peculiar responses; and as a fortunate and wonderful consequence, the invention of these methods of preservation has simultaneously given him the idea and the power of artificially developing and enriching the fragments of poetic life with which his nature from time to time presents him. He has learned to retrieve from the flight of time, and to detach from events, these miraculous, fortuitous forms and perceptions which would have been irrevocably lost if the ingenious and sagacious mind had not helped the mind of the moment—had not brought the aid of its inventions to the purely sensitive *self*. All the arts have been created to perpetuate and change, each according to its essence, an ephemeral moment of delight into the certainty of an infinity of delightful moments. *A work is no more than the material instrument of this potential increase or reproduction.* Music, painting, architecture are the different means corresponding to the different senses. Now among these means of producing or reproducing a poetic world, of organizing it so as to endure, and of amplifying it by conscious work, the most ancient, perhaps the most direct, and certainly the most complex, is language. But on account of its abstract nature and its more particularly intellectual—that is, indirect —effects, and its practical origins or functions, language sets the artist who is concerned with employing and fashioning it into poetry a curiously complicated task. There would have been no poets if there had been any awareness of the problems to be solved. (No one would learn how to walk if walking demanded that one realize and grasp as clear ideas all the elements of the smallest step.)

But we are not here to write verse. On the contrary, we are trying to consider verse as impossible to write, so as to admire more clearly the efforts of poets, to conceive of their temerity, their fatigues, their risks, and their virtues, and to wonder at their instinct.

I shall therefore try to give you in a few words some idea of these difficulties.

As I said just now: language is an instrument, a tool, or rather a collection of tools and operations formed by practice and subservient to it. It is, then, a necessarily clumsy means that everyone uses, adapts to his current needs, alters according to circumstances, and adjusts to his physiological personality and psychological history.

You know what tests we put it to sometimes. The values and meanings of words, their rules of agreement, their pronunciation and spelling are at once our playthings and instruments of torture. No doubt we have some regard for the decisions of the Academy; no doubt, too, teachers, examinations, vanity in particular, set up certain obstacles to the exercise of individual fancy. In modern times, moreover, typography has a very powerful influence on the preservation of these conventions of writing. For this reason, alterations of a personal origin are to a certain extent delayed, but the most important qualities of language for the poet, which are obviously, on the one hand, its musical properties or possibilities and, on the other, its unlimited signifying values (those which preside over the propagation of ideas derived from an idea), are those least protected from the caprice, initiative, actions, and dispositions of individuals. Each man's pronunciation and particular psychological "store" introduce into communication by language an uncertainty, chances of misunderstanding, and an unexpected character that are quite inevitable. These two points should be noted: apart from its application to the simplest and most common needs of life, language is the opposite of a precision instrument. And apart from certain extremely rare coincidences, certain happy combinations of expression and material form, it has none of the characteristics of a poetic vehicle.

To sum up, the poet's bitter and paradoxical destiny forces him to use a product of current practical use for exceptional and nonpractical ends; he must borrow means of statistical and anonymous origin to accomplish his aim of exalting and expressing the purest and most individual aspect of his personality.

*　　*　　*

Nothing gives a better idea of the difficulty of his task than a comparison of his basic material with what the musician possesses. Consider what is given to each one at the moment when he is about to set to work and pass from intention to execution.

Happy musician! The evolution of his art has given him a privileged position. His means are well defined, the substance of his composition lies elaborated before him. One can compare him to the bee when she is concerned only with her honey. The regular combs and waxen cells are all laid out before her. Her task is well gauged and restricted to the best of herself. Such is the composer. One might say the music pre-exists and awaits him. It has been formed for a long time!

How did this institution of music come about? We live by ear in the universe of noises. From the mass of them is detached a group of particularly simple noises, that is, particularly recognizable by the ear and serving it as landmarks: these are the elements whose mutual relations are intuitive; *these exact and remarkable relations are perceived by us as clearly as the elements themselves.* The interval between two notes is as perceptible to us as a note.

Hence the tonal units, these *sounds*, are capable of forming connected sequences, continuing or simultaneous systems whose structure, links, implications, and intersections appear to us and make themselves felt. We clearly distinguish *sound* from *noise*, and we then perceive a contrast between them, which is a very important impression, for this contrast is that of the pure and the impure, which comes down to that of order and disorder, which itself, no doubt, derives from the effect of certain laws of energy. But let us not go so far.

So, this analysis of noises, this discernment which made it possible for music to be constituted as a separate activity and an exploitation of the universe of sound, has been accomplished, or at least controlled, unified, and codified, thanks to the intervention of physical science, which itself was at the same time revealed and acknowledged as a science of measurement that since antiquity has been able to adjust measure to sensation and obtain the essential result of producing the sensation of sound in a constant and identical fashion by means of instruments that are, in reality, *measuring instruments*.

The musician thus possesses a perfect collection of well-defined means that exactly match sensations with acts; all the elements of his activity are before him, counted and classified, and this detailed knowledge of his means, which he has not only learned but by which he is penetrated and intimately equipped, permits him to foresee and build, without any anxiety about the substance and general mechanics of his art.

As a result, music possesses a realm that is absolutely its own. The world of musical art, a world of sounds, is quite separate from the world of noises. Whereas a noise merely evokes in us some isolated event, *a produced sound in itself evokes the whole musical universe.* If in this hall where I am speaking, where you hear the noise of my voice together with various other auditory events, a note were suddenly heard— if a tuning fork or a well-tuned instrument began to vibrate —the moment you were affected by this unusual noise, *which cannot be confused with the others,* you would immediately have the sensation of a *beginning.* A quite different atmosphere would be immediately created, a special state of expectation would be felt, a new order, a *world,* would be announced, and your attention would be organized to receive it. Moreover, your attention would tend of itself somehow to develop these premises and to provoke further sensations of the same kind and of the *same purity* as the first.

And the counter proof exists.

If, in a concert hall, while the symphony resounds and dominates, a chair should fall, a person should cough, or a door slam, we at once have the feeling of a kind of rupture. Something indefinable, like a spell or a crystal, has been shattered or cracked.

This atmosphere, this strong and fragile spell, this universe of sounds, is offered to any composer by the nature of his art and by the immediate assets of that art.

Far different, infinitely less favorable is the poet's equipment. Pursuing an object that is not so very different from that of the musician, he is deprived of the immense advantages I have just been showing you. He must continuously create or re-create what the other finds ready to hand.

In what an adverse and disordered state the poet finds things! He has before him this everyday language, this collection of means so crude that all precise knowledge rejects them in order to create its own instruments of thought; he must avail himself of this collection of traditional and irrational terms and rules, modified by everybody, oddly created, oddly interpreted, oddly codified. Nothing is less suited to the artist's design than this primal disorder from which he must continually select the elements of the order he wishes to produce. For the poet, there was no physicist to determine the constant properties of these elements of his art, their relations, and the conditions of their identical emission. No tuning forks, no metronomes, no inventors of scales and theoreticians of harmony. No certainty, unless it be that of the phonetic and semantic fluctuations of the language. Moreover, language does not act, like sound, on a single sense, that of hearing, which is the supreme sense of expectation and attention. On the contrary, it forms a mixture of perfectly incoherent sensory and psychic stimuli. Each word is a momentary collection of unrelated effects. Each word couples a sound and a meaning. I am wrong: there are at once several sounds and several meanings. *Several sounds*, as many sounds as there are provinces in France and, almost, as there are men in each province. This is a very serious circumstance for the poets, whose desired musical effects are corrupted or disfigured by the action of their readers. *Several meanings*, since the images suggested to us by each word are generally somewhat different and their secondary images infinitely different.

Speech is a complex thing; it is a combination of properties at once linked in fact and independent by nature and function. A discourse may be logical and full of sense, but without rhythm or measure; it may be agreeable to the ear, and completely absurd or meaningless; it may be clear and useless, vague and delightful. . . . But to grasp its strange multiplicity, it is enough to enumerate all the sciences created to deal with this diversity, each to exploit one of its elements. One may study a text in many independent ways, for it falls successively under the jurisdiction of phonetics, semantics, syntax, logic, and rhetoric—not forgetting metrics and etymology.

Here, then, is the poet at grips with this shifting and adulterated matter, forced to speculate by turns on the sound and the meaning, on the musical phrase, and again on various intellectual conditions such as logic, grammar, the poem's subject, figures, ornaments of all kinds—not to mention conventional rules. Consider what effort is implied in the undertaking to finish satisfactorily a discourse in which so many requirements must be miraculously satisfied at the same time!

Here begin the uncertain and painstaking operations of the literary art. But this art presents two aspects; there are two great methods which, at their extremes, are opposed, but which, however, meet and are linked by a host of intermediate degrees. There is *prose* and there is *verse*. Between them are all the mixtures of the two, but it is in their extreme forms that I will consider them today. One might illustrate this opposition of extremes by a slight exaggeration: one might say that the bounds of language are, on the one side, *music* and, on the other, *algebra*.

*   *   *

I shall have recourse to a comparison I have often used in

order to make what I have to say on this subject easier to grasp. One day when I was speaking of all this in a foreign city, and had used the same comparison, one of my listeners sent me a remarkable quotation, which made me see that the idea was not a new one. Or rather it was new only to me.

Here is the quotation. It is an extract from a letter from Racan to Chapelain, in which Racan tells us that Malherbe likened prose to walking and poetry to dancing—as I am about to do:

Give what name you please [said Racan] to my prose—gallant, simple, sprightly. I am resolved to hold to the precepts of my first master, Malherbe, and never to strive after number or cadence in my periods nor for any other ornament than the clarity that may express my thoughts. This good man compared prose to ordinary walking and poetry to dancing and used to say that in the things we are obliged to do we may tolerate some carelessness, but in those we do from vanity it is ridiculous to be no more than mediocre. The lame and gouty cannot help walking, but nothing compels them to dance a waltz or a cinquepace.

The comparison that Racan attributes to Malherbe, and which I for my part had easily perceived, is a direct one. I will show you how productive it is. It can be extensively developed in astonishing detail. It is perhaps something more than a surface likeness.

Walking, like prose, always has a definite object. It is an act directed *toward* some object that we aim to reach. The actual circumstances—the nature of the object, my need, the impulse of my desire, the state of my body and of the ground —regulate the rhythm of walking, prescribe its direction, speed, and termination. All the properties of walking derive from these instantaneous conditions, which combine *in a novel way* each time, so that no two movements of this kind are identical, and each time there is special creation, which is each time abolished and as it were absorbed in the completed act.

Dancing is quite different. It is, of course, a system of acts, but acts whose end is in themselves. It goes nowhere. Or if it pursues anything it is only an ideal object, a state, a delight, the phantom of a flower, or some transport out of oneself, an extreme of life, a summit, a supreme point of being. . . . But however different it may be from utilitarian movement, this essential yet infinitely simple observation must be noted: *that it uses the same limbs, the same organs, bones, muscles, and nerves as walking does.*

It is exactly the same with poetry, which uses the same words, the same forms, the same tones as prose.

* * *

Prose and poetry are distinguished, therefore, by the difference between certain laws or momentary conventions of movement and function, applied to identical elements and mechanisms. This is why one must be careful not to think about poetry in the way one thinks about prose. What is true of the one has often no meaning when one seeks it in the other. And for this reason (to give an example), it is at once easy to justify the use of inversions; for these alterations of the customary and, in some ways, elementary order of words in French have been criticized at various periods, very superficially in my opinion, for reasons that come down to this unacceptable formula: poetry is prose.

Let us go a little further with our comparison, which can bear extension. A man is walking. He moves from one place to another, following a path that is always the path of least action. Note here that poetry would be impossible if it were confined to the rule of the straight line. One is taught: "Say it is raining if you mean that it is raining!" But a poet's object is not and never can be to tell us that it is raining. We do not need a poet to persuade us to take our umbrella. Think what would become of Ronsard and Hugo, what would become of the rhythm, images, and consonances of the finest verses in the world once you subjected poetry to the system of "Say it is raining!" It is only by clumsily confusing genres and occasions that one can blame a poet for his indirect expressions and complex forms. One fails to see that poetry implies a decision to change the function of language.

I return to the man walking. When this man has completed his movement, when he has reached the place, the book, the fruit, the object he desired, this possession immediately annuls his whole act, the effect consumes the cause, the end absorbs the means, and whatever the modalities of his act and steps, only the result remains. Once the lame or gouty, of whom Malherbe spoke, have painfully reached the armchair at which they were aiming, they are no less seated than the most alert man, who might reach the chair with a quick and light step. It is just the same with the use of prose. Language I have used, which has expressed my aim, my wish, my command, my opinion, my question, or my answer, language that has fulfilled its office, vanishes once it has *arrived*. I sent it forth to perish, to be irrevocably transformed in you, and I shall know I am *understood* by the remarkable fact that my discourse no longer exists. It is entirely and definitively replaced by its *meaning*, or at least by a certain meaning, that is, by the images, impulses, reactions, or acts of the person to whom one speaks; in a word, by an inner modification or reorganization of that person. But if someone has not understood, he preserves and *repeats the words*. The experiment is simple....

You can see then that the perfection of that discourse

whose sole aim is comprehension obviously consists in the ease with which it is transmuted into something quite different, into nonlanguage. If you have understood my words, those very words are now less than nothing to you; they have disappeared from your minds, and yet you possess their counterpart, you possess in the form of ideas and associations enough to reconstitute the significance of these remarks *in a form that may be quite different.*

In other words, in the practical or abstract uses of language that is specifically *prose*, the form is not preserved, does not outlive understanding, but dissolves in the light, for it has acted, it has made itself understood, it has lived.

*   *   *

But the poem, on the contrary, does not die for having been of use; it is purposely made to be reborn from its ashes and perpetually to become what it has been.

Poetry can be recognized by this remarkable fact, which could serve as its definition: it tends to reproduce itself in its own form, it stimulates our minds to reconstruct it as it is. If I may be permitted a word drawn from industrial technology, I should say that poetic form is automatically salvaged.

This is an admirable and uniquely characteristic property. I would like to give you a simple illustration. Think of a pendulum oscillating between two symmetrical points. With one of these points, associate the ideas of poetic form, the force of rhythm, the sonority of syllables, the physical act of declamation, and the natural psychological surprises caused by the unexpected association of words. With the other point, the acnode of the first, associate the intellectual effect, the visions and feelings that, for you, make up the "content," the "meaning" of the given poem, and then observe that the movement of your mind, or of your attention, when sub-jected to poetry, and submissive and docile to the successive impulses of the language of the gods, goes from the *sound* to the *sense*, from the container to the contained, everything happening at first as with the ordinary use of speech. But then the living pendulum is brought back, at each line, to its verbal and musical starting point. The sense that is presented has as its sole issue, its sole form, the very form from which it proceeded. So between the form and the content, between the sound and the sense, between the poem and the state of poetry, an oscillation is set up, a symmetry, an *equality of value* and of power.

This harmonious exchange between impression and ex-pression is in my eyes the essential principle of the mechanics of poetry, that is, of the production of the poetic state through speech. The poet's profession is to find by good fortune and to seek with industry those special forms of language whose action I have tried to analyze for you.

Thus understood, poetry is radically different from all prose: in particular, it is clearly opposed to the description and narration of events that tend to give the illusion of reality, that is, to the novel and the tale when their aim is to give the force of truth to stories, portraits, scenes, and other representations of real life. This difference has even physical signs, which can be easily observed. Consider the comparative attitudes of the reader of novels and the reader of poems. They may be the same man, but he is entirely different as he reads one or the other work. Watch the reader of a novel plunge into the imaginary life his book shows him. His body no longer exists. He leans his forehead on his two hands. He exists, moves, acts, and suffers only in the mind. He is absorbed by what he is devouring; he cannot restrain himself, for a kind of demon drives him on. He wants the continuation and the end; he is prey to a kind of madness; he takes sides, he triumphs, he is saddened, he is no longer himself, he is no more than a brain separated from its outer forces, that is, given up to its images, going through a sort of *crisis of credulity*.

How different is the reader of poems.

If poetry really affects someone, it is not by dividing him in his nature, by communicating to him illusions of a fancied and purely mental life. It does not impose on him a false reality that demands the docility of the mind and hence the absence of the body. Poetry must extend over the whole being; it stimulates the muscular organization by its rhythms, it frees or unleashes the verbal faculties, ennobling their whole action, it regulates our depths, for poetry aims to arouse or reproduce the unity and harmony of the living person, an extraordinary unity that shows itself when a man is possessed by an intense feeling that leaves none of his powers disengaged.

In fact, the difference between the action of a poem and of an ordinary narrative is physiological. The poem unfolds itself in a richer sphere of our functions of movement, it exacts from us a participation that is nearer to complete action, whereas the story and the novel transform us rather into slaves of a dream and of our faculty of being hallucinated.

But I repeat that innumerable degrees and transitional forms exist between these two limits of literary expression.

Having tried to define the realm of poetry, I ought now to try to consider the actual work of the poet, the problems of composition and execution. But that would be to take a thorny path. One meets endless torments there, disputes with no solution, tests, enigmas, cares, and even despairs, which make the poet's craft one of the most uncertain and exhausting. Malherbe, whom I have already quoted, used to say that after finishing a good sonnet, an author has the right to ten years' rest. And he even implied that the words, *a finished sonnet*, meant something. . . . As for me, I hardly understand them. . . . I translate them by *abandoned sonnet*.

Let us, however, touch on this difficult question: Writing verse. . . .

Now you all know that there exists a very simple way of writing verse.

It is enough to be *inspired*, and things happen of themselves. I only wish it were like that. Life would be bearable. Let us take this naïve notion and examine its consequences.

If anyone is satisfied with it, he must admit either that poetic production is a result of pure chance or that it proceeds from a kind of supernatural communication; both hypotheses reduce the poet to a wretchedly passive role. They make of him a kind of *urn* in which millions of marbles are shaken, or a *talking table* possessed by a "spirit." A table or a jug, in fact, but not a god—the opposite of a god, the opposite of a *Self*.

And the unfortunate author, who is no longer an author but a signatory, and responsible only in the same way as a newspaper editor, is forced to say to himself: "In your works, my dear poet, what is good is not by you, and what is bad is indisputably yours."

It is strange that more than one poet should have been content—if, indeed, he was not proud—to be no more than an instrument, a temporary *medium*.

Now, experience and reflection both show us, on the contrary, that those poems whose intricate perfection and felicitous development give their wonder-struck readers most strongly the notion of a miracle, a stroke of fortune, a super-human accomplishment (because of an extraordinary assembly of virtues that one may wish but not hope to find together in a work), are also masterpieces of labor and are, too, monuments of intelligence and sustained work, products of the will and of an analysis that exacts qualities too multifarious to be reduced to those of a machine for recording enthusiasms or ecstasies. Faced with a beautiful poem of some length, one is well aware that the chances are infinitesimally small of a man's being able to improvise, without second thoughts and without any other exertion than that of writing or dictating what comes into his mind, this singularly sure discourse, furnished with continuous resources, a constant harmony, and perpetually felicitous ideas—a discourse which never fails to charm, in which there are no rough spots, no marks of weakness and impotence, none of those tiresome incidents that break the spell and ruin the poetic universe I was speaking of just now.

It is not that something more is not needed to make a poet, some *virtue* which cannot be broken down, which cannot be analyzed into definable actions and hours of work. *Pegasus-power* and *Pegasus-hours* are not yet legal units of poetic force.

There is a special quality, a kind of individual *energy* proper to the poet. It appears in him and reveals him to himself at certain infinitely precious moments.

But these are only moments, and this higher energy (higher, that is, in that all man's other energies cannot make up or replace it) *exists and can act only in brief and fortuitous manifestations.*

It must be added—and this is rather important—that the treasures it illuminates in our own mind's eye, the ideas or forms it produces within ourselves are very far from having the same value in the eyes of others.

These infinitely precious moments, these instants that lend

a kind of universal dignity to the relations and intuitions they provoke, are no less fruitful in illusory or incommunicable values. *What is of value to us alone has no value.* This is the law of literature. These sublime states are really "absences" in which natural marvels are met with that are found only there —but those marvels are always impure, I mean mixed with base or useless things that are insignificant or incapable of withstanding the outer light, or impossible to catch or keep. In the glare of exaltation, all that glitters is not gold.

To sum up, certain instants betray to us the depths where the best of ourselves is found, but in pieces embedded in shapeless matter, odd or rough in appearance. We must separate these elements of noble metal from the mass, and take care to fuse them together and fashion some ornament.

If one cared to develop rigorously the doctrine of pure inspiration, one would arrive at very curious conclusions. One would necessarily find, for example, that a poet who limits himself to transmitting what he receives and to delivering to strangers what he gathers from the unknown has no need to understand what he writes under this mysterious dictation.

He has no effect on the poem of which he is not the source. He can be utterly alien to what flows through him. This inescapable consequence makes me think of what, in other days, was widely believed about diabolical possession. In old documents telling of the inquests into witchcraft, one reads that people were often proved to be possessed of the devil and were condemned on that score because, although ignorant and unlettered, they had during their crises disputed, argued, and blasphemed in Greek, Latin, and even Hebrew before their horrified inquisitors. (I should imagine that this was not Latin without tears.)

Is this what one demands of the poet? Certainly an emotion characterized by the spontaneous power of expression it arouses is of the essence of poetry. But the poet's task cannot consist in merely undergoing it. These expressions, springing from emotion, are only accidentally *pure;* they bring with them much dross, contain many faults whose effect is to hinder the poetic development and interrupt the prolonged resonance that is to be evoked in another's mind. For the poet's desire, if he is aiming at the heights of his art, can only be to introduce some stranger's spirit to the divine duration of his own harmonious life, in which all forms are composed and measured, and *responses* are exchanged between all his sensitive and rhythmic powers.

But inspiration belongs to and is meant for the reader, just as it is the poet's task to make one think of it, believe in it, to make sure that one attributes only to the gods a work that is too perfect or too moving to be the product of a man's uncertain hands. The very object of an art, the principle of its artifice, is precisely to impart the impression of an ideal state in which the man who reaches it will be capable of spontaneously producing, with no effort or hesitation, a magnificent and wonderfully ordered expression of his nature and our destinies.

The Necessity of Poetry

BEFORE I speak of poetry, allow me to say a few words about a poet who has just died, a great poet and for forty years a friend of mine; a French poet of his own will, although a native and citizen of the United States. I refer to Francis Vielé-Griffin, who recently died at Bergerac, and whose death is a great loss. I speak of him this evening because there is a certain justice to be done him. This poet, who for many years lived in retirement, first in Touraine and then in Périgord, had taken France for his chosen homeland; he has a most honorable place in the very honorable list of foreign poets who have written in our language and won distinction by their verse.

You are not unaware that French poetry, since Baudelaire, has exercised a peculiarly strong and glorious influence on all poetry and that this influence has not been confined to creating readers and admirers of our authors, but has also brought forth poets. France has been enriched by authors of high rank, some of whom have not failed in their turn to exercise a real influence on our art. The great English poet Swinburne, who wrote several poems in French, is one of the first to be mentioned.

From Swinburne to Rainer Maria Rilke, the German poet, the list is embellished by those who have paid our language the tribute of devoting their talent to it. I will merely remind you of such famous men as Gabriele D'Annunzio, and pass to those who have uninterruptedly and almost exclusively written in French and become French poets. Together with the Flemings Van Lerberghe, Maeterlinck, and Verhaeren, I shall mention Jean Moréas, my old comrade Stuart Merrill, and lastly Francis Vielé-Griffin.

Vielé-Griffin was born in the United States. His father, a general in the Northern army during the War of Secession, was at the siege of Charleston at the moment of his son's birth. Francis Vielé-Griffin came to France at an early age to pursue his studies; he was the intimate friend of Henri de Régnier, and we knew him among the faithful followers of Mallarmé, in the eager and interesting milieu of Symbolism, pursuing researches into poetry that at that time were very diverse. He was trying to combine certain qualities of Anglo-Saxon poetry, rare in our own, with the forms of the latter. Having first, as is right, composed regular verse, he found a delightful expression in free verse.

Before going on to my subject for today, I shall allow myself to read to you, in commemoration and salute to his noble memory, the funeral poem *Thrène*, which he composed upon the death of Stéphane Mallarmé:

> *Si l'on te disait: "Maître!*
> *Le jour se lève;*
> *Voici une aube encore, la même pâle;*
> *Maître, j'ai ouvert la fenêtre,*
> *L'aurore s'en vient encor du seuil oriental,*
> *Un jour va naître!"*
> *Je croirais t'entendre dire: "Je rêve."*

Si l'on te disait: "Maître, nous sommes là,
Vivants et forts,
Comme ce soir d'hier, devant ta porte;
Nous sommes venus en riant, nous sommes là,
Guettant le sourire et l'étreinte forte,"
On nous répondrait: "Le Maître est mort."

Des fleurs de ma terrasse,
Des fleurs comme au feuillet d'un livre.
Des fleurs, pourquoi?
Voici un peu de nous, la chanson basse
Qui tourne et tombe,
Comme ces feuilles-ci tombent et tournoient,
Voici la honte et la colère de vivre
Et de parler des mots—contre ta tombe.

These few words, this poem, will serve most naturally as an introduction to the other few words I have to say about poetry and, if you will, about what may be called "the necessity of poetry."

*   *   *

The memory I have just evoked leads us to ponder a little on this *necessity of poetry*. I must first tell you the meaning I attribute to this phrase.

You have often heard people called *bourgeois*—it is an expression that dates from Romanticism. This term, which was once an honorable one, was transformed about 1830 into a contemptuous epithet, applied to anyone suspected of knowing nothing about the arts. Then politics adopted it and turned it into what you know. But that has nothing to do with us.

Now, I believe that the idea the Romantics formed of this horrible bourgeois was not quite accurate. The bourgeois is not at all a man insensitive to the arts. He is not impervious to letters, or music, or any cultural values. There are very cultured bourgeois: some have excellent taste; most of them like music and painting, and some are even amazingly *advanced*, and proud of it. The bourgeois is not necessarily what in classical times was called a Boeotian. You will easily recognize the bourgeois (granted that he still exists, which is not certain) by the fact that this man (or this woman), who may be well educated, full of taste, knowing well how to admire the works that should be admired, has nevertheless no *essential need of poetry or art.* . . . He could, at a pinch, do without them; he could live without all that. His life is perfectly well organized independently of this strange need. His mind appreciates art; it does not live by it. Its essential and immediate food is not the particular food of poetry.

Such is the bourgeois, but, as you can see, he is not at all the man without eyes or ears of whom we were told; he is merely the man who is not tormented by "what exists only in the forgetting of what exists," who is not harassed by a mad desire to live as though the luxuries of the mind were a necessity of life itself.

In saying this, I think of my youth. I lived among young people for whom art and poetry were a kind of essential nourishment impossible to forego, and indeed something more: a supernatural food. In those days—some who are still living will remember—we had the urgent impression that a sort of cult or new kind of religion was about to be born, that would give shape to the quasi-mystical state of mind which reigned at that time and which was inspired in or communicated to us by our extremely intense awareness of the universal value of the emotions of Art.

*   *   *

When one looks back to the youth of that epoch, to that time more charged with intellect than the present, and to the way in which we faced life and the knowledge of life, one can see that all the conditions were present for some development or creation almost religious in character. Indeed, there reigned at that moment a kind of disillusion with philosophic theories, a contempt for the promises of science, that had been very ill interpreted by our predecessors and elders, the realist and naturalist writers. The religions had experienced the assault of philological and philosophical criticism. Metaphysics seemed to have been destroyed by Kant's analyses. Before us was a white, blank page, and we could inscribe on it only a single affirmation. This seemed to us indisputable, being founded neither on a tradition, which can always be contested, nor on a science, whose generalizations can always be criticized, nor on texts, which can be interpreted at will, nor on philosophical reasoning, which lives only on hypotheses. Our certainty was in our emotion and our feeling for beauty; and when we met on Sundays at the Lamoureux concerts, where the young and their masters came together, when we listened to the whole series of Beethoven's symphonies or dazzling fragments of Wagner's dramas, an extraordinary atmosphere arose. We left the hall as fanatics, devotees, proselytes of art; for there was no subterfuge, doubt, or obstruction between us and our vision. We had *felt;* and what we had felt gave us the strength to resist all waste of our powers and all the nonsense and malice of life. . . . We met together with souls enlightened and intellects filled with faith; what we had heard appeared to us as a kind of personal revelation and a truth essentially our own.

* * *

I do not know how things are today. I know young people, of course; but one never thoroughly knows the life of young people, even those one knows best. One can know of men only what they themselves know, and they know themselves only when they are finished.

What nowadays is the burning question—the spur that pricks the inmost substance of the young and incites them to rise above what they are? I do not know....

Of course, material preoccupations and political disputes unfortunately occupy most of the mind, so that the seriousness and absolute values that formerly attached to the mysteries and promises of art are necessarily—alas!—transferred to cares of quite another order and, principally, to the problems of life.

But one can also say (I have already spoken here on this theme) that our age shows evidence of an undeniable debasement of the mind, a lessening of the need for poetry. Why? Why is there a weakening of the need and the power of the beautiful which have existed even among the people, which have so keenly existed among the people that they, in the course of the ages, have produced many admirable works? The crafts were creative.

I advise you, when you are walking about Paris, to linger in our old streets, the Rue Mazarine or the Rue Dauphine or perhaps the Rue du Marais; there you will notice the little wrought-iron balconies attached to the old houses of the sixteenth and seventeenth centuries. Each of these forms a simple and original design that is never repeated; the iron-smith who could make these things was a creator in a somewhat difficult art.

The artisans felt themselves masters, and were inventive in their own sphere without trying to leave it. In those days there was no Exhibition; but there were artisan artists, which is as good, surely, as an Exhibition.

The people produced, as they have not produced for a good century and a half, poems and songs, a complete creation that has entirely vanished. Popular poetry and melody are things of the past. There is absolute sterility in that direction.

And finally there is degradation of verbal invention. Certainly the people still invent words, but these words are generally ugly and unwelcome; they borrow terms from the various techniques of the age. Some are fairly picturesque, but they have not that particular flavor which formerly impregnated the language of the crafts.

In this connection I can quote you definite facts that I have observed—and I am not alone—in an almost official capacity: one must note, as well as the birth of more or less felicitous terms, the death of charming words, which existed in our language and which are of completely popular origin.

*   *   *

As you know, the French Academy is a kind of registry where we record without haste the birth, and with melancholy the death, of *words*. It constantly happens in our work on the Dictionary that we examine words that have to be expunged, however charming their form and poetically popular their appearance, since none of us has ever heard them! Now the edition we are dealing with is scarcely forty or fifty years old. So here we have words which forty or fifty years ago were living . . . speaking words, words made for poetry, which today are dead, quite dead!

The case arises fairly often. It is not the actual disappearance and substitution of terms that is serious. That is the very life of language. But the quality of those which have disappeared and that of the newly born are hardly comparable. Last year, in spite of some opposition, we admitted the word *mentalité*, which is not very attractive, and the word *mondial*. But what can we do? . . .

*   *   *

This example, from among many others, shows that the

substance of poetry and of language is undergoing a change that is not favorable to the poet's art. Another observation is perhaps more profound and more serious: one notices the increasing disappearance of legends; legends are losing their force and their charm, and even in the countryside, where they could formerly be found living, they are perishing and being preserved in the scrapbook of folklore. This is a bad sign! In a collection as rich, as curiously rich as *The Thousand and One Nights*, of which there is no single text but a thousand and one texts, variation is almost a rule with each storyteller. Each storyteller lends his expression, adds and transforms, introduces local allusions, new incidents, and his own images. It is the life of a work developing from mouth to mouth. But here everything becomes fixed; we see the poetic value of legends disappear; they belong more and more to the domain of studies at the Sorbonne and pass from the vigor of life to the inert condition of a document.

These are very serious signs. What have we to exchange for these creations, to compensate for these losses, since people can no longer draw their enchantments from themselves, enjoy their own language, and take pleasure in speaking it? Nowadays this pleasure gives way to haste; our speech is no more than a hurried indication as bare and rapid as possible. We are very nearly speaking in initials. Incidentally, the drafting of a telegram bears out this point, and the telephone cannot be said to be an instrument of fine language.

So on that side there is an obvious loss. Now we can only wonder how and why so much helplessness has abolished so many ornaments of life's leisure.

* * *

Artistic crafts are now hardly more than luxuries, occasionally supported by the state or by a generous Maecenas. They no longer supply language with those racy words and turns of speech which have been replaced by the bizarre or revoltingly abstract terms inflicted on us every day by politics and technology. I will even say that it is not poetry alone which is endangered; the very integrity of the mind is at stake; for all these words of our day, all these abstractions of an inferior quality (since they are not defined) are content with a crumbling logic....

We constantly hear reasoning that is nothing of the kind; the critical spirit is becoming weaker. In most of the articles we read, the logical framework, the solidity of the reasons put forward, the worth of the facts—all is mere appearance; squeeze these texts, and you will be surprised at how little remains in your grasp.... All this contributes to a general degradation of language, but in particular corrupts it in its natural poetic functions.

Well, we must look for something to replace them. What has replaced this innate, natural, and popular poetry that was in our language, and within many persons, a century and a half ago? Let us see what amuses people, what their desires and pleasures are. It must be recognized that in this connection we have made immense progress. Modern methods manufacture, on an industrial scale (this is the word) and at high pressure, a kind of poetry that requires no effort, no creating of value on the part of him who receives it; no direct participation, but a minimum of himself; and this form of poetry is reduced to a more or less powerful sensation, which today can be quashed by means that physics and technics put at the disposal of modern man.... We have extraordinary spectacles, orchestras summoned by a gesture. Each one of us might be a Mephistopheles. We could, tomorrow, call up at will a vision of what is happening at the ends of the earth.

Intellectual and emotional excitements are overcome by the intoxication of speed: people go so fast that on their way they by-pass both thought and pleasure.

I hope there are no architects in the audience, because I do not want to get myself murdered, but a few days ago I was saying to one of my friends who is an architect: "You have powerful materials; what you do is paradoxical. You have cements that permit overhangs of 120 feet! This is all very well, and I congratulate you. You build extraordinary sky-scrapers; but, my dear fellow, I shall never pause before a skyscraper to enjoy some detail, whereas I stop in front of an old house or a village church, because there is a stone there which repays an hour's pause; there is invention, an idea, a solution here and there that catches the eye and the mind. But I shall never stop in front of your six-hundred-foot sky-scraper because with a ruler and a compass I could make one in my own room, and I shall see that skyscraper in Tokyo and Vancouver, as well as in Honolulu and Marseille, without its making any difference.

"I know that there is poetry in this skyscraper. Everyone admires the sky line of New York. But, you see, the sky-scraper and that powerful architecture are made to be seen at seventy miles an hour, and if you were to stop at the foot of one of these monuments to study it a little, an hour would be a good deal too long to think about it."

* * *

We have, then, substituted very powerful tools for the pow-ers of action we formerly sought within ourselves, and there happens in the sphere of the mind what happens in the sphere of physical life. There are perhaps several people here who never use their legs, on the excuse that there are automobiles and lifts. . . . Perhaps you have your car, perhaps you will have a machine for carrying your umbrella. The muscles become useless, and one is obliged to take to sport, to golf or tennis, so as not to let them fall into disuse. It is the same with all the needs of the mind. One fills it with easy amusements and even learning without tears. One gives it a ready-made, powerful poetry, indeed too powerful, that triumphs over our poetry of the days of rhyme, which did not possess landscapes, things themselves, life itself ! But this great force, this possession of the tangible world, is not without some cost to us. . . . I sometimes have the impression that we lose by it. . . . Shall I speak as in *Faust?* We lose our soul by it, assuming that we have one, which more than one person makes me doubt !

It is against this, then, perhaps that we must react. . . . No, *react* is not the word. *React* is too little. We must act. It would be enough to become conscious of what is happening to one, and to keep an account of one's mind, to have a little notebook and write: "Today I lost so much . . . *a little poetry*, a little of the power of my mind. I accepted. I merely accepted!"

But let us return to the old poetry, so as to explain how it can still serve us. You know that this word *Poetry* has two meanings. You know that by the word *Poetry* one understands two very different things, which are nevertheless linked at a certain point. In the first meaning of the word, poetry is a particular art based on language. Poetry also bears a more general meaning, more widespread, difficult to define because it is more vague; it indicates a certain state that is at once receptive and productive, as I was trying to explain to you just now. It is productive of fiction, and note that fiction is our life. As we live, we are continually producing fictions. . . . You are at present thinking of the longed-for moment when

I shall have finished speaking. . . . It is a fiction ! We live only by fictions, which are our projects, hopes, memories, regrets, etc., and we are no more than a perpetual invention. Note well (I insist) that all these fictions necessarily relate to *what is not*, and are no less necessarily opposed to *what is;* besides, which is curious, it is *what is* that gives birth to *what is not*, and *what is not* that constantly responds to *what is*. You are here, and later on you will no longer be here, and you know it. *What is not* corresponds in your mind to *what is*. That is because the power over you of *what is* produces the power in you of *what is not;* and the latter power changes into a feeling of impotence upon contact with *what is*. So we revolt against facts; we cannot admit a fact like death. Our hopes, our grudges, all this is a direct, instantaneous product of the conflict between *what is* and *what is not*.

But this is all intimately bound up with the profound state of our powers. We cannot live without these contrasts and these variations that command all the fluctuations of the intimate source of our energy and are reciprocally commanded by them. From that, our actions arise or cease. But among these actions, among the actions that result from this constant production of things which are not, or which respond to them, there are some that stand out by their immediate and vital interest. These are the ones that tend to modify, for our needs, the things around us. "I am thirsty, I shall have a glass of water": I act. I first of all think that I am thirsty, then I act by getting water. That is a useful action, or at least I think so, which suffices! I modify both the glass's situation and my own. But among these actions there are those which arise from another form of sensibility. There are productions of ideas or acts whose aim is not to modify the things around us but to modify ourselves, to dispel a kind of interior discomfort, a sickness that no act relieves *directly*. Laughter, tears, and cries are among these actions with no exterior object. They come under the category of *expressions*. These utterances constitute an elementary language, for they are contagious, like laughter and yawning, or *sympathetically* felt, like tears and complaints. Spoken language itself, when spontaneous, is an explosion that relieves us of the weight of some impression. Now, these characteristics of emotions and impressions have been exploited by culture, and means have been invented, actions have been applied to external matter so as to make an object that can be preserved and that, like an instrument or a machine, can be used to revive a state of mind and reconstruct a phase of our emotion. If I write a piece of music or a dance, I fix a certain action that can be reproduced at will. The musician writes actions for a virtuoso who is ready to reproduce them. If I write a poem or some music, if I paint a picture, I tend to fix, to discharge my emotion, to make a lasting object, indefinitely capable, if it is put into action, of making you hear the poem, hear the music, rediscover the picture; the object will fulfill its role and give back what was entrusted to it . . . if it is capable of giving anything back! . . . But the initial emotion, even if it were very powerful and extremely profound, will not be identically restored, even in the most favorable circumstances: we want to remain the masters; we are quite willing to suffer by art, and to be moved, but only to a certain point; we wish only to pass our finger through the candle flame. This is one of the most curious characteristics of art, which gives us a felt effect, but not of the same order of sensibility as that of the original feeling. Consequently art gives us the means to explore at leisure that part of our own sensibility that remains restricted in its relation to reality. It revives our emotions, but

not in all their individual detail. Finally, it offers us something
else as well, in the search for this means. I allude to quite
different gifts. Art, poetic or any other, is led to develop
certain initial materials, which I will call raw materials, that
are the spontaneous products of sensibility. Art begins by
working upon some form of matter: language, if a poem is
in question; pure sounds and their arrangement, if it is a
musical work; clay, wax, stone, and colors, in the domain of
sight. But then all the techniques of the crafts, the methods
employed for effective manufactures, lend their aid to the
artist. He borrows from them the means to master matter
and to make it serve ends that are not utilitarian. But again,
action brings into play no longer the bare, simple sensibilities,
the direct expression of emotions, but what is called *intelligence*,
that is, the clear and distinct knowledge of separate means,
the calculation of foreseeing and combining. We become the
masters of the actions that work on matter. We analyze,
classify, define, and this allows us to reach the results—such
as expert composition—which we could not expect from
sensibility alone. Why? Because sensibility is momentary; it
has neither usable duration nor possibilities of continuous
construction; we are therefore obliged to ask our faculties of
judgment and co-ordination to intervene, not so as to dominate sensibility, but to make it yield all it contains.

* * *

I conclude by saying that, in short, poetry and the arts have
sensibility as beginning and end, but between these two extremes, the intellect, all the resources of thought—even of
the most abstract thought—and all the resources of technique
may and must be used.

The poet is often reproached for his researches and his

reflections, for meditating on his means; but who would dream of reproaching the musician for the years he has devoted to studying counterpoint and orchestration? Why does one wish poetry to need less preparation, less artifice, and less calculation than music? Can one reproach a painter for his studies in anatomy, drawing, and perspective? No one dreams of it.... As for poets, it would seem that they should compose as they breathe.... This is simply an error, which is not a very old one, and which arises from a confusion between the immediate facility that provides us with the products of a moment—the worst and the best in their chaotic state—with that other facility which is acquired only by a sustained exercise of the mind.... You will see it in La Fontaine as much as in Victor Hugo.

Besides, there is no need to point out to ladies that beauty itself demands laborious aid, exquisite care, long consultations before the mirror.

The poet looks at his work on the page and retouches, here and there, the original face of his poem....

Notes on Tragedy and a Tragedy

FABRE appears, disappears, and reappears in the world of Letters. One suspects, one knows, that between two manifestations of his literary self he has accomplished work of a very different kind, created a huge factory, directed a railway company, managed a mill, set a failing business on its feet, and each time has shown a new aspect and a new employment of his practical talents.

But the diversity becomes marked, and the astonishment of the observer is the sharper for noticing that the purely intellectual productions which from time to time arise from the same center of activity, between those plunges into the Universe of Utility, are no less varied than his enterprises as an engineer or an industrialist. One day Fabre offers us an early account of the theory of relativity; another time it is a collection of poems, and a few years later a very long novel full of extraordinary life and vigor, forceful in its depiction of a drama of material interests and in its realization of a hero of that redoubtable species which reminds one of Balzac. But after a silence, briefly broken by an analysis of Laughter, fundamentally different from that of M. Bergson, a profusion of dramatic works is suddenly announced. Only one of these has so far been given to us, under the enigmatic title of *God Is Innocent*.

* * *

The title alone astonishes, makes one stop and inquire; and one begins, in a way, to muse, to raise in one's mind the question of what it signifies and to what realms of thought it may lead.

One thinks of I know not what enormous *responsibility*.

Man has forever been complaining, a complaint against the unknown, a complaint that narrows down to a complaint against the unknowable—if that be a narrowing down.

Can we do otherwise? Are we not beings constitutionally simple enough to adopt or submit to the crude and almost reflex idea of *cause*, which can only have meaning within very narrow limits? Once it is no longer a question of what determines the action of a living being and of the immediate results of that action, the idea of cause vanishes from the universe—which itself is a way of speaking not translatable into precise knowledge. . . .

But being unable to free himself from the idea of cause, Man seeks and finds a supreme cause of the evil and unhappiness of which he has always complained. If he personifies it, he accuses *God*. But how to presuppose in a God the infinite heinousness that the existence of evil in an all-powerful, conscious will would require? The Ancients, *already* much embarrassed by this problem, brought in here the strange, yet natural, idea of "Fate." I call it *natural*, and this is indeed the attribute that fits it. The contemplation of the mechanical heavens, of the periodicity they reveal, that of the seasons, the remarkable coincidences that occur in them, the chronological relationships revealed by these accumulated observations, all gave rise to the thought of a transcendent necessity that imposed itself even on the godhead, for all its immortality and sovereignty. I do not undertake to reconcile these ideas. . . .

Besides, if one attempts to set forth the few *words* that man traditionally uses to express as well as he can what the vicissitudes and contrasting circumstances of his life, the constraints of his condition, and the drama of his essential incomprehensibility suggest to him, one quickly discovers *four terms,* no doubt created independently of each other, and which no one has been able either to reconcile in a coherent system or even to define with any precision: God, FATE, *Freedom, Chance* are invoked or used according to circumstances. These are four "products of the mind"—or, if you like, "products of causality," *no one of which,* any more than it can be defined, *can be adopted and retained to the very end of an attempted explanation of our condition....*

It follows from these remarks that the notion of moral responsibility and metaphysical justice does not come to mind without at once arousing those jealous powers which are our sensibility, reason, and acquired experience. If we are told that "our actions follow us," we are tempted to ask whether they do not rather precede us—in potentiality? If it is alleged that we bear the deadly burden of our ancestors' immemorial faults, which we are reproached with having committed even before birth, we feel like the lamb created to be eaten because everyone must live, and we then think that by going back from culprit to culprit, one necessarily arrives at the prime author....

True—that is, observable—freedom is the sensation of our general power of action when nothing is urging us to act. But this would not explain the extraction from us, without direct physical pressure, of certain acts or abstentions from action which an alien will tries to impose on us. It has not been sufficiently remarked that metaphysical freedom is nothing but our (variable) capacity for obeying a will that is not ours: I mean one such that we would not have invented what it commands, for I believe that if we are anything definable, we are only what we may will at each moment.

In reality, all these questions arose from the need to "justify" what seems unjust in the human condition, and also to provide some kind of foundation other than force for the social necessity of smiting those who infringe the laws. But on this last point and in support of what I said earlier—touching, or rather brushing, the problem of responsibility—it is remarkable that the jurists have never been able to agree on the significance to be given to legal sanctions. Some talk of *the exemplary value of the penalty:* they think to make crime scarcer through fear of punishment; others, with no illusions about example, confine themselves to looking on the criminal as a noxious animal and treating him accordingly. These are the utilitarians. Yet others, animated by a spirit at once theological, popular, and commercial, see in punishment the payment of a debt, a kind of vengeance, and a satisfaction given to World Order, which was offended by the act of some being.

If we are "free" (in the philosopher's sense), I do not see what more fatal gift could have been made us than this freedom which reduces us to envying animal innocence, the clarity and simplicity of a condition that is always pure, with no inward shadows, with no cruel thoughts, with no hatred or remorse, but affording a life made up of precise and uniform reactions, liable and submissive to the fluctuations of the statistical equilibrium said to exist between the "devouring species and the devoured species." This innocence is reminiscent of that which disported itself in Eden up to the fateful moment when we learned that we possessed freedom and were immediately punished for exercising it.

* * *

The sole object of these speculations, which cannot be gone into very deeply here—and besides, I lack the preparation— is to introduce the order of ideas whose immemorial power Lucien Fabre wished to demonstrate through the theater. From the ancients he has taken the most sinister of criminal cases, the story of a man hurled from one crime to another like a top rebounding from the raised edge of a table or like a drunken man reeling from one wall to another without being able to stop himself.

Infanticide, parricide, incest, suicide, and self-mutilation —none of these is missing in and around Oedipus. This wretched man might cry out with Gide (but with infinitely more justification): Families, I hate you. Yet Oedipus has for this reason become one of the most celebrated heroes of the world of legend and of literature. Several great poets have sung the horror of his fate, in which all that was lacking was the supreme outrage that it has received in our time, that of being the prey and pabulum of the fanciful methods of psychoanalysis.

* * *

I was struck by the extreme energy of Fabre's work, its hard and close-knit form—I would say *too hard* and *too close-knit*, but without that *too* being a criticism, that is, without meaning by it that I would rather he had softened either the wording or the effects of his work. I mean that the *first* impression I formed was one of an excess that was *then* resolved into a judgment admitting that this excess was profoundly necessary and that the author's plan could be carried out only at this cost. The play had to be a sum of crimes weighing on certain persons, *quite apart from their respective places in time*. In metaphysics, time has no effect on the harshness of forfeits. By abandoning his child, Laius has as it were transmitted an unending evil to his descendants, and the defeated Sphinx does not cease to affect even the living substance of its conqueror. If we protest, as we always do, against a moral responsibility prolonged beyond the term of the individual on whom it devolves, we are unhappily forced to acknowledge the sad reality of pathological heredity. This remark suggests another, which I offer to Lucien Fabre: one can conceive of a drama modeled on his, but a drama in which one or several "diatheses" and their terrifying metamorphoses, replacing the factors of criminality that develop and combine in his play, would develop and combine within the characters, with all the severity and all the diversity of horror and suffering which "humoral" fatality, changing its mask but not its cruel face, pursues from generation to generation through as many victims as are engendered before it.

I said that I was struck. . . . This is also because the author has concentrated in the play and in its single action all that we know of Oedipus and his family through the ancient dramatists, each of whom took only his share of the abominations. He has thus brought about an almost unbearable concentration of violence, terror, and despair. Here, I thought, the engineer reveals himself. He knowingly and skillfully puts us under a pressure of anguish and emotion that grows pitilessly from scene to scene. Fortunately the engineer has not killed the poet, and this poet inserts admirable passages in the play: the dialogue in the first act between Creon and his son Hemon contains some fine astropoetical beauties. . . . Knowledge of the starry sky plays a magnificent part in the exposition of the drama, and being insensibly diverted toward astrology, it guides the mind toward the predestination that is confirmed from one scene to the next as inexorably as the march of the celestial bodies. . . .

* * *

What can I say of the dramatic machinery? Confronted by even the most trivial spectacle, I feel I am the least qualified of men to understand "how it is done." How matters are assembled, how managed, how one makes the characters enter, leave, behave, how one ties the knots that are later to be untied, I do not know. I can certainly write for several voices, having tried it; but action, situations, combinations, and solutions seem to me to require miraculous gifts that never cease to make me envious.

Since I am so inexpert, I shall confine myself to a mention of the altogether "classic" unity that Fabre has imposed on his play. The place, time, and theme are as though blocked out, forming a system of links by whose intimate connection the formal conditions of a dramatic work and the intrinsic conditions of the subject are made to correspond exactly.

What happens, what has happened, what may happen— this is what defines the *moment* of the drama (which is not an "infinitely small" moment). Now, in this particular work the subject requires that what may happen *must* happen, since fatality is the very essence of the subject and prints its in- effaceable mark on the development of the play; but it is no less necessary, for the play's existence, that the people con- cerned should retain and communicate their feeling of free- dom, between two encounters with . . . themselves. Just as the mirror shows us *someone*, who at first is merely *someone*, but who then can be *explained only as ourselves* and hence can give *us* the shock of a contradiction, so the meeting with our past actions in the shape of present consequences—*even if only as extremely precise memories of those acts, strongly aroused by some circumstance!*—divides us against ourselves. . . . But is not this kind of inner division latent within the very notion of meta- physical liberty?

* * *

There is tragedy (in the formal meaning of the term), then, in Fabre's work and moreover it is under this name, *tragedy*, that he presents the work. He has, however, refrained from writing it in verse. . . . Should not a play of this type, of such high aims, of this continuous tension and distance from us in time, raise itself to the traditional language of writers of tragedy and force itself to submit to the noble fate of meter and rhyme? In principle it should do so. But I must confess that if he had consulted me as a friend on what decision to take, I should, as a friend, have advised him to do nothing of the kind. Today, versifying for the theater involves something of a risk. The public nowadays is used to the scamped language of the film, which abolishes all literary form. The true lovers of poetry, on their side, have doubtless been made more exacting by researches into "pure poetry." As I once wrote: "What must be said (in poems) is almost impossible to say well." Moreover, one would have to find a verse style that was happily equidistant from the classic type and from the romantic: neither *Phèdre* nor *Ruy Blas*. . . . I do not say that no one will revive, by re-creating, the real verse theater. Who would dare to lay upon the future the judgment of impotence? But I think I can see all the difficulty of the undertaking.

*   *   *

I must now try to express another thought, about the very notion of *tragedy*.

This word (whose ancestor is the goat) was at a very early stage committed to designating only those works in which the extremes of passion and the pressure of situations and events drag people into intentions or acts that are either inhuman or too human, and always terrible or sinister. Violent death hovers over the tragic stage. Panic, horror, despair, hate, jealousy, every means of torturing the soul, and everything that impels it toward a wish to destroy life are the essential elements of this form of art, which seems made to arouse exclusively painful feelings in the spectator, either anxious tension or pity leading to tears, and this course, sometimes almost unbearable, is sustained, shaken, torn by surprises that are rarely happy, so much does the action seem to proceed toward its end *by dint of shocks.* . . . I apologize for this regrettable expression, which nevertheless seems to me explicit. Add that these intense effects are greatly reinforced by the number of those who experience them in common, every breath suspended, every heart wrung, every eye near tears.

Thus a whole type of "entertainment" was based on the exploitation of the nervous dynamics of real suffering, *exacerbated* by the presentation of fictitious events. The problem is, then, to produce in the spectator—who is the "subject" of an experiment—the sensation of participating in a reality that changes him in so far as it forces him to identify himself with a witness or an actor in the very action which is proceeding before his eyes, *starting from a situation presented as unstable.* It is strange that man should find pleasure in these spectacles; but man is not averse to feasting on the sight of other people's misery. Ladies, two centuries ago, went to see people put to the torture. However that may be, it seems that the tragic genre is completely opposed to producing in the soul the most elevated state that art can create there: the contemplative state—a state of sensitive awareness in which all those notions and emotions that cannot compose a momentarily harmonious life are abolished in us.

This is where the most artistic of peoples intervene. I know of nothing more exalted in the annals of the *aesthetic-in-action* than what the Greeks did when, putting on the stage the most hideous stories in the world, they imposed on them all the purity and perfection of a form that insensibly communicates, to the spectator of the crimes and baleful acts shown to him, an inexplicable feeling of watching these dreadful disorders with a godlike eye. . . . Between us and horror are interposed the power of intellectual awareness and the rich combinations of creative sensibility, and we can always return from emotion to understanding, from disproportion to proportion, from the exceptional to the normal, and from disordered nature to the unchanging presence of the profound order of the world.

* * *

There are other methods besides the Greek for dealing with the problem of playing with horror. There is French tragedy, which stirs or terrifies according to stricter rules and insists on the alexandrine. There is English drama, which denies itself nothing, and its romantic derivatives, which tail off into melodrama.

Fabre has followed none of these models. Besides, none of them lent itself to his metaphysical aim. He took from each what he needed to strengthen the fateful impression he wished to convey. He understood how the restrictions decreed by the classic theater's famous system of unities could serve his purpose, which was, I think, to bring about a strategic concentration of the different moments or aspects of the story of Oedipus that the old poets offer to us separately. He undertook to unite and compose them, as, sometimes in a museum, the disjointed fragments of an antique sculpture are assembled. This was a remarkable effort, a labor of the will, which gives an effect of power. This effect is perhaps too intense in the second act—at least for my nerves. . . . In my opinion the first act is entirely fine. The dialogue between Creon and his son

is admirable. The latter character, incidentally, is a true creation—and I think the one that most interests me. His complexity marks him out. He seems to me to present a figure of much
richer depths, and one who is consequently unhappier, perhaps, than Oedipus: he has, I should say, more *dimensions*
than the latter.

Antigone is as pure and touching as can be.

*   *   *

I end by murmuring that Fabre has only half convinced me
of the innocence of God.

The Poetry of La Fontaine

LA FONTAINE is, with the exception of Malherbe, the only French poet of the first rank in the seventeenth century who did not devote himself to dramatic art.

He is also the only great poet of whom certain works have attained that rare and more or less desirable species of fame— that of being, with the nation's universal consent, dedicated, as it were, to the earliest poetic education of childhood, so that the author's name is forever associated with the idea of the simplicity of the very young, as though he had written especially with a view to childish recitations and had expended much art and wit for the sake of the tenderest age. He is thus the most used of our poets and the one of whom everyone in France knows a few verses *by heart*. An air of negligence, sometimes studied perhaps, in his style, and the image of him one easily forms from what one thinks one knows of his life, habits, tastes, and indifferences have given him in the general opinion the appearance of a "dreamer," a man who abandons himself to the passing cloud, to what momentarily amuses his mind, and who as freely becomes uninterested as interested, without caring too much for the unequal weight of reality in the successive objects of his thought. This very simple judgment is worth what it is worth as far as La Fontaine's apparent character is concerned, but an examination of his works leads, and indeed obliges, us to consider him as an author who is an *artist*, that is, who does not confine his action to gathering the spontaneous fruits of the moment. Where one saw only reverie, there was meditation—that is, inner labor. The error arose because there are two kinds of absent-mindedness, one indicating the absence of cares or their slight persistence, the other, on the contrary, consisting of perseverance in care.

The poetic work of La Fontaine comprises (to count only what counts) several compositions, of which the *Adonis* is the most remarkable; a novel partly in verse, *Psyche;* the *Fables;* and the *Tales.* There can be no hesitation as to the relative importance of these various works; if he had not written his *Fables,* La Fontaine would today be, if not altogether forgotten, at least rather poorly placed—that is, placed according to his *Tales.* But his *Fables* have won him the fame and popularity we have mentioned; he is the supreme fabulist. A whole literature—imitations, glosses, commentaries, works of scholarship—has found in these *Fables* its excuse or its sustenance, showing us the curious variety of ways to exploit a collection of apparently simple little poems. But every reputation demands that its reality be re-examined in every age: is it reduced to a kind of traditional tribute, or is it kept alive by an ever fresh virtue?

Here an essential question must be asked: what is the *true current worth* of La Fontaine's work, and particularly of his *Fables,* their *living importance*, if one eliminates from this attempted evaluation everything deriving from their didactic use and from the ambitions connected with it, whose mainspring is not, perhaps, a pure love of poetry? In other words, can one today find real pleasure in reading the *Fables* as though they had been quite newly composed? Further, what profit for his art can be drawn from this reading by the artist in

243

verse? The lover of poems and the poet are, indeed, the only two persons who can give a meaning to the expression "true value" and who can be recognized by this: that for them poetry is an immediate need that can be satisfied only by the actual sensation of the singing language, without any explanation, whether scholarly or not, intervening between the body and soul of the discourse, that is, between the *sound* and the *sense*. A poem exists only in this state, that is, in *action*. To consider these elements separately is in a sense to murder poetry, an assault and an absurdity that are unfortunately in constant, almost obligatory, use in the teaching of Letters. If, then, we repeat to ourselves some fable by La Fontaine as cultivated but passionate lovers of poetry—who, *by definition*, have read and appreciated the many excellent poets who have arisen since the time of those *Fables* and who have brought so many new fashions and such clever combinations—shall we still be sensitive to the voice of the lamb, the pigeon, the ass, or the shepherd? And will that voice teach us something that may help us develop our own industry as versifiers? Such are the questions that each can resolve in his own way but upon which for each one the true life of La Fontaine's poetry depends.

A Fable, according to its style, is made of a little story or apologue, generally borrowed, whose recital turns into a moral lesson—more or less moral. We will not linger on this moral, saying only this: it sometimes borders on politics and reveals the author's feelings. There is no doubt that he felt only moderate enthusiasm for the autocratic regime. The Fouquet affair, brutally conducted, must have left a painful impression on him. In the *Fables* many strokes are aimed at the "great," the court, and justice. The abuses of the old law are wonderfully accentuated in a living and perfect tale such as that entitled "The Gardener and His Lord." Our so-called absent-minded man was a pitiless observer of the system and manners of his time, perhaps as little dazzled, perhaps as fundamentally bitter, as his friend Molière. In these two great men can be felt a rebellious mental reservation, and in both, the same significant approval of the simple wisdom and rustic judgment of the common people.

La Fontaine having borrowed a "subject" from someone else, Aesop or Phaedrus, his creative act consists in the *invention of a form*, and it is by this that he reveals himself and becomes the very great and finished artist who sets himself his conditions, discovers his means, and tends ever more surely toward a state of full possession and toward the balance of his powers. This progress may be seen in the successive collections of *Fables* (1668, 1678, 1694). The form created by him is astonishingly supple. It allows of every tone of speech, moves from the familiar to the solemn, from the descriptive to the dramatic, from the amusing to the pathetic, and arranges these modulations in every degree according to the breadth or narrowness of the theme to be used. One of the happiest successes of this freedom of execution may be seen in the unexpected combination of the keenest and most just observation of the ways and characters of animals with the human sentiments and human remarks which, on the other hand, they must affect. It has become a commonplace to remark on the treatment of the apologue as a comedy, sometimes a very light comedy, but always one full of admirable life and truth. Sometimes this little theater, in which the producer presented and moved his furred and feathered marionettes and made them speak, suddenly expanded and rang with lyric accents of the highest resonance.

But all this was possible only by virtue of that poetic form which is and remains La Fontaine's incomparable creation. It is to the system of "varied verse" that we allude. Since the introduction of "free verse" into our poetry, a novelty that appeared around 1880, one generally thinks only of the contrast of "free verse" to "regular verse," without noticing that this is a very summary and superficial classification. The principal laws for regular verse are equality in the number of syllables, or the periodic return of like meters, and the obligation of rhyme. Free verse is exempt from these restraints. But its very freedom places it entirely at the mercy of diction, and without the artifice of unequal lines it would often be prose, from which it does not compel the voice to rise. Moreover, it hardly impresses itself on the memory. Two centuries before free verse was introduced in France, La Fontaine had created the poetic manner that we have named "varied verse" and which wonderfully unites the qualities of regular verse with the true advantages of free verse. In varied verse, the poet arranged the succession of meters to suit himself, but he rhymes and observes the caesuras. This system is the richest and most supple we have. One may wonder that it has not been used by any of our great poets since this one. It is not without interest to remark that this varied verse lends itself as well to the expression of the simplest, most familiar things as to that of the most abstract that poetry can admit without ceasing to be poetry. The proof of this proposition is to be found in the collection of *Fables* itself, from which it is enough to compare one of the slightest with the "Letter to Mme de La Sablière" to find our remark verified. As for musical power, one example will bring out all the worth of the method in question. I have taken it from the end of Fable IX of Book X, "The Shepherd and the King." The shepherd, a dismissed vizier, gives up power gracefully and puts on his rags again:

Doux trésors, se dit-il, chers gages qui jamais
N'attirâtes sur vous l'envie et le mensonge,
Je vous reprends: sortons de ce riche palais
Comme l'on sortirait d'un songe.

This line of eight syllables is an admirable conclusion to the well-formed and divided alexandrines that precede it.

Actually there is in La Fontaine no lack of less finished verses, and there are some whose facility can be accounted for only by the necessity of telling a story. Every story is thought out in prose and then put into verse: putting into verse is the most antipoetic operation there is. But a story comprises both description and dialogue, which provide fortunate lyric and dramatic opportunities for a poet to seize. All who have written about La Fontaine have with justice praised his exquisite art of setting the stage and producing his animal, rustic, or mythological comedies. No one has drawn animals better in fewer words or given them speech with a truer awareness of the character that would be theirs if they were what they seem to be. Even the vegetation has its specific eloquence: look at the famous fable "The Oak and the Reed." One cannot finally leave the *Fables* without saying something more about their beauty of form. We have mentioned the "varied verse," but the alexandrine is itself varied verse when it obeys a master who makes it yield up all its resources of rhythm and tone. This verse, which is called monotonous and which can indeed be so, becomes in La Fontaine's hands the most sensitive, and the richest in varied figures, of all the modes of poetic expression. There are some of a great and solemn fullness, others lively as a sudden movement, others again whose sound is an image of the sense, like this one:

Prends ce pic et me romps ce caillou qui me nuit....

These remarks on the *Fables* enable us to reply as follows to the two questions we set down at the beginning of the present study: we can find true pleasure in reading the *Fables* without being lured into it by a scholastic tradition of admiration; but the prerequisite of this true pleasure is that *we should know how to read*, and it is the opposite of this that is taught in school. Finally, what we said about varied verse indicated what profit for his art a poet of today could draw from a study of the *Fables*.

We must now speak of the *Tales*, La Fontaine's other important work. What they are is well known: that is, short stories taken from many authors, from Boccaccio, Ariosto, from our own fables, from Rabelais, even from Anacreon and Petronius. This simple list is enough to define the genre. There is no literature that does not contain in its penumbra or in its shadows many erotic works of differing worth, and their undoubted existence could give rise to many a question. Criticism hardly risks dealing with them for fear of itself appearing to belong to the same suspect and special category. I shall confine myself to mentioning one point suggested by works of the type of La Fontaine's *Tales*: how is it that love can be treated in a farcical manner and used to produce comic effects when, in reality, it comprises pathetic and tragic forces that trouble or obsess every life? This attitude cannot help but give to these works an air of vulgarity that is all the more displeasing since these works are in verse. It is all very well for La Fontaine to say with exquisite elegance:

> *Nuls traits à découvert n'auront ici de place;*
> *Tout y sera voilé, mais de gaze et si bien*
> *Que je crois qu'on n'y perdra rien.*

Qui pense finement et s'exprime avec grâce
Fait tout passer....
Vous ne faites rougir personne
Et tout le monde vous entend....

It is no less true that the conjunction in his *Tales* of poetic form, erotic implications, burlesque aims, and the prosiness, even the platitudes, inevitable when any story is put into verse, does not make a happy composition. From the artistic point of view, one may here remark on the frequent use of the ten-syllable line rhyming sometimes in couplets, sometimes alternately. Its use gives an impression of monotony and of facility that can quickly become unbearable for the modern reader:

Le roi de Naple avait lors une fille,
Honneur du sexe, espoir de sa famille..., etc.

It must be admitted that lines of this kind, which are not lacking in the *Tales*, add nothing to La Fontaine's reputation. However, they were popular in their time. As for the subjects, whose bawdy and bantering character we have mentioned, one may recall in the author's defense that he did no more than continue a very ancient tradition to which, I know not why, the epithet *Gallic* is attached.

Psyché is a novel partly in verse. A charming work, whose theme, taken from Apuleius, appears only as a reading given by a supposed author to three of his friends. Under the name of Polyphile the author is La Fontaine himself. As for the others, it has been suggested that they are Racine, Molière, and Boileau, but the attribution is not clear, and it is still debated. . . . But, in our eyes, the preface to *Psyché* is a document of high literary importance, a simple examination of which entirely destroys the idea of a lazy, careless La Fontaine.

Indeed, nowhere else do we see such a clear avowal of the price paid for attention to form, such detailed comments on the process of writing and on the choice of a "form" appropriate to the effect one wishes to obtain. This remarkable text is not sufficiently known.

This survey must be ended and summed up by some formulation of La Fontaine's sensibility, which may be deduced from his language and from its musical characteristics. This language holds every tone, from the simplest to the most subtle, from the most familiar to the noblest; the vocabulary embraces the archaism and sometimes the technical term; the syntax, which is most supple, often ventures into peculiar constructions (. . . *Et, pleurés du vieillard, il grava sur leur marbre* . . .). Finally, the invention of "varied verse" bears witness to the variety of modes in our poet's inner life. His acknowledged gift of animating his characters, great or small, and of turning into real comedies the treatment of slender moral theorems, joined with his other gift of building and handling with grace and grandeur passages of alexandrines in the finest style, reveal a most finished artist. There is something of Molière in him, in his rather bitter sense of comedy (and moreover in his being a rather severe critic of his age, of whose artifice he was aware, under its pomp); and there is something of Racine, antedating Racine, prefigured in the lines of *Adonis*.

Victor Hugo, Creator through Form

VICTOR HUGO is said to be dead, to have been dead for fifty years. . . . But an impartial observer would not be so sure. Only the other day he was being attacked just as though he were alive. An attempt was being made to destroy him. That is a strong proof of existence. However, I grant that he is dead: though not, I am convinced, to the point some say he is and wish he were.

When, half a century after his disappearance, a writer still provokes heated discussion, one may be free from anxiety about his future. There are centuries of vigor ahead of him. His future will settle down into a fairly regular cycle of phases of *indifference* and phases of *favor*, moments of devotion and periods of neglect. For the duration of fame this is a stable condition. It has become *periodic*.

And so one author takes his place as a sun or planet in the literary firmament, whereas another, who was his rival and who originally shone no less brightly than he, passes by and escapes us—like a meteor, a luminous incident that will never recur.

Victor Hugo, a meteor in 1830, did not stop growing and shedding light until his death. At that time one might have wondered what would become of the prodigious phenomenon of his renown and influence. Time seemed, at first, to work against them. Other poets appeared; they created new poetic fashions and new desires in the public. On the other hand, critics, men of various degrees of intelligence, dared to examine the enormous work without indulgence. What would become of that immense, almost monstrous glory?

We now know. Hugo, the meteor, the dazzling phenomenon who filled a whole century with his extraordinary radiance, but who, as has happened with so many others, might have gradually become dimmer and burnt out and entered forever the night of oblivion—Hugo today appears to us one of the greatest stars in the literary sky, a Saturn or a Jupiter in the system of the world of the mind.

When a man's work has reached this exalted rank, it acquires this very remarkable characteristic, that all the attacks of which it may henceforth be the object, the denunciation of the errors that sully it (and they are made the most of), the blemishes one finds in it, are infinitely more helpful than harmful. It is not hurt by them so much as revived and as it were rejuvenated. Its enemies are only apparent enemies; in reality, they aid it powerfully to attract still more attention and to overcome once more the truly great enemy of the written word: *oblivion*. Once a certain threshold is crossed, therefore, all the effort expended against a man's work only strengthens its established existence, directs public opinion to it, and forces the public once more to recognize in it *a certain enduring principle* against which objections, mockery, analysis itself, can do nothing.

Further, one could well assert that at this stage the faults of the work, when they are as outstanding as the work itself, act as foils to its beauties and, moreover, provide criticism with opportunities for easy triumphs, for which in the end the work may be grateful.

But what is this enduring principle, this curious quality which preserves writings from being entirely effaced, endows them with a value very similar to that of gold, since, sustained by it, they oppose the effects of time by some kind of marvelous incorruptibility?

Here is the reply, whose excellent formula I take from Mistral. "Form alone exists," said the great poet of Provence. "Only form preserves the works of the mind."

To demonstrate the truth of this simple and profound saying, it is enough to notice that primitive literature, which is not *written*, which is kept and transmitted only by the actions of a living being, by a system of exchanges between the speaking voice, the hearing, and the memory, is necessarily a rhythmical, sometimes rhyming, literature, provided with every means that words afford for creating a memory of itself, for getting itself retained and imprinted on the mind. Everything that seems precious enough to preserve is put in the form of a poem, in epochs that do not yet know how to invent material signs. In the form of a poem: that is, one finds *rhythm*, *rhymes*, *meter*, *symmetry of figures*, *antitheses*, and all those means which are the essential characteristics of *form*. The *form* of a work, then, is the sum of its perceptible characteristics, whose physical action compels recognition and tends to resist all those varying causes of dissolution which threaten the expressions of thought, whether it be inattention, forgetfulness, or even the objections that may arise against it in the mind. As stress and weather perpetually tax the architect's building, so time works against the writer's productions. But time is only an abstraction. It is the sequence of men, events, tastes, fashions, and ideas which act on the work and tend to render it uninteresting or naïve or obscure or tedious or absurd. But experience shows that all these causes of neglect cannot destroy a really assured form. Form alone can indefinitely guard a work against the fluctuations in taste and culture, against the novelty and charm of works produced after it.

Finally, so long as the last judgment of works by the quality of their form has not been made, there exists a confusion of values. Does one ever know who will endure? A writer may, in his day, enjoy the greatest favor, excite the liveliest interest, and exert immense influence: his final destiny is not in the least sealed by this happy success. It always happens that this fame, even if justified, loses all those reasons for existing which depend only on the *spirit* of an age. The *new* becomes *old; strangeness* is imitated and surpassed; *passion* changes its expression; *ideas* become widespread; *manners* worsen. The work that was only *new, passionate, significant of the ideas* of a period can and must perish. But, on the contrary, if its author has been able to give it an effective form, he will have built upon the constant nature of man, on the structure and function of the human organism, on life itself. He will thus have forearmed his work against the diversity of impressions, the inconstancy of ideas, the essential mobility of the mind. Nay, more, an author who imparts to his compositions this deep-seated power thereby shows an unusual vitality and physical energy. A vitality and energy that involve sensuousness, an abundance of dominant bodily rhythms, the unlimited resources of the individual being, confidence in his strength and intoxication with the abuse of strength—are not these the very characteristic powers of Victor Hugo's genius?

Hugo can risk all the darts of criticism, face all the reproaches, present his adversaries with many arguments against himself, be prodigal of errors; one may well point out in his work many weaknesses and blemishes, even great ones.

Thanks to the magnificence of what remains, these are only spots on the sun.

What is more, this work and this fame have often, and without perishing, undergone the severest test that can affect a man's work and fame. Even before the poet's death, other poets, lesser perhaps, but poets of the rarest quality, were already publishing works of a delicacy or violence or profundity or a new magic that one did not find in his. One might think that this novelty, these marvels of perfection or surangeness or charm, would attenuate, would weaken the great man's dominion over poetry. This result was all the mere probable in that they all derived more or less openly from him. Everyone knows that to aim at not following or imitating someone is still in some way to imitate him. The mirror reverses images.

Hugo, however, endures and has power still. My invariable experience confirms this: each time I happen— *I who was so charmed, forty-five years ago, by the magic of the enchanters of that epoch*—each time I happen to open a volume by Hugo, I always find, in turning over a few pages, enough to fill me with admiration.

But I must explain in a few words how this great poetic force began, established, and developed itself.

In the first half of the nineteenth century, the matter of form, whose importance I have tried to show, was widely neglected. Purity, richness, and propriety of language, and the musical quality of verse were little sought after. Facility won the day. But facility, when it is not divine, is disastrous. The romantics generally were concerned with acting almost exclusively on the first impulse of the soul, whose emotions they tried to communicate without considering the reader's resistance, without bothering about the formal conditions I have mentioned. They put their trust in vehemence, intensity, singularity, the naked force of their feeling: they did not wait to organize its expression. Their verses are astonishingly unequal, their vocabulary vague, their images often imprecise or traditional. The immense resources of language and poetics were unknown to them; or else they thought them hindrances, bars to the possession of genius. These are naïve conceptions —of a detestable slackness. We recognize today to what extent very great poets, men like Lamartine, Musset, Vigny himself, suffer and will suffer more and more from having neglected all these things. This is easily verified by considering the events that followed. One then observes that although these poets have given rise to innumerable imitators, they have found no one to *continue* their *work;* that is, no one could develop the ideas and technical qualities that they did not possess. They gave us something to imitate but nothing to learn.

But Hugo arose among them. He noted their verbal insufficiency and the decadent state of the art of verse that all the triumphs of his rivals did not hide from so profound a connoisseur. For that is what Hugo is. Nothing is more significant than his choice of his true masters: Virgil and, above all, Horace, among the Latin authors. In France he cultivated most fruitfully the most substantial and the richest writers we have, of whom many are little known and read, some literally unknown. I refer to the poets and prose writers of the end of the sixteenth century and the beginning of the seventeenth, whose influence on Hugo is undoubted and from one of whom, the obscurest of all, he even borrowed one or two pages. If one goes back from Racine to Ronsard, one notices that the vocabulary is richer, the forms are firmer and more varied. Corneille, du Bartas, d'Aubigné were for Hugo models that in his mind he must have opposed to Racine. Hugo, like all true poets, is a critic of the first rank. His criticism is exerted through fact, and the fact is that he very soon opposed to the weaknesses of his rivals the resources of an art that he was to develop by incessant exercise until the end of his career.

Yes, in him the artist is dominant. For more than sixty years he spent from five until noon each day at his poet's workbench. He spent himself in assaults on the ease and difficulties of a calling that came more and more to be his own creation. Picture this inventor at work. I mean just that: inventor; for with him the invention of form is as stimulating and urgent as the invention of images and themes. From the time of the *Odes* and the *Orientales*, he seems to take pleasure in imagining unusual and sometimes baroque types of poems. But he thus trained himself in all the possibilities of his art. Madame Simone will recite the *Djinns* to you wonderfully. This poem is one of the many exercises he performed in order to become master of the universe of verbal effects. Sometimes he reaches an extreme and, indeed, somewhat perilous point. He came to be able to solve, or to think he could solve, all problems not only of art but of thought through the action and artifices of his rhetoric. Just as he knows how to describe, or rather to create, the prodigious presence of all visible things, and makes a sky, a tempest, a Cirque de Gavarnie, a Titan, so he boldly deals with the Universe, God, life, and death with extraordinary and sometimes stupefying freedom. Here criticism gets its chance. It can easily point out monsters of absurdity and puerility in these sequences of magnificent alexandrines. But perhaps in its zeal it does not see that a very profound lesson is hidden in this sometimes startling manner of attacking, or rather of assaulting, every possible question and of resolving them between two rhymes, usually rich. Indeed, whatever may be the problems that puzzle the mind, whatever the solutions it decides to give them, they are in the end (if it is able to give them expression) only combinations of words, arrangements of terms whose elements lie in the alphabetical chaos of a dictionary. Mallarmé said to me one evening, rather jestingly, that if there were a world mystery it could be contained in an article of the *Figaro*. Hugo, perhaps, flattered himself unconsciously that he had written or could one day write that particular page....

Although he did not write it, he wrote others. This man ran through the whole universe of vocabulary; he tried every genre, from the ode to the satire, from the drama to the novel, criticism, and oratory. Nothing, indeed, is finer than to see him unfold his incomparable faculty of organizing verses and words. In our language the capacity for saying everything in correct verse has never been possessed and exercised to the same extent. To the point of abuse, perhaps. Hugo is, in a way, too strong not to abuse his power. He transmutes everything he wishes into poetry. In the use of poetic form he finds the means of imparting a strange life to everything. For him there are no inanimate objects. There is no abstraction he cannot make speak, sing, lament, or threaten, and yet with him there is no verse that is not a verse. Not one error of form. This is because with him form is the supreme mistress. The action that makes form is entirely predominant in him. This sovereign form is in some way stronger than himself; he is as it were possessed by poetic language. What we call Thought becomes in him, by a strange and very instructive reversal of function ... thought becomes in him the means and not the aim of expression. Often with him the development of a poem is visibly deduced from a wonderful accident of language that has occurred in his mind. The case of Hugo merits long and deep reflections that I cannot even touch upon here.

But how can one, in speaking of this extraordinary man, conclude without invoking his own voice, surely the finest verses he wrote and perhaps the finest ever written. Here they are: they end the piece he wrote, at the age of seventy, on the death of Théophile Gautier:

> *Passons, car c'est la loi; nul ne peut s'y soustraire;*
> *Tout penche, et ce grand siècle avec tous ses rayons*
> *Entre en cette ombre immense où, pâles, nous fuyons.*
> *Oh! quel farouche bruit font dans le crépuscule*
> *Les chênes qu'on abat pour le bûcher d'Hercule!*
> *Les chevaux de la Mort se mettent à hennir*
> *Et sont joyeux, car l'âge éclatant va finir;*
> *Ce siècle altier qui sut dompter le vent contraire*
> *Expire...O Gautier! toi, leur égal et leur frère,*
> *Tu pars après Dumas, Lamartine et Musset.*
> *L'onde antique est tarie où l'on rajeunissait;*
> *Comme il n'est plus de Styx, il n'est plus de Jouvence.*
> *Le dur faucheur avec sa large lame avance,*
> *Pensif et pas à pas, vers le reste du blé;*
> *C'est mon tour; et la nuit emplit mon œil troublé*
> *Qui, devinant hélas! l'avenir des colombes*
> *Pleure sur des berceaux et sourit à des tombes.*

Victor Hugo's Finest Stanza

Reply to an Inquiry

YOU ASK me, most politely, to do something I disapprove—
that is, to pluck from Victor Hugo's writings some fragment
that seems to me of especial excellence. I do not at all like this
process of detaching from a work the purest or happiest portion of it. Is this not treating poems as children treat cakes—
picking out the almonds to crunch and giving the rest to
the dog?

There is nothing more contrary to a sense of the true
nature of poetry, or more harmful to the education of the
public in this regard, than to subject the structural whole
intended by the poet to this quite arbitrary reduction. Would
amateurs of architecture and lovers of music put up with
having a building reduced to half a dozen capitals and *Tristan*
to a thematic table?

And yet, where hapless Poetry is concerned, the practice
exists, in France, of killing a poem with its own "finest lines,"
without anyone's being moved to cry murder. It is made a
kind of parlor game; people play at deciding by statistics "*the
finest alexandrine*" in the French language. I realize that you
are asking for a little more: a whole stanza. But, my good
friend, I shall not let you have it. Believe me, statistics of

opinion and the decomposition of poems require completely antipoetic states of mind.

The thing that is truly superior and extremely rare in poetry is not the *fine line*, or even the *percentage of fine lines* which people think they can point to in a work and deliberately single out from the whole; it is, in my opinion, the composition of that whole, by which I do not at all mean the logical sequence and abstract hierarchy of ideas, but the composition which ordains the succession of forms, images, tones, rhythms, and sonorities, and which alone makes of the poem a unity that is indivisible. . . . I almost said, *substantial. This unity must be experienced, precisely as one experiences the unity of one of the "fine lines" that may be so lightly extracted from it.* I admit that to the majority it is imperceptible, and that more than one person confuses it with the "lyrical movement" that surges through certain works. This misunderstanding and confusion are but the fruits of the absurd methods by which, from our childhood, we are initiated and instructed in poetry. We must not forget that France is the only place in the world where one does not learn in school *to speak French*. One can learn it in Vancouver, in Quito, in Johannesburg, yet not in Lille or Carcassonne.

But on this subject I should never have done. . . .

Fountains of Memory

POETRY needs no announcement. It is a fact, which either exists or does not. It must come into being with no promises and must penetrate, just as it is and by its own efforts, the world of a mind—as a pure sound suddenly occurs. A pure sound suddenly rises and dominates us, it destroys the bizarre babble of human words, sweeps before it the airy disorder of noises in a room of people, the creaking of doors and chairs, and the murmur of all the accidental movements of persons and things through which silence gropes, as it were, to find itself.

To put in, to mutter a little prose at the beginning of a book of verse seems to me, in general, to be a fault. I have committed this fault more than once, but always with regret. Nothing disturbs and annoys one's conscience more than the feeling of committing a sin one does not like.

But it can happen that an unusual, even quite exceptional, circumstance arises, of which the reader must be advised so as to dispose him to special attention—which justifies a short preface to the poems, to be forgotten as soon as read.

* * *

There is among women no lack of poets, even of poets in the grand style. Although it is remarkable, very mysterious and yet very certain, that nothing essential has so far been accomplished by a woman in the field of musical composition, in Poetry, on the other hand, there are, one knows, many excellent works by women, some of which are brilliant.

But there are poets and poets, and more than one type of poetry. If, instead of considering poetic production as a whole, one distinguishes between those poets whose works seem to develop of themselves at the bidding of an immediate emotion, and those who restrain their first impulse of expression, who do not wish to confuse force with form, and who hold that it is not enough to feel in order to arouse feeling nor enough to arouse feeling once, and as though by surprise, in order to prolong that feeling indefinitely and more and more fully—then it would appear that nearly all women whose talent has compelled recognition belong to the first kind. They dislike offering resistance to their genius, having second thoughts, controlling their spontaneity, submitting to impersonal constraints whose profound virtue is hidden from them. They do not admit that the duration and effect of a production depend on work at least as much as on a few wonderful moments. They do not understand that "inspiration" should be nothing more than their "material."

*   *   *

I was able to observe in one of them, one of the most generously endowed, how astonishingly difficult it was for her to reconsider a poem whose beauties would not allow her to abandon it, although she was very conscious of its obvious defects. She did not know where to apply her effort nor how to handle the verbal figure that had first come to her mind, all glowing with freshness and ease, with the kind of coolness and freedom necessary if one is not to remain a slave to detail.

An expression whose spontaneity has enchanted you is never more than a presage or a promise: the end is the *whole* of the poem. But the person I am speaking of would not understand that the poet's task does not so much consist in receiving gifts from an unknown god as in striving to bestow them himself —making them as divine as he can—on entirely unknown people. One should do what is needed to impart to these people the awareness of a certain *poetic necessity*, which can reside only in form, and form demands a continuity of felicitous expression.

But there come into play here the considered purpose and the desire to penetrate further than the flash and very instant of "genius" can, into the duration of an enchantment; and they must do so to the point of effacing finally all traces of their effort.

This is what is rare in the poetic works of women and what, to my pleased surprise, I recognize in the work of Madame Yvonne Weyher.

* * *

Her book opens, and the eye falls first upon *Eight Poems in Chant Royal*.

The square appearance of these poems, their arrangement in massive and almost solid stanzas, gives pause.

This did not come about of itself. . . .

I confess that before beginning to read, I spent some time examining this "frame," and I was interested for my own pleasure in the structure of these extraordinarily complete elements whose formal symbols, if rendered by a kind of diagram, would be reminiscent of certain pages of algebra, or skillfully and strictly constructed music.

Five stanzas of *Eleven* lines, completed by a final strophe of *Five* lines as an envoi; and these *Sixty* lines constrained to rhyme in only *Five* syllables, whose sounds follow or alternate according to a strict formula—such is the hard rule of this type of ode. (In each stanza four of the five rhymes are used in pairs, the fifth recurring three times. These rhymes are *alternate* in the first quatrain, *couplets* in the second, whose last line forms, with the three following, a new quatrain of alternate rhymes.)

I can think of no more rigorous scheme. Compared with the chant royal, the sonnet is child's play.

* * *

I know of few poets since Marot who have cudgeled their brains to observe the laws of the chant royal. Mention of these rules is enough to arouse all the disgust of the moderns toward deliberate and considered arbitrariness, to which they oppose unconsidered arbitrariness.

It is not unknown how much importance I attach to discipline in art, if the artist imposes it on himself, not from imitation or from belief in the virtue of tried formulas, but because he himself, through meditation on his great desire, has rediscovered, as though he had invented it in a few moments, the idea of conventional structures analogous to those we derive from age-old experience. If he thinks about it a little more, he may judge it unnecessary to create new ones. I have sometimes wondered (ignorant as I am of music) why no one since Bach has sought another formula than the fugue; but I am told that it is adequate to provide the systematic difficulty necessary to teach natural liberty how to follow a liberty of a superior kind.

As for the unconsidered arbitrariness I mentioned, although I am not unaware that everything begins with it and that it carries with it inestimable beauties, I observe that it offers these only by a happy accident and that one cannot delude oneself that it provides us with a whole poem—one of those poems from which no fragment can be detached without destroying the rest and which cannot be reduced to a few dazzling lines.

But for me, the great task in poetry, now that so many experiments and exciting novelties have enriched almost to excess the treasury of expressions and possible forms of verse, is *finally* to seek more skillful compositions. Nothing is rarer in our art. Nothing is more difficult, if by "composition" in poetry one means something quite different from what one means by that word in relation to prose works.

Neither the chronology of a story nor the pure succession of situations nor the "logical" development of "ideas" nor even of "sentiment" is enough to give a poem the . . . substantial unity, the continuity, the indivisibility which would make of it the "glorious and incorruptible body" that one can imagine. This subtle conception excludes the too conscious pursuit of the "fine line," that great enemy of the poem which encourages the reader to destroy it in order to steal the diamonds.

Nevertheless, there is a means of resolving this problem of composition without infinite trouble—a means so subtle and so difficult to express that many great poets seem not to have been aware of it: the use of stanzas, but of stanzas that are linked together and can give the impression of a series of magical transformations of the same emotive substance.

This point of view is sharply opposed to free development, in which one ventures to throw in everything, and which procures the illusion of richness by means of the unlimited abundance of what costs nothing. The poetic player can choose his game: some prefer roulette, others chess.

* * *

Madame Yvonne Weyher has no less merit for having conceived and willed what she has done than for having put it into execution. But it is the execution itself that we must look at now.

One must picture clearly the difficulty of fulfilling the rigorous, almost inhuman rules of the chant royal, together with the aim of moving the human soul as delicately and deeply as those poets try to do who allow themselves every liberty. To sing of the most sensitive aspects of life without letting it appear for a single moment that one is loaded down with chains; while observing wholly abstract laws, to construct forms that compel Tenderness, Sadness, the noble bitterness of Regret, the depth of Memory; to lose nothing of the nuances of reverie while seeing to the accuracy of the arrangement and forcing oneself not to stray outside one of the severest of programs—this is the extraordinary achievement on which I wanted to beg the reader to fix his attention.

It is not that Madame Weyher's collection does not contain other pieces than those in chant royal form, or that one will not find excellent poems in various other forms, but their charm does not demand a special preface. If I thought I must write this one, it was, I admit, to express my contentment at seeing a thesis that is dear and familiar to me verified by a most happily successful experiment. I have often wondered why accepting clearly defined conventions should be more shocking in Literature than it is in Music or Architecture. One should not imagine that the will to do so is opposed to what is called "Life." Life itself goes on only in a framework of terribly narrow conditions, and it is only its most superficial manifestations that seem free and capricious. This flower is formed of a certain number of petals. My hand has five fingers, which I might consider to be an arbitrary number:

it is for me to find some freedom in the exercise of this hand with five fingers, and the most agile and adroit actions that I shall obtain from it will be due only to the consciousness of that limitation and to the efforts I shall make to supplement by art and exercise the small group of *given* means. Now consider language....

A Solemn Address

THE COMÉDIE FRANÇAISE had the idea—the very beautiful idea—of giving you today an opportunity of hearing a collection of poems, chosen from among the treasures of French poetry, from its origins to the first years of the present century.

You are aware that this is no ordinary occasion of poetry reading and that this Sunday is not like one of our Saturdays. Circumstances have given this gathering an almost solemn character.

We are at war. . . . The whole atmosphere of life has changed. All human feelings and values are transformed, exalted, or dominated by the strong awareness of the enormous and formidable presence of the war. Nothing can remain as it was. And now everything in our system of existence, as it was until a few days ago, must justify itself before that mysterious and incorruptible judge within us which is the nation's conscience, stirred to its depths and poised for our struggle.

Must even poetry justify its coming forward and showing itself in such a critical hour? May we now admire and breathe in these flowers of personal passion, contemplation, or reverie? Shall we taste the fruits of the poet's free inspiration or of the subtle luxury of his toil, works of pure beauty, when armies are engaged, peoples in anguish, and every destiny dependent on events?

This is what I must consider in a few words: on one side is the war, that is, France and her peril; on the other French poetry, that is, France and the noblest emanations of her spirit. I ask myself: what is becoming of the latter at this very moment, and what business here has the enchantment of verse, what business here have the rhythm and winged thought of our poets, when our men are on the frontiers and our hearts are so warmly with them and as it were far from ourselves?

I will tell you what I feel. My explanation will be short; it can be easily reduced to an extremely simple reflection on the very nature of poetry.

What is poetry? It is an art whose productions are made of words and forms of speech: an art of language. And here is an immediate consequence of this obvious remark: of all arts, poetry is the one most essentially and eternally linked to a people, who are the principal author of the language it uses.

Whereas the painter, the sculptor, and the musician may reach a foreign public, may be understood far beyond the boundaries of their own country, create an international work, a poet is never profoundly, intimately, and completely understood and felt but by his own people: he is inseparable from the speech of his nation. But for him this speech is more living than for his fellows; he guesses at and uses its most special resources and neglected musical riches; he makes precious objects out of qualities of speech to which the majority are insensitive and which he reveals through his art. He pays back to his country in currency of gold what he had received in ordinary speech. But all this restricts him still more to the special fact of belonging to his country. You will observe, indeed, that the prose writer, the novelist, the philosopher, the moralist can be translated, and often are, without too much damage. But to the poet belongs the privilege and the inevitable disadvantage that his work cannot be translated either into prose or into a foreign language. A true poet is strictly untranslatable; with him form and thought are equally powerful; the virtue of the poem is one and indivisible. Our art, then, is made of the body and spirit of the French language, and this truth, so palpably felt, leads us to apprehend the true function of a poet, the very real importance of his role, both as I have defined it and in the preservation of the homeland.

I used the word *poet*. But it must be understood that under this title I comprise the glorious assembly of our great poets from the most ancient to the quite modern, from the time of the trouvères to our own. I make one mighty poet from all our poets, forming a single being; or rather this being takes shape of itself from this simple fact: that we can all read and understand them, that they are associated in our admiration, in spite of chronology; for their perfections, felicities, and beautiful ideas are ageless. Picture this immense poet, this millennial creator of poetry who from century to century has discovered so many resources in our language, who has displayed to everyone's gaze all its strength and grace, developed all its seeds of music and all its powers of charm. He has chosen, refined, and made lustrous in immortal works the most enchanting inventions or the happiest accidents of the language we speak. He has raised the common language to the highest pitch of purity, elegance, or energy; and in so doing, he has presented to each of us the inestimable gift of a spiritual substance to which we can perpetually return in the anthology of recollection. How wonderful that we should be able to carry deep within us certain especially favorite stanzas; that we should be able to repeat or murmur them to ourselves or recite them among friends, among companions in travel or in the vigils of war. To possess this privilege is to be no longer entirely separated from the world of ideal forms and infinite overtones. It is to keep with oneself the best part of the life of so many admirable men, the most exquisite distillation of their emotions, the noblest and surest expression of our country's sensibility. Our Poetry marches with us, but not as a shadow; it beguiles the tedium of the way; it replaces the gloomy thoughts born of fatigue and the long road. There is no solitude whose bitterness cannot be relieved by this return of the most beautiful verses we know to our memory, which is suddenly peopled by their echoes.

Yes, it is a miracle that we should carry within us, in the shape of harmoniously arranged syllables, the essence and, as it were, the real presence of the poetic power of France; that we can quote in our minds Villon, Ronsard, Racine, or La Fontaine; and that if our lips give them the air we breathe, they at once revive; and the words they uttered to themselves, the rhythms that haunted them, the sounds that charmed them, that they combined, essayed, and fixed, ring out in the atmosphere of our day as richly, beautifully as they have rung through the air of the centuries and on the lips of these famous dead.

After all, ladies and gentlemen, whatever the individual worth of a poet, he is never more than one of those voices— the purest, no doubt, and the most cunningly wrought voices in the world—but only one of that immense choir, the choir of the living and the dead, formed by all French voices since there has been a France and she has thought and spoken. It is from this choir that our admirable, our incomparable language was formed. There are some languages that are better suited to facile poetry. There is none whose richness is more complete. From age to age, from century to century, French poetry has never ceased to exist and to renew itself. From

Théroulde to Hugo, from Villon to Baudelaire, always something beautiful, always something new. One may run over this keyboard, pass from one to the other, from Ronsard to Banville, from d'Aubigné to Victor Hugo, from Racine to Verlaine—what variety is sustained and poured out by this language of ours, which is sometimes alleged to be unfavorable for poetry because it is excellent for prose! No, I am sure that nowhere in the world is there poetry more richly diverse than ours. And I may add that it would be very strange if it were otherwise.

France is essentially varied; from Lille to Marseille, from Nantes to Strasbourg everything changes, but everything holds together. It must be admitted that a country that invented the Crusades and the Rights of Man, where *Gargantua* and the *Discourse on Method* were written, and Chartres and the Trianons built, is not a country ruled by uniformity nor a country that is easily disciplined, yet it leaps forward when it must under a supreme and luminous authority. At such times it needs no exaggerated speeches, no convulsive rhetoric or extravagant invective: it needs only a white poster on the walls, a few clear, simple explanations, and it is on the march.

Well, I was saying that our poetry is as varied as ourselves; it is, in a way, as eventful as our history, which, as even foreigners admit, is the noblest in the world, being alas! the most dramatic, the richest in personalities and tragic situations, as can easily be seen by noting the number of subjects borrowed by the literature of all countries, from Joan of Arc to Charlotte Corday and Napoleon. Among other things, our poetry invented what is known as classicism, which on this stage I do not need to define; but it also created modern poetry. Modern poetry, with its oddities, bold experiments, theories, and forays into the obscurest domains of sensibility, is entirely and incontestably of French origin; and a great connoisseur—he was called Victor Hugo—recognized this when he wrote to the author of *Les Fleurs du Mal*, "You have created a new thrill." This thrill has spread throughout the universe of literature: from Paris it has reached all the leading poets of the world.

Ladies and gentlemen, everything I have said can be summed up in one word. Poets are sometimes interviewed and asked curious questions to which they must give immediate answers. One is asked, for example, whom one considers to be the greatest French poet. I have my answer ready; it is comprised in what I have just been telling you. I reply, "The greatest poet—but, good heavens, it's obvious—is France."

And to prove this, it is enough to know or to suspect that the chief ambition of every poet is to leave his nation's language a little richer, that is, a little better known in its resources than it was at the beginning of his career.

I conclude.

This occasion of September 24, 1939, is therefore not so much a spectacle as a celebration, not so much a literary entertainment as a very solemn act. It affirms our will to preserve, in the midst of the preoccupations, torments, threats, and burdens imposed by the war, a part of that higher freedom of the mind for which, let it not be forgotten, we are fighting, and without which the French nation would find life unworthy to be lived. That in itself is an essential characteristic of this nation's well-marked personality, one that can be found on every page of its history and proved by the whole development of its poetry.

An After-Dinner Speech

To the PEN Club

THIS IS a mere guest rising to his feet. . . . Until a few days ago I was unaware even of the existence of the PEN Club. Now I marvel at this magnificent reunion, where I see men like Galsworthy, Pirandello, Unamuno, Kuprin, together with other writers of all nations mixing with many writers of our own.

But allow me to tell you what a strange feeling I have, and what an odd idea comes into my head as I contemplate your assembly.

I find this meeting almost inexplicable. There is something paradoxical about it.

Literature is the art of language. It is an art concerned with the means of mutual comprehension.

One can understand that mathematicians, economists, or manufacturers of all races should with advantage gather together, since they are dedicated to those studies or hold those interests whose aims are one and identical.

But writers! . . . Men whose business is based directly on their native tongue, *whose art, as a result, consists in developing what most clearly — and perhaps most cruelly — separates one people from another people!* . . . What means this reunion of those who, in every nation, necessarily labor to maintain, strengthen, and perfect just those most palpable obstacles, just those most remarkable and precise differences, which isolate that nation from all others? How is this meeting possible?

Here, gentlemen, one must invoke the miraculous. I mean, of course, the miracle of love.

The different literatures are amorous of each other. And this miracle is not a recent one. Virgil yearned towards Homer. And what have we French *not* loved? Italy, in Ronsard's day, Spain in Corneille's, England in Voltaire's, Germany and the Near East with the Romantics, America with Baudelaire, and always, from century to century, like mistresses enjoyed with more constancy, Greece and Rome.

I consider Greece and Rome simply as nations a little farther away than others. Homer is still only a few billion kilometers from here. He must be excused, on account of the distance, for not being among us tonight.

These amorous literatures have wooed and ardently desired each other; but you know, gentlemen, that lovers always embrace what they do not know, and perhaps there would be no love without that essential ignorance which gives, and which, indeed, alone can give, infinite worth to the beloved object.

However perfectly we know a foreign language, however deeply we penetrate into the intimacy of a people that is not our people, I think it impossible to flatter ourselves that we understand its language and literary works as a native of that country may. There is always some fraction of meaning, some delicate or faraway echo that escapes us; we can never be sure of full and unquestionable possession.

Between these literatures, as they embrace, there remains always some inviolable tissue. It may be worn extremely thin, reduced to the utmost fineness; it can never be broken. But, for a wonder, the love-making of these impenetrable literatures is no less fruitful for that. On the contrary, it is more fruitful than if we understood each other perfectly. Creative misunderstanding is at work, and the result is an endless progeny of unforeseen values. Our Shakespeare is not the Shakespeare of the English, and, indeed, Voltaire's Shakespeare is not Victor Hugo's. There are in the world twenty Shakespeares who multiply the original Shakespeare and develop from him unexpected resources of glory.

That is one of the wonderful consequences of imperfect understanding....

It is furthermore a quite adequate justification for this reunion, which even a little while ago seemed to me so astonishing.

* * *

But one can consider it from another, and doubtless more elevated, point of view.

Such an assembly of the writers of all races, being held this time in Paris, reminds me of the structure of France herself. There is no nation in the world more heterogeneous than ours, and yet our unity is complete.

Is not France a kind of figure of what a united Europe might be?

Allow me, gentlemen, in conclusion, to remind you of an idea held by a man I greatly loved and passionately admired. Mallarmé, who as you know thought profoundly about matters of literature, had made for himself a whole metaphysics of our art.

He could not bring himself to regard it merely as an entertainment that writers give the public.

Rather, he believed with all his heart that the universe could have no other object than that of finally producing a complete expression of itself. "The world," he used to say, "is made to result in a splendid book." He found no other meaning in it, and thought that as everything was bound to end by being expressed, all who *express*, all who live for the increase of the powers of language, are laboring at that great work, each executing some small part of it.

That book, gentlemen, is in all languages.

I drink to that splendid book.

Spiritual Canticles

I suggest that lovers of the beauties of our language should henceforth consider one of the most perfect poets of France in the person of the Reverend Father Cyprian of the Nativity of the Virgin, a Discalced Carmelite, hitherto almost unknown.

I discovered him at least thirty years ago: a small discovery, no doubt, but similar to many a great one in having been, as they say, due to chance. I came across a rather large book, which was not of the kind I usually read or need to consult. It was an old quarto with faded red edges, bound in gray parchment, one of those massive volumes which one too readily assumes contain only a waste of dead sentences, one of those books which arouse pity in libraries, whose walls are made of their backs turned on life. However, it may happen at long intervals that, with pious intent, I open one of these literary tombs. Indeed the mind is wrung by the thought that never again will anyone read those thousands of tomes so carefully preserved for fire and worm.

But I had no sooner noticed the title of this volume than it held my attention. It announced: THE SPIRITUAL WORKS OF THE BLESSED FATHER JOHN OF THE CROSS, *First Discalced Carmelite of the Reformed House of Our Lady of Carmel, and Coadjutor to the Holy Mother Teresa of Jesus, etc., etc. The Whole*

Translated into French by the Reverend Father Cyprian of the Nativity of the Virgin, Discalced Carmelite, 1641.

I am not a great reader of mystical works. One must oneself, I think, be on the road they map and trace, and indeed well advanced on it, to give full meaning to a work which admits no "skimming" and whose worth is revealed only by a profound and, as it were, endless penetration of its workings. It requires a vital participation, which is quite different from a simple understanding of its text. Understanding is, of course, necessary: it is very far from being enough.

That is why I would have done no more than open and close the old book if the illustrious name of the author had not invited me to linger over it. There were happy surprises in store for me.

The favorite theme of St. John of the Cross is a state that he calls the "Dark Night." Faith exacts or creates this night, which must be the absence of all natural light and the reign of that darkness which only supernatural light can dispel. It is, therefore, of the first importance for faith to strive to preserve this precious obscurity, to guard it from all figurative or intellectual clarity. The soul must *absent itself from everything that suits its nature, that is, the sensible and the reasonable.* It is only on this condition that it can be led to *the highest contemplation.* To dwell in the Dark Night and sustain it within oneself must, therefore, consist in yielding nothing to ordinary knowledge—for *all that the understanding can encompass, the imagination forge, and the will savor is very unlike and out of scale with God.*

There follows a most subtle analysis, which I was quite astonished to find perfectly clear or to think I understood. It sets out and defines the difficulties, chances of error, confusions, dangers, "natural or imaginary apprehensions," which can change the tenebrous purity of this phase and degrade the perfection of this mystic void where nothing must be produced or propagated that comes from the sensual world or from the abstract faculties as applied to it.

Finally there are described the signs that will show that one is passing without illusion, without question, from the state of meditation, which one has to leave and which is imbued with inferior lights, into the state of contemplation.

It is not for me to deal with such lofty matters. This doctrine is essentially different from all "philosophy," since it has to be verified by an experience, and this experience is as remote as possible from all describable and cognate experiences; whereas a philosophy can aim only at presenting the latter to the intelligence by as comprehensive and expressive a system as possible, and confines itself to moving between language, the world, and reflective thought, organizing all the exchanges between these three around one person, who is *the Philosopher*.

However, imperfect reader though I was of these sublime pages, I could wonder at the observations on inner speech and memory that I read in *The Ascent of Mount Carmel* and *The Dark Night of the Soul*. In them is the testimony of an awareness of self, and of a power of describing intangible things, of which literature—even that particularly devoted to "psychology"— offers few examples. It is true, as I have said, that my knowledge of mystical works and of mysticism itself is extremely limited; I cannot compare these analyses by St. John of the Cross with others of the same kind, and there is every chance that I am wrong.

I come now to what struck me as the singularity of these treatises: both are *commentaries on poems*. These poems are three Spiritual Canticles: one sings of the soul's happy adventure in "passing through the Dark Night of Faith, in nakedness and purgation, to union with her Well-Beloved; another is the song of the Soul and her spouse Jesus Christ; finally comes the song which celebrates the soul in intimate union with God." In all, there are 264 lines, if I have counted correctly, and these lines of seven or ten syllables are arranged in stanzas of five. On the other hand, the commentary surrounding them is extensively developed, and the glosses forming it fill the large volume in question. The poetic expression, therefore, serves here as a text to be interpreted, a program to be developed, as well as a symbolic and musical illustration for the treatise of mystical theology that I touched on above. The sacred melody is accompanied by a skillful counterpoint, which weaves around the song a whole system of inner discipline.

This set purpose, very new to me, made me think. I wondered what effects would be produced, in secular poetry, by this remarkable method which links to the poem its explanation by the author, even admitting that the author had something to say about his work, a fact that would rarely fail to be counted against him. However, there would be some advantages, perhaps of a kind that would result in developments in the art of literature hitherto impossible or very hazardous. The substance or poetic efficacy of certain subjects or of certain ways of feeling or apprehending is not always immediately revealed to inadequately prepared or informed minds, and the majority of readers, even scholars, will not accept that, to be appreciated, a poetic work should exact real mental labor or more than superficial knowledge. Both the poet who assumes that these conditions have been fulfilled and the poet who tries to write them into his poem expose themselves to formidable judgments, which attack obscurity in the one case and didacticism in the other.

Plato, indeed, mingles a very delicate poetry with his Socratic arguments; but Plato is not writing in verse and is handling that most supple form of expression, the dialogue. Verse does not easily tolerate whatever is limited to signifying something and whatever does not rather try to create its equivalent in feeling. An object is merely an object, and its name merely a word among words. But if the value of recollection or foresight attaches to it, then you have a resonance that involves the soul in the poetic universe, as a pure sound among mere noises makes us aware of a whole musical universe. This is why the man who claimed that "his verse, *good or bad*, always said something" was talking nothing but nonsense, made worse by that abominable "good or bad." When one thinks that for more than a century this saying has been inculcated into French youth, while the language's powers of charm were systematically misunderstood, and the speaking of verse unknown or prohibited or confused with declamation, one is no longer surprised that, during this period devoted to the absurd, our authentic poetry could manifest itself only through a succession of revolts, not merely against the arbiters of public taste but against the greater part of that public which had become all the more insensitive to the essential graces of poetry for having been the more instructed in Letters, pompously and ridiculously styled "Humanities."

There is, in fact, nothing against thinking that the method adopted by St. John of the Cross to communicate what one may call the harmonics of his mystical thought, while the thought itself is openly expressed close at hand, could be used in the service of all abstract or deep thought of the kinds that can nevertheless provoke emotion. There are such thoughts, and there does exist a sensibility of intellectual things: pure thought has its poetry. One may even inquire whether speculation does not always have some kind of lyricism that gives it the necessary charm and energy to induce the mind to engage in it.

The commentary surrounding the Spiritual Canticles was essential, for these pieces are clear enough of themselves at first reading but do not immediately reveal their second meaning, which is mystical. The outward appearance of these poems is that of a very tender song, which first of all suggests some ordinary love and a kind of gentle, pastoral adventure lightly sketched by the poet in almost furtive and occasionally mysterious terms. But one must not stop at this initial lucidity: one must, through the gloss, come closer to the text and invest its charm with a depth of supernatural passion and a mystery infinitely more precious than any secret of love dwelling in a human heart.

The model of the genre is undoubtedly the Song of Songs, which, like the poems of St. John of the Cross, cannot dispense with an explication. Dare I admit here that all the beauties of that intensely rich poem leave me somewhat sated with metaphor and that the many gems that load it end by antagonizing my Occidental soul and a certain abstract tendency of my mind? I prefer the pure style of the work I am discussing.

Enough of my own taste: it is of little importance. I mention merely that the Song attributed to Solomon has created an allegorical genre particularly suited to the expression of mystical love, which takes its place among the other literary genres created or disseminated by the Old Testament. The Psalms, for example, are of the nature of both hymn and elegy, a combination that forms a remarkable alliance between collective sentiments lyrically expressed and those which proceed from a person's inner being and faith.

I may now introduce Father Cyprian of the Nativity of the Virgin, the admirable translator of the works of St. John of the Cross, of which latter I had first to say a few words. I should doubtless never have read very far in the old volume I was leafing through had my eyes not chanced to light on some verses facing a Spanish text. I saw, I read, I at once murmured to myself:

> *A l'ombre d'une obscure Nuict*
> *D'angoisseux amour embrasée,*
> *O l'heureux sort qui me conduit,*
> *Je sortis sans estre avisée,*
> *Le calme tenant à propos*
> *Ma maison en un doux repos....*

"Oh," I said, "but this sings!"

There is no other test of poetry. For poetry to be a certainty (or at least for us to feel ourselves in imminent danger of poetry), it is necessary, and indeed sufficient, for the simple arrangement of words, which we have been reading as spoken, to compel our voice, even the inner voice, to leave the tone and rhythm of ordinary speech and to enter a quite different key and, as it were, a quite different *time*. This inner coercion to a pulse and a rhythmical action profoundly transforms all the values of the text that imposes it. All at once this text is no longer one of those intended to teach us something and to vanish as soon as that something is understood; its effect is to make us live a different life, breathe according to this second life; and it implies a state or a world in which the objects and beings found there, or rather their images, have other freedoms and other ties than those in the practical world. The names of these images henceforth play a part in their destiny: and thoughts, also, often follow the fate assigned to them by the sonority or number of syllables of these names, being enriched by the likenesses and contrasts they themselves awaken; all this gives us the idea of an enchanted nature, subjected as by a spell to the whims, the magic, and the powers of language.

Having read and reread these verses, I had the curiosity to look at the Spanish, which I can understand a little when it is extremely easy. The charming stanza I quoted is a translation of the following:

> *En una noche oscura,*
> *Con ansias en amores inflamada,*
> *¡O dichosa ventura!*
> *Salí sin ser notada,*
> *Estando ya mi casa sosegada.*

It is impossible to be more faithful—even though our reverend translator has modified the type of stanza. He has adopted our octosyllabics instead of following the variations of the original meter. He realized that prosody must suit the language, and unlike other translators (particularly in the sixteenth and nineteenth centuries), he has not attempted to impose on French what French does not itself impose on or propose to the French ear. This is really to *translate*, which is to reconstitute as nearly as possible the *effect* of a certain *cause* —here, a text in Spanish—by means of *another cause*, a text in French.

In doing this, Father Cyprian has enriched our poetry, although in the most discreet (and until now almost imperceptible) way by a very slender collection, which is, however, of a most assured and pure quality.

What followed overwhelmed me. I read with delight:

> *A l'obscur, mais hors de danger,*
> *Par une eschelle fort secrette,*
> *Couverte d'un voile estranger*
> *Je me derobay en cachette,*
> *(Heureux sort!) quand tout à propos*
> *Ma maison estoit en repos.*
>
> *En secret sous le manteau noir*
> *De la Nuict, sans estre apperceuë,*
> *Ou que je peusse apercevoir*
> *Aucun des objects de la veuë....*

This was like nothing else; it was made from very little and completely ravished me without my being able to resolve the composition of its spell, in which the utmost simplicity and the most exquisite "distinction" were joined in admirable proportion.

I thought: how is it possible that this monk should have acquired such lightness of form and phrasing, and should have immediately grasped the melodic line of his words? There is nothing surer, freer, more natural, and hence more accomplished in French poetry. Did ever a more flowing song—flowing but not slack—escape more happily from silence, even in La Fontaine or Verlaine?

> *Dans mon sein parsemé de fleurs,*
> *Qu'entier soigneuse je luy garde,*
> *Il s'endort....*

And again:

> *Morte bise arreste ton cours:*
> *Leve-toi, ô Sud qui reveilles*
> *Par tes soufles les saincts amours....*

Or take this fragment of landscape delicately painted in sound:

> *Allons...*
> *Au mont d'où l'eau plus pure sourd,*
> *Au bois plus espais et plus sourd....*

In poetic matters my vice is to be unable to love (or indeed to tolerate) what does not give me the feeling of perfection. Like so many other vices it gets worse with age. Whatever I feel I could easily change in a work is the enemy of my pleasure, that is, the enemy of the work. It is no use dazzling or surprising me at certain points only; if the rest does not link these up, if the rest may be freely forgotten, I am angry. And the more precious those scattered pleasures were, the angrier I am. It annoys me that beauties should be accidents and that I should find before me the opposite of *a work*.

Even the accumulation of grand effects, astonishing images and epithets, wonderfully fetched from afar, and compelling us to admire the author and his resources at the expense of the work itself, obscures the *whole* of the poem—the father's genius is fatal to the child. Too great a variety of values, the use of too much rare knowledge, too frequent and systematic starts and surprises, give us the idea of a man intoxicated by his abilities and developing them in every possible way, not in the style and order of a single design but in the unbounded space of every mind's inexhaustible incoherence. This exciting idea is the opposite of the impression produced by a work unified within itself, creating an inconceivable charm, *and as though without an author*. Besides, a work should inspire the wish to reread it, to recite its lines over and over, to carry them within oneself for perpetual inner use; but in persistent reading and repetition, the attractions of contrast and intensity vanish: novelty, strangeness, and shock exhaust their quite relative effect, and what remains, if anything remains, is only what withstands repetition, as does our own inner expression, what we can live with, our ideals, our truths, and our chosen experiences—in a word, everything we like to find in ourselves in the most intimate, that is, the most lasting, state. It seems to me that the soul, when alone with itself, speaking to itself from time to time between two *absolute* silences, uses only *a small number of words, none of them extraordinary.* This is how one recognizes that *there is a soul* at that moment, if one also experiences the sensation that everything else (everything that would demand a wider vocabulary) is only pure possibility....

I prefer, therefore, those poems which produce (or seem to produce) their beauties as if they were the delicious fruits of their seemingly natural course, the necessary products of their own unity or of the idea of fulfillment which is their sap and their substance. But this apparent marvel can never be got without its entailing extremely hard work, and all the more sustained since, to be finished, it must strive to cover up its own traces. The purest genius is revealed only on reflection: it never projects onto its work the laborious and excessive shadow of a particular person. What I call *Perfection* eliminates the person of the author, and therefore does not fail to arouse a certain hint of mysticism—as does every quest whose bounds are deliberately set "at infinity."

Nothing is less modern, for nowadays almost the only thing of importance is to *become known:* this immediate aim is reached by every possible means, and the imperfections of the man and his work, when properly handled and exploited, are not the slightest handicap.

The person of Father Cyprian is curiously invisible; yet the world is even less aware of this work, whose merits I am trying to establish, than of him. It has remained until our time so obscure that even my much-regretted friend Henri Bremond seems to have been totally unaware of it, and mentions our Carmelite only incidentally in connection with other works, translations, and biographies to which he gives a few lines in his vast *Histoire littéraire du sentiment religieux en France*. Bremond, who felt and eagerly showed a deep tenderness for poetry, would not have failed to mark out and love the poetry I am discussing unless it had inexplicably escaped the eye of that passionate lover of belles-lettres. It should have belonged to that creator of literary values to bring to light Father Cyprian's *Canticles:* for Bremond's capital work, indeed, constitutes a real and very precious anthology, a selection of admirable fragments from writers whom no one reads, but who are, for all that, masters such as are no longer seen (and cannot today possibly appear) of the high art of construing in simple and so to speak organic terms the forms and parts of abstract thought in religious matters.

A few verses from the *Canticles* would not have marred that collection of noble pieces of prose.

But here is what is known about Father Cyprian, which I learned from a note written for me by M. Pierre Leguay, of the Bibliothèque Nationale, to whose kindness and erudition I appealed. Our author, born in Paris on November 25, 1605, was known in the world as André de Compans. To begin with, he held a financial post *in regio aerario praefectus*. He learned several languages and traveled in the Orient. It was in 1632, at the age of twenty-seven, when he appeared to be well established in his career, *in saeculo fortunam constituisse videbatur*, that he entered the Discalced Carmelites. He made his profession in Paris on September 18 of the following year. He took up preaching and wrote many works. He died in Paris on September 16, 1680.

It *now* appears—or at least I think so—that this contemporary of Richelieu and Descartes, this former Inspector of Finances or high official of the Treasury turned Carmelite, was accomplished in the fine art of writing verse in the pure state. I say *writing verse in the pure state*, and by that I mean that in the work I am discussing, his share is limited to fashioning the form. All the rest—ideas, images, and choice of terms—belongs to St. John of the Cross. The translation being extremely faithful, all that remained for the versifier was the quite restricted freedom jealously allowed him by the severity of our language and the strict rules of our prosody. It was like having to dance loaded down with chains. The more one considers this problem, the more one admires the grace and elegance with which it was solved: the most exquisite poetic gifts had to be exercised under the most adverse conditions. I must explain this a little, which will explain my admiration in so far as admiration can be explained.

In general, a poet can accomplish his work only if he can command his first or guiding thought, impose on it all the modifications (sometimes extensive) suggested to him by his desire to satisfy the demands of execution. Thought is a provisional activity, intermingled with a diversity of inner speech, fitful gleams, and beginnings with no future; but it is also rich with possibilities, often so abundant and tempting that they hinder the thinker rather than help him to his end. If he is a true poet, he will nearly always sacrifice to form (which, after all, is the end and act itself, with its organic necessities) any thought that cannot be dissolved into the poem because it requires him to use words or phrases foreign to the poetic tone. An intimate alliance of sound and sense, which is the essential characteristic of poetic expression, can be obtained only at the expense of something—that is, thought. Conversely, all thought which has to define and justify itself to the extreme limit dissociates and frees itself from rhythm, numbers, and resonance—in a word, from all pursuit of the sensuous qualities of speech. A proof does not sing. . . .

Father Cyprian, then, presents a really unusual case. He had not the slightest access to the ease afforded by possible variations of thought, which allow one to say somewhat differently what one wanted to say, to defer or cancel it. He did not allow himself the joy of discovering within himself the unexpected beauties which the dialogue between the idea and the mind gives rise to. On the contrary. . . . His originality is: to admit of none; and yet he makes a kind of masterpiece by producing poems whose substance is not his own and each word of which is prescribed by a given text. I can hardly refrain from claiming that the merit of completing such a task so successfully is greater (as it is rarer) than that of an author entirely free to choose his means. The latter sings what he will, as he may, whereas our monk is compelled to contrive grace under the utmost constraint.

When I read this, for example,

> Combien suave et plein d'amour
> Dedans mon sein tu te réveilles
> Où est en secret ton séjour,

or this,

> En solitude elle vivoit,
> Son nid est dans la solitude,
> En solitude la pourvoit
> L'Auteur seul de sa quiétude,

I cannot but perceive the artist's extreme sensibility. But a certain amount of reflection is needed for entirely appreciating delicate values of this kind. One finds that neither the "canon" of the stanza, whose quatrain is in alternate rhymes and the distich a couplet, nor the rhyme itself, nor the necessity of very close translation hinders the gentle movement of the discourse, and that the meter beats time as easily as if nature itself were dividing the song according to the sense and at the same time according to the voice—which is indeed a miracle of harmony when such harmony is prolonged; and it does not cease throughout these poems. One then notices that although nothing seems easier than this continuity, although nothing is more seductive to hear, more desirable to reread for a better appreciation, nothing can have been more difficult to obtain. On reflection the height of art is revealed in this: that what was so natural should be seen to be so accomplished.

Modest though Father Cyprian was, he did not want his reader to think that his poetic translation had cost him nothing. He says in his preface:

As for the verses of the Canticles, much work was required to give them to you in their present state, on account of the obligation to follow the meaning and spirit the Author put into them, seeing that they contain the subject and substance of his books; and yet one could hardly make omissions without their being important. For the work I put into them, I will say little so as not to lack charity or contravene humility...yet...I will pay this homage to the truth, which is that the labor whose fruits you are now enjoying in the form in which you have the version of these works is a hidden matter and one that can never be known save by those who will take pains to confront the whole original with the French....

And he adds that "in particular the *Spiritual Canticle*... could well pass for a new work."

For exactly three hundred years now this "new work"

has remained in obscurity, which has preserved it in the condition of a relatively new work, for the first modern edition, in 1917, by Art Catholique, which quickly went out of print, could reach only a few people, and in spite of the number of anthologies of our poetry published since then, it does not appear that the existence of Father Cyprian's Canticles has received the slightest mention. I have said what a high opinion I have of them. Others may say that I am mistaken and that other eyes do not see what I think I see in these few short stanzas. For me poetry should be the Paradise of Language, in which the different virtues of this *transcendent* faculty, united in their use, but as foreign to each other as the tangible is to the intelligible and as the immediate force of sound is to the development of thought, can and must come together to form for a time an alliance as intimate as that between body and soul. But this perfect union, which, we must admit, has against it the convention of language itself, is seldom realized and sustained for more than a few lines. I very much fear that one may count on one's fingers the number of poets in whom delight in continuous melody begins with the poem and ends only with it. That is why Father Cyprian's astonishing success in his undertaking has delighted me to the point I have said.

Variations on the *Eclogues*

ONE OF my friends asked me, on behalf of certain persons who wish to produce a fine book, to translate the *Eclogues* in my own fashion. And desiring a symmetry that would make visible to the eye their plan to compose noble, firm, and well-balanced pages, they decided that it would be well if the Latin and French were to correspond line for line. They therefore set me this problem of the equality of appearance and numbers.

*   *   *

Latin is, in general, a more compact language than our own. It has no articles; it is chary of auxiliaries (at least during the classical period); it is sparing of prepositions. It can say the same things in fewer words and, moreover, is able to arrange these with an enviable freedom almost completely denied to us. This latitude is most favorable to poetry, which is an *art of continuously constraining language to interest the ear directly* (and through the ear, everything sounds may provoke of themselves) *at least as much as it does the mind.* A *line* is both a succession of syllables and a combination of words; and just as the latter ought to form a *probable meaning*, so the succession of syllables ought to form for the ear a kind of *audible shape*, which, with a special and as it were peculiar compulsion, should impress itself simultaneously on both voice and memory. The poet must therefore constantly fulfill two separate demands, just as the painter must present to the *simple vision* a harmony, but to the understanding a likeness of things or people. It is clear that freedom in arranging the words of a sentence, to which French is curiously hostile, is essential to the game of verse making. The French poet does what he can within the very narrow bounds of our syntax; the Latin poet, within the much wider bounds of his own, does almost what he will.

*   *   *

As I therefore had to translate Virgil's famous text into French, line for line, and as I was inclined to allow, from myself as from others, only the most faithful translation that the differences in language would admit, my first impulse was to refuse the proposed task. Nothing marked me out for it. My small amount of schoolboy's Latin had faded, after fifty-five years, to the memory of a memory; and as so many men, among them the most scholarly and erudite (not to mention others), had toiled in the course of three or four centuries at the translation of these poems, I could only hope to do much worse what they had accomplished so well. In addition, I must confess that bucolic themes do not excite my interest uncontrollably. Pastoral life is quite foreign to me and strikes me as tedious. Agricultural industry requires precisely the virtues I lack. I am depressed by the sight of furrows—including those made by my pen. The recurrence of the seasons and of their effects illustrates the stupidity of nature and of life, which can persist only by repeating itself. I think, too, of the monotonous efforts required to trace lines in the heavy soil, and I am not surprised that the obligation inflicted on man of "earning his bread by the sweat of his brow" should be considered a harsh and degrading punishment. This rule has always seemed to me ignominious. If I am reproved for this sentiment, which I confess and which I do not pretend to excuse, I shall say that I was born in a port. No fields round about, only sand and salt water. Fresh water had to be brought from a distance. No cattle were seen except as cargo, when the poor beasts, more dead than alive, hung between heaven and earth, dangling their hooves in the air, as they were hoisted rapidly up and deposited, all bewildered, on the dusty quayside. They were then driven in a herd to the dark trains, trotting and stumbling over the rails, urged on by the sticks of fluteless herdsmen.

But in the end the sort of challenge posed by the difficulties I have mentioned, together with the very comparisons to be feared, acted as incentives, and so I yielded. My habit is to give way to those agents of fate known as "Others." I have no will, except on two or three absolute and deep-rooted matters. For the rest, I am pliable to the point of weakness and stupidity, as a result of a curious indifference that is founded, possibly, on my conviction that no one knows what he is doing or what he will become, and that to will one thing is at once to will an infinity of other things that will inevitably, when their time comes, appear on the horizon. All the events of my life, though apparently my own acts, were the work of some other, and each is signed with a name. I have observed that there is scarcely more advantage than disadvantage in doing what one wants, and this leads me to ask and to refuse as little as possible. The most reasonable decision, in view of the complexity and confusion of things, is no different from the toss of a coin; if you do not realize it the same day, you will a month later.

* * *

So I again opened my school Virgil, where, as is usual, there was no lack of notes revealing the erudition of some professor but revealing it to him alone, for on the whole they are wonderfully calculated to entangle the innocent pupil in philology and doubts—if, that is, he should consult them, which he is careful not to do.

O classroom Virgil, who would have thought that I should have occasion to flounder about in you once more?

*   *   *

Having sworn on this childhood Virgil to be as faithful as possible to the text of these occasional pieces which nineteen centuries of fame have rendered venerable and almost sacred, and in view of the condition I mentioned of the correspondence line for line between Virgil according to Virgil and Virgil according to me, I decided to write a verse for a verse, an alexandrine opposite each hexameter. However, I did not even consider making the alexandrines rhyme, for this would undoubtedly have led me to make too free with the text, whereas I allowed myself scarcely more than a few omissions of detail. Again, here and there the practice of writing verse made easier, and as it were more natural, the pursuit of a certain harmony, without which, where poetry is concerned, fidelity to meaning alone is a kind of betrayal. How many poetic works, reduced to prose, that is, to their simple meaning, become literally nonexistent! They are anatomical specimens, dead birds! Sometimes, indeed, untrammeled absurdity swarms over these deplorable corpses, their number multiplied by the teaching profession, which claims them as food for what is known as the "Curriculum." Verse is put into prose as though into its coffin.

This is because the finest verses in the world are trivial or senseless once their harmonic flow has been broken and their sonorous substance altered as it develops within the time peculiar to their measured movement, and once they have been replaced by an expression of no intrinsic musical necessity and no resonance. I would even go so far as to say that the more an apparently poetic work survives being put into prose and retains a certain value after this assault, the less is it the work of a poet. A poem, in the modern sense (that is, appearing after a long evolution and differentiation of the functions of speech), should create the illusion of an indissoluble compound of *sound* and *sense*, although there exists no rational relationship between these two constituents of language, which are linked word by word in our memory; that is, by chance, to be called on at need—another effect of chance.

* * *

I shall now relate quite simply my impressions as a translator, but, according to my peculiar habit of mind, I shall not be able to help first laying down a few principles and turning over a few ideas—for the pleasure of it. . . . Πρὸς Χάριν.

* * *

Writing *anything at all*, as soon as the act of writing requires a certain amount of thought and is not a mechanical and unbroken inscribing of spontaneous inner speech, is a work of translation exactly comparable to that of transmuting a text from one language into another. This is because, within the range of any one language, used by everybody to meet the conditions of the moment and of circumstance, our interlocutor, our simple or complex intent, our leisure or haste, and so on, modify our speech. We have one language for ourselves, from which all other ways of speaking differ more

or less. One language for our friends, one for general intercourse, one for the rostrum. There is one for love, one for
anger, one for command, and one for prayer. There is one
for poetry and one of prose, if not several in each category,
and all this with the same vocabulary (more or less restricted
or extended as the case may be) and subject to the same
syntax.

* * *

If the discourse is a considered one, it is as though composed
of halts; it proceeds from point to point. Instead of embracing
and permitting the utterance of what comes to it as an immediate result of a stimulus, the mind thinks and rethinks (as
though in an *aside*) the thing it wishes to express, which is not
yet in language, and this takes place *in the constant presence*
of the conditions it has set itself.

A man writing verse, poised between his ideal of beauty
and his nothingness, is in a state of active and questioning
expectation that renders him uniquely and supremely sensitive to the forms and words which the shape of his desire,
endlessly resumed and retraced, *demands from the unknown*,
that is from the latent resources of his constitution as a speaker.
Meanwhile, an indefinable *singing force* exacts from him what
the bare thought can obtain only through a host of successively tested combinations. The poet chooses among these,
not the one which would express his "thought" most exactly
(that is the business of prose) and which would therefore repeat what he knows already, but the one which a thought by
itself cannot produce, and which appears to him both strange
and a stranger, a precious and unique solution to a problem
that is formulated only when it is solved. This happy formulation communicates to the poet the same state of emotion

which suddenly engendered the formulation: it is not a constructed expression, but a kind of propagation, a matter of resonance. Here language is no longer an intermediary annulled by understanding, once its office is accomplished; it acts through its form, and the effect of form is to be immediately reborn and recognized as itself.

The poet is a peculiar type of translator, who translates ordinary speech, modified by emotion, into "language of the gods," and his inner labor consists less of seeking words for his ideas than of seeking ideas for his words and paramount rhythms.

*   *   *

Although I am the least self-assured of Latinists, the slender and mediocre knowledge of the language of Rome that I still retain is very precious to me. One can quite easily write in ignorance of that language, but I do not believe that, if one is ignorant of it, one can feel that one is constructing what one writes as well as if one had a certain awareness of the underlying Latin. One may quite well draw the human body without having the least knowledge of anatomy, but he who has this knowledge is bound to profit somewhat by it, if only by abusing it in order more boldly and successfully to distort the figures in his composition. Latin is not merely the father of French; it is also its tutor in matters of the grand style. All the foolishness and extraordinary reasoning that have been put forward in defense of what are vaguely and untruthfully called the *Humanities* do but obscure the evidence of the true value for us of a language to which we owe what is most solid and dignified in the monuments of our own tongue. Latin is related to French in two ways, a fact in itself both remarkable and unusual. First of all, Latin gave birth to French through a succession of imperceptible self-modifications, during which evolution a good many other factors and borrowings were irregularly annexed and incorporated down the ages. Later, when our French language was well established and quite distinct from its parent stock, learned men and the most notable authors of their time chose out of the long history of literary Latin one period, rather short but rich in works of the first order, which they hailed as the epoch of perfection in the arts of speaking and writing. One cannot prove that they were right, since this is not a field in which proofs can be made, but it would be easy to show that the close study and assimilation of the writings of Cicero, Livy, or Tacitus were essential to the formation of our abstract prose in the first half of the seventeenth century, which contains the finest and most substantial works produced by France in the realm of Letters. Poor Latinist though I am, this is what I feel.

But I should be dealing with poetry and with Virgil.

* * *

After a while, as I went on with my translation—making, unmaking, remaking, sacrificing here and there, restoring as best I could what I had first rejected—this labor of approximation with its little successes, its regrets, its conquests, and its resignations, produced in me an interesting feeling, of which I was not immediately aware and which it would be better not to confess, if I cared about other readers than those reflective enough to understand it.

Faced with my Virgil, I had the sensation (well known to me) of a poet at work. From time to time I argued absently with myself about this famous book, set in its millennial fame, with as much freedom as if it had been a poem of my own on the table before me. At moments, as I fiddled with my translation, I caught myself wanting to change something in the venerable text. It was a naïve and unconscious identification with the imagined state of mind of a writer in the Augustan age. This lasted for one or two seconds of actual time and amused me. "Why not?" I said to myself, returning from this short absence. Why not? At bottom there are always the same problems—that is, the same attitudes: the "inner" ear alert for the possible, for what will murmur "of itself" and, once murmured, will return to the condition of desire; the same suspense and the same verbal crystallizations; the same oriented sensitivity of the *subjective* vocabulary, as though all the words in the memory were watching their chance to try their luck in reaching the voice. I was not afraid to reject this epithet, to dislike that word. Why not?

* * *

Two coincident remarks may serve to justify this involuntary amusement. As a diversion the critic may explain himself to himself.

First of all, there is the fact that the *Eclogues* are a work of youth. Then, there is the state of Latin poetry at the time of their composition. The man was young, but the art of verse in Rome had reached the point where it was so conscious of its means that the temptation to employ them for the pleasure of it and to develop them to the limit outran the true, primitive, and simple need of self-expression. The taste for producing the effect became the cause: put a weapon into the hands of a boy, and flee from him. This is because awareness of strength urges us to use it, and abuse of power is inevitably suggested by the knowledge that one has it. So, in the arts, there appear the virtuosos with their superb indifference to the subject they have to treat or interpret.

But to produce this mental state it is not necessary that

technical ability, the possession of supple means, and the free play of an articulate mind be really as assured as the budding artist imagines after making a few attempts whose daring and novelty astonish and enrapture him. It is almost enough to have some inkling of them, and to feel in himself the necessary audacity, for him to experience the sensation of wresting from his probable genius one or two secrets of producing Beauty....

* * *

I have gone into this subject because anything useful I have to say about Virgil I have gathered from some experience of his craft. Indeed, erudition (which I do not possess) can only point out amid so much uncertainty a few landmarks of biography, reading, or the interpretation of terms. This has its importance, but it is mainly external. It would doubtless be interesting to know whether the poet practiced the kind of love he attributes to some of his shepherds, or whether a certain plant named in his verse has its equivalent in French. Philology can ponder laboriously, and even brilliantly, over these problems. But for myself, I can only wander along quite different paths. I proceed, as is my method, from the finished poem, crystallized as it were in its fame, back to its nascent state. I agree that this is a matter of pure imagination, but imagination tempered by reliable memories.

* * *

I cannot, then, think of Virgil as a young poet without remembering the time when I, too, was a beginner. The work of translation, done with regard for a certain approximation of form, causes us in some way to try walking in the tracks left by the author; and not to fashion one text upon another, but from the latter to work back to the virtual moment of its formation, to the phase when the mind is in the same state as an orchestra whose instruments begin to waken, calling to each other and seeking harmony before beginning their concert. From that vividly imagined state one must make one's way down toward its resolution in a work in a different tongue.

The *Eclogues*, drawing me for a moment out of my old age, took me back to the time of my first verses. They seemed to give me the same impressions. I believed I could see in the text a mixture of perfections and imperfections, of felicitous combinations and graces of form together with palpably clumsy expressions and sometimes rather surprising common-places, of which I shall give an example. I recognized in this unevenness of execution a talent in its youth, and one, more-over, that had budded at a critical age of poetry. When I was twenty, our own poetry, after four centuries of magnificent production, was prey to a restless search for entirely new developments. The widest variety of forms and modes of expression was permitted, and our art was given over to every possible experiment that could be suggested, by both the wish to break with the poetic systems followed till then and the positive idea of enriching it with inventions that were sometimes bizarre, born of the subtlest analyses of the stim-ulating powers of language.

I was attracted by research of this kind. Soon I had more liking for it than was perhaps necessary merely for the mak-ing of verse. My passionate interest in the creative process itself detached me from the initial motive of works, now be-come a pretext, and in the end gave me a sensation of freedom toward "ideas," and of the supremacy of form over them, which satisfied my belief in the sovereignty of the mind over its functions. I made up my mind that thought is only an accessory to poetry and that the chief thing in a work in verse, a thing proclaimed by the very use of verse, is the *whole*, the power resulting from effects compounded of all the attributes of language.

* * *

These explanations, far too personal perhaps, are intended to show that I found myself assuming an attitude of familiarity, rather shocking but inevitable, towards a work of my own trade.

I might also observe that Latin verse differs much more from prose than does French verse, which grazes it and even blends too easily with it, in spite of being subject, in general, to the law of rhyme, which is unknown in "classical" Latin. French verse will stand being made from a verbal substance that does not necessarily display the musical quality of the "language of the gods." Our syllables follow one another without any rules requiring them to do so as harmoniously as possible. This was where Malherbe and Boileau erred, forgetting the essential part of their code while proscribing the unfortunate *hiatus*, and thus sometimes making life very difficult for us and depriving us of charming effects such as the most necessary *tutoiements*. Only a few poets have spent their energy in the search for continuous euphony in their verses, which in most cases is infrequent and almost incidental. I admit that I have attached prime importance to euphony and made great sacrifices to obtain it. I have often said: for me, since the language of the gods should be as distinct as possible from the language of men, all means of differentiating it should be retained as long as they also conduce to harmony. I am a partisan of inversions.

* * *

Being imbued with these sentiments, I could not help looking at the text of the *Eclogues*, as I translated them, with the same critical eye as at French verse, my own or another's. I may disapprove, may regret, or may admire; I may envy or delete; I may reject, erase, then rediscover, confirm my discovery, and looking on it with more favor the second time, adopt it.

When an illustrious work is in question, this way of treating it by analogy may, and indeed probably does, appear naïve and presumptuous. I can only contend that it was quite natural for me to do so, for the reasons I have mentioned. Moreover, I thought that by thus imagining the still fluid state of a work now far beyond being merely completed, I could most feelingly share in the very life of that work, for a work dies by being completed. When a poem compels one to read it with passion, the reader feels he is *momentarily its author*, and *that is how he knows the poem is beautiful*. Finally, my illusory identification all at once dispelled the schoolroom atmosphere of boredom, the recollection of wasted hours and rigid programs that brood over those unhappy shepherds, their flocks, and their loves (of various kinds), and which the sight of my "classic" brings back to me. I know of nothing more barbarous, pointless, and consequently more stupid than a system of education that confuses the so-called acquisition of a language with the so-called comprehension and enjoyment of a literature. Marvels of poetry or prose are droned out by children who stumble over each word, lost in a vocabulary and syntax that teach them nothing but their ignorance, whereas they know only too well that this forced labor leads to nothing and that they will abandon with relief all these great men who have been turned into instruments of torture for them and all these beauties whose too early and peremptory acquaintance engenders, for the most part, nothing but distaste.

* * *

Let us now face the *Eclogues* as readers tempted to play the poet. One needs some courage to be this particular poet. In age he is between a youth and a young man. He knows the pleasure of writing verse. He is already able to sing of whatever he likes; he finds a thousand "motifs" in his Italic countryside—both nurse and mother. He is its son and lives by it, body and soul. Besides being well versed in letters, he is more familiar than anyone with the people, the customs, the works and days of this very varied land, where wheat and vines are cultivated, where there are fields and marshes, wooded mountains and bare, stony patches. The elm and cypress grow there, each in its own particular majesty. There are also oaks, sometimes struck by lightning—which signifies something. Moreover, the whole region is haunted or inhabited by deities or divinities who each have some part to play in the strange economy of nature found in Latium, which was a singular combination of the mystical and practical sides of existence. The common task of this mythical population was to animate men's relations with the products, metamorphoses, caprices and laws, benefits and hardships, regularities and irregularities they observed in the world around them. In those days nothing was inanimate, nothing was senseless and deaf unless deliberately, for those Latin peasants, who gave their real names to the springs, the woods, and the grottoes and knew how to speak to things, to invoke and adjure them and call them to witness. So between things and men there grew up an intercourse of mystery and service that we cannot call to mind without thinking: "Poetry"—thus eliminating the whole value and seriousness of this system of exchanges. But what we call "Poetry" is in fact only what remains to us of an epoch that knew only how to create. All poetry derives from a period of innocent creative awareness and has gradually emerged from a primary and spontaneous state in which thought was fiction in all its force. I fancy that this power has become progressively weaker in towns, where nature is ill received and badly treated, where fountains obey the magistrates, nymphs have dealings with the vice squad, satyrs are looked at askance, and seasons are thwarted. Later on, the countryside also became depopulated, not only of its charming and redoubtable ghosts but also of its credulous and dreaming men. The peasant became an "agriculturist."

But, to return to our poet of the year 40 B.C., it must be admitted that one sings of Fauns, Dryads, Silenus, and Priapus more gracefully when one believes much less in their existence than in the magic of accomplished verse and in the charm of exquisitely formed figures of speech.

* * *

Virgil, the small landowner—though very different from many modern ones, who are moved only by the conversion of their toil and sweat into hard cash, and who cut down a fine tree on the edge of a field as though the preservation of that magnificence were a crime against their virtuous economy —Virgil, who felt himself divided between the different ways of looking at the country around him, Virgil, whose view was double, sometimes invested the countryside with the contentment, fears, and hopes of a man who possesses and is often obsessed by the cares of the property that provides him with a living. At other times a different consideration assailed him. His ambitions ceased to be rural; he was no longer a simple man; there emerged in him a polished spirit, learned in Greek refinements and attracted by subtler compositions than these songs of the artless herdsmen. He could have written an eleventh eclogue between him and himself. But then he was, or had just become, a victim of the disorders that civil war and its brutal consequences had brought into the orbit of his life.

So: a poet, whose desire and artifices are developing, a man of the fields, yet a man threatened with expropriation and practically ruined by the exactions of the victorious soldiery, reduced to appealing to the powers of the day and arranging for protectors—such is the threefold state of the author of the *Eclogues*. Virgil's whole poetic career was to be the most graceful development of the Latin language and its musical and plastic means in a field of political forces, with his native soil at once a foster mother, a bearer of history or legend, and a treasure house of images, furnishing him with the different pretexts, settings, episodes, and personages of his successive works.

* * *

This would be a good place for a short consideration of the poet's relations with the authorities. It is a vast subject, a perennial question. If I had not so often teased History, I should suggest a thesis or treatise: *On the Relations of Poetry with Various Regimes or Governments*. One could also conceive of a Fable in the manner of La Fontaine: "The Poet and the State," on the lines of "The Cobbler and the Financier." Or make a commentary on the famous saying of the Gospel: "Render unto Caesar," etc.

This problem admits of as many solutions as the mood

and state of each man, or the circumstances, suggest. There are economic solutions—for one must live. Others are of a moral order. And some are purely affective. A regime attracts either by its material perfections or by its glory and triumphs; one leader by his genius; another by his liberality, sometimes a mere smile. In other cases opposition is provoked by the state of public affairs. The man of intellect rebels more or less openly or shuts himself up in a work that secretes a kind of intellectual insulation about his sensibility. In fact, every type can be observed. Racine adores his King. Chénier curses his tyrants. Hugo goes into exile. Corneille begs proudly. Goethe prefers injustice to disorder. Majesty dazzles. Authority impresses. Freedom intoxicates. Anarchy terrifies. Personal interest speaks with its powerful voice. One must not forget, either, that every individual distinguished by his talents places himself in his heart among a certain aristocracy. Whether he wishes it or not, he cannot confuse himself with the masses, and this unavoidable feeling has the most various consequences. He notices that democracy, egalitarian in its essence, is incapable of pensioning a poet. Or else, judging the men in power and the men dominated by these, he despises both but feels the temptation to appear in politics himself and to take part in the conduct of affairs. This temptation is not infrequent among lyric poets. It is remarkable that the purest of human occupations, that of taming and elevating beings by song, as Orpheus did, should so often lead to coveting the impurest of occupations. What is one to think? There are examples of everything, since we are speaking of History....

* * *

Virgil cannot stand disorder and exactions. He sees himself plundered, torn from his home, deprived of his means of existence by measures of political expediency. He sees a threat to his leisure to be himself and to become what he dreams of —that most precious possession, that treasure of free time, rich in latent beauties that he is sure of bringing forth. He sees no further. How should one expect him not to welcome the favors of a tyrant, not to sing of the man who assures him peaceful days and thus restores his reason for living?

Ludere quae vellem calamo permisit agresti

Virgil did not hesitate between the independence of the citizen and that of the creator of poems. Perhaps he did not even think that he was sacrificing anything in professing to praise Caesar, even to deifying him:

Erit ille semper deus. . . .

Just imagine all the sentences that could be written for or against that attitude, according as one judged as a modern or took account of the relativity of feelings and circumstances. In those days there was yet no question of the Rights of Man.

The problem of conscience that might be introduced here, insoluble though it is, becomes particularly interesting if it is transformed into a problem of values. If the submission to a despot, the acceptance of his favors, which degenerates into, or reveals itself in, expressions of gratitude and praise, is a condition of the production of works of the first order, what is one to decide, to do, to think? This problem is hardly introduced before it develops into endless arguments. I shall take care not to enter upon them.

APPENDIX

Sur la Technique Littéraire

...LA LITTÉRATURE est l'art de se jouer de l'âme des autres. C'est avec cette brutalité scientifique que notre époque a vu poser le problème de l'esthétique du Verbe, c'est-à-dire le problème de la Forme.

Etant donnés une impression, un rêve, une pensée, *il faut* l'exprimer de telle manière, qu'on produise dans l'âme d'un auditeur le maximum d'effet—et un effet entièrement calculé par l'Artiste.

Cette formule donne, par déduction, quelques notions très nettes sur le Style: le style n'est pas un rite invariable, un éternel moule définitivement coulé—même par un Flaubert—il doit se plier au dessein de l'auteur et servir uniquement, à préparer le *feu d'artifice* final. Il le faut adéquat à l'objet. Enfin, l'écrivain devra posséder diverses notes dans le clavier de l'expression, afin de produire de multiples effets—comme le musicien a le choix entre un certain nombre de timbres et de vitesses rythmiques.

Et, ceci nous amène naturellement à une conception toute nouvelle et moderne du poète. Ce n'est plus le délirant échevelé, celui qui écrit tout un poème dans une nuit de fièvre, c'est un froid savant, presque un algébriste, au service d'un rêveur affiné. Cent vers tout au plus entreront dans ses plus longues pièces. . . . Il se gardera de jeter sur le papier tout ce que lui soufflera aux minutes heureuses, la Muse Associa-

On Literary Technique

... LITERATURE is the art of playing on the minds of others. It is with this scientific brutality that the problem of the aesthetics of the Word, that is to say the problem of Form, has been set for our age.

Given an impression, a dream, a thought, one *must* express it in such a way as to produce the maximum effect in the mind of a listener—an effect entirely calculated by the Artist.

From this formula one can deduce several definite ideas about Style: style is not an unchanging rite, an everlasting mold cut once and for all—even by a Flaubert; it must adapt itself to the author's design and serve solely to prepare the final *fireworks*. It must be adequate for its object. Finally, the writer must be master of various notes in the scale of expression so as to produce multiple effects—just as the musician has the choice of a certain number of notes and tempos.

And this leads us naturally to a totally new and modern conception of the poet. He is no longer the disheveled madman who writes a whole poem in the course of one feverish night; he is a cool scientist, almost an algebraist, in the service of a subtle dreamer. A hundred lines at the most will make up his longest poems. ... He will take care not to hurl on to paper everything whispered to him in fortunate moments by the Muse of Free Association. On the contrary, everything he has imagined, felt, dreamed, and planned will be passed

tion-des-Idées. Mais, au contraire, tout ce qu'il aura imaginé, senti, songé, échafaudé, passera au crible, sera pesé, épuré, mis à la *forme* et condensé le plus possible pour gagner en force ce qu'il sacrifie en longueur: un sonnet, par exemple, sera une véritable quintessence, un osmazôme, un suc concentré, et cohobé, réduit à quatorze vers, soigneusement *composé* en vue d'un effet final et foudroyant. Ici, l'adjectif sera impermutable, la sonorité des mètres sagement graduée, la pensée souvent parée d'un *Symbole*, voile qui se déchirera à la fin. . . .

Je viens d'écrire le mot de symbole et je ne puis m'empêcher en passant de toucher à cet incomparable mode d'expression artistique. Après avoir été chez tous les peuples mystiques d'un quotidien emploi, il a disparu devant le rationalisme et le matérialisme. Les artistes ont oublié la beauté de l'allégorie, et cependant, comme l'a écrit Charles Baudelaire, c'est une forme esthétique *essentielle*.

Aujourd'hui des poètes de la valeur de Sully Prudhomme et de Mallarmé ont montré tout le parti que la littérature contemporaine pourrait tirer du symbolisme remis en honneur. . . .

. . . Ainsi, le poème, selon nous, n'a d'autre but que de préparer son dénouement. Nous ne pouvons mieux le comparer qu'aux degrés d'un autel magnifique, aux marches de porphyre que domine le Tabernacle. L'ornement, les cierges, les orfèvreries, les fumées d'encens—tout s'élance, tout est disposé pour fixer l'attention sur l'ostensoir—sur le dernier vers! La composition où cette gradation fait défaut a un aspect fatalement monotone, si riche et savamment ciselée soit-elle. C'est, à notre avis, le grand défaut des sonnets de de Heredia—par exemple—qui sont *trop beaux*, tout le long, d'un bout à l'autre. Chaque vers a sa vie propre, sa splendeur particulière et détourne l'esprit de l'ensemble.

through a sieve, weighed, filtered, subjected to *form*, and condensed as much as possible so as to gain in power what it loses in length: a sonnet, for example, will be a true quintessence, a nutrient, a concentrated and distilled juice, reduced to fourteen lines, carefully *composed* with a view to a final and overwhelming effect. Here the adjective will be impermutable, the sonority of the meters carefully graduated, the thought often adorned by a *Symbol*, like a veil that in the end will be torn away....

I have just written the word *symbol*, and I cannot help incidentally commenting on that incomparable mode of artistic expression. Having been in everyday use among all mystical peoples, it vanished in the face of rationalism and materialism. Artists forgot the beauty of allegory, and yet, as Charles Baudelaire wrote, it is an *essential* aesthetic form.

Today poets of such merit as Sully Prudhomme and Mallarmé have demonstrated all the advantages that a renewed respect for symbolism could bring to contemporary literature....

... So, in our opinion, the poem's only aim is to prepare its climax. We cannot find a better comparison than the stair to a magnificent altar with steps of porphyry surmounted by the Tabernacle. The ornaments, the candles, the golden vessels, the clouds of incense—everything rises towards and is arranged to draw one's attention to the monstrance, to the last line! The composition that lacks this progression has a fatally monotonous appearance, however rich and cunningly wrought it may be. In our opinion this is the great fault of the sonnets of de Heredia, for example, which are *too fine* the whole time, from one end to the other. Each line has its own life, its particular splendor, and distracts the mind from the whole.

. . . Quand le poème a une certaine étendue, une centaine de vers, je suppose, l'artiste doit s'ingénier à retenir la pensée sur quelques points importants qui, rapprochés et fortifiés à la fin, contribueront puissamment à l'éclat dernier et décisif. Ceci m'amène à parler de la Poétique si originale d'Edgar Poe; je dirai ensuite quelques mots d'une théorie musicale dont la connaissance est à mon avis très suggestive pour quiconque s'occupe de littérature.

Edgar Allan Poe, mathématicien, philosophe et grand écrivain, dans son curieux opuscule *la Genèse d'un poème*— the philosophy of composition—démontre avec netteté le mécanisme de la gestation poétique, telle qu'il la pratique et qu'il l'entend.

Aucune de ses œuvres ne renferme plus d'acuité dans l'analyse, plus de rigueur dans le logique développement des principes découverts par l'observation. C'est une technique entièrement *a posteriori*, établie sur la psychologie de *l'auditeur*, sur la connaissance des diverses notes qu'il s'agit de faire résonner dans l'âme d'autrui. La pénétrante induction de Poe s'insinue dans les intimes réflexions du sujet, les prévient, les utilise. Connaissant bien la part immense que l'habitude et l'automatisme ont dans notre vie mentale, il préconise des procédés que, depuis les anciens, on avait abandonnés aux genres inférieurs. La répétition des mêmes mots que les Egyptiens avaient paraît-il, employée, il la ressuscite. Il prévoit, à coup sûr, l'effet accablant d'un morne refrain, d'allitérations fréquentes:

And the Raven, never *flitting*, *still is sitting*, *still is sitting*.

De même, le désolant Nevermore, revient à chaque strophe; d'abord sans signification morale; peu à peu opposé à des phrases de plus en plus douloureuses, de plus en plus sonnant un glas de désespoir, jusqu'au dénouement:

When the poem is of a certain length, about a hundred lines I suppose, the artist must manage to concentrate our attention upon several important points, which, brought together and strengthened at the end, will powerfully contribute to the last, decisive flash. This leads me to speak of the extremely original poetic theory of Edgar Poe. Later, I shall say a few words on a musical theory, the understanding of which is, in my opinion, very suggestive for anyone occupied with literature.

Edgar Allan Poe, mathematician, philosopher, and great writer, clearly demonstrates in his curious little work "The Philosophy of Composition" the mechanics of poetic creation as he understands and practices it.

None of his works contains more acute analysis or a more strictly logical development of the principles discovered by observation. It is an entirely *a posteriori* technique, based on the psychology of the *listener*, on the knowledge of the different notes that must be sounded in another's soul. Poe's penetrating induction insinuates itself into the reader's intimate reflections, anticipates and uses them. Well knowing the great part played in our mental life by habit and automatism, he postulates methods that since the ancients had been relegated to the inferior genres. He revives repetition of the same words, which, it seems, was an Egyptian practice. He predicts with certainty the overwhelming effect of a bleak refrain, or of frequent alliterations.

And the Raven, never *flitting, still is sitting, still is sitting*.

Similarly, the desolate"Nevermore"returns in each verse; first of all, with no moral significance; then gradually opposed to lines ever more painful, ringing ever more loudly the knell of despair, until the climax:

Et mon âme de cette ombre qui gît à terre—ne s'élancera Jamais plus! Nevermore!

Tous ceux qui ont lu le splendide morceau intitulé le Corbeau (surtout dans le texte) auront été frappés de la force du refrain artificieusement employé. On peut dire que dans la poésie française l'emploi (j'entends l'emploi judicieux, en vue d'un effet) n'en a jamais été fait, du moins d'une façon délibérée et réellement savante....

Supposons qu'au lieu d'un refrain unique et monocorde, on en introduise plusieurs, que chaque personnage, chaque paysage, chaque état d'âme ait le sien propre; qu'on les reconnaisse au passage; qu'à la fin de la pièce de vers ou de prose, tous ces signes connus confluent pour former ce qu'on a appelé le *torrent mélodique* et que l'effet terminal soit le fruit de l'opposition, de la rencontre du rapprochement des refrains, et nous arrivons à la conception du *Leit motiv* ou motif dominant qui est la base de la théorie musicale wagnérienne.

Croit-on impossible d'appliquer ces principes à la littérature? Croit-on qu'ils ne renferment pas tout un avenir pour certains genres, tels que la Ballade en prose, création de Baudelaire, perfectionnée par Huysmans et Mallarmé?

... Et ici, ne pas prononcer le mot de Décadence, qui ne signifie rien: aux vieilles sociétés qui ont des siècles d'analyse intérieure et de production littéraire, il faut des plaisirs nouveaux, toujours plus aigus! Pour nous, nous ne nous plaindrons jamais de vivre en un temps où l'on voit coexister des Hugo, des Flaubert, des Goncourt, où la maladive sensibilité d'un Verlaine fait face à l'énorme vitalité d'un Zola, où l'on peut jouir de ce rare spectacle: la brutalité de la concurrence vitale, du mercantilisme, de l'effacement de la

And my soul from out that shadow that lies floating on the floor
  Shall be lifted—nevermore!

Everyone who has read the splendid piece called *The Raven* (particularly in the original) will have been struck by the power of the artificially employed refrain. One may say that use (I mean judicious use, for effect) has never been made of it in French poetry, at least in a deliberate and truly knowing way....

Let us suppose that instead of a single, monotonic refrain, several are introduced, and that each character, each landscape, each state of mind has its own; that they are successively recognizable; that at the end of the piece of verse or prose, all these known signs flow together to form what has been called the *melodic torrent;* and that the terminal effect is the fruit of the opposition and encounter of this meeting of refrains—then we arrive at the conception of the *Leitmotiv* or dominant theme, which is the basis of Wagnerian musical theory.

Is it considered impossible to apply these principles to literature? Are they believed not to contain a whole future for certain genres, such as the prose ballad, created by Baudelaire and perfected by Huysmans and Mallarmé?

... Let not the word *Decadence*, which is meaningless, be uttered here: old societies which have behind them centuries of inner analysis and literary production require pleasures ever new, ever keener! For ourselves, we will never complain of living in an age in which such men as Hugo, Flaubert, the Goncourts coexist, in which the effete sensibility of a Verlaine opposes the enormous vitality of a Zola, in which one can enjoy the rare spectacle of the brutality of the life struggle, of commercialism, of the effacement of personality, contrasted

personnalité, opposée au féminisme, à l'alanguissement exquis des artistes et des raffinés dilettanti. Nous nous plaisons à cette sublime antithèse : la grandeur barbare du monde industriel vis-à-vis des extrêmes élégances et de la recherche morbide des plus rares voluptés.

Et nous aimons l'art de ce temps, compliqué et *artificiel*, trop vibrant, trop tendu, trop *musical*, d'autant plus qu'il devient plus mystérieux, plus étroit, plus inaccessible à la foule. Qu'importe qu'il soit fermé à la plupart, que ses ultimes expressions demeurent le luxe d'un petit nombre, pourvu qu'il atteigne chez les quelques *justes* dont il est le divin royaume, le plus haut degré de splendeur et de pureté !

Novembre 1889

with feminism and the exquisite languor of artists and refined dilettanti. We take pleasure in this sublime antithesis: the barbarous grandeur of the industrial world faced with the extremes of elegance and the morbid search for the rarest pleasures.

And we love the art of this age, complicated and *artificial*, too vibrant, too tense, too *musical*, and all the more as it becomes more mysterious, narrower, more inaccessible to the crowd. What matter if it be closed to the majority, if its ultimate expressions remain the luxury of a small number, provided that with the few *elect*, whose divine realm it is, it reaches the highest degree of splendor and purity!

November 1889

NOTES

NOTES

THE explanatory notes are limited, with a few exceptions, to those allusions which a French reader might be expected to catch and an American or English reader might not. The bibliographical notes indicate for each essay its first publication and, if republished, one later collection where it may be found. The publisher is Gallimard and the place of publication is Paris unless otherwise stated. The French title of each essay is given after the English title. Except where otherwise noted, all translations are the editor's.

3. PREAMBLE: "Préambule," preface to Valéry's *Poésie, essais sur la poétique et le poète*, with eight engravings by the author (Bertrand Guégan, 1928). This collection of essays on "poetics and the poet," conceived and arranged by Valéry, has served as a model for the present collection.

8. CONCERNING 'ADONIS': "Au sujet d'Adonis," preface to La Fontaine's *Adonis* (Collection "Le Florilège Français"; Devambez, 1921); previously in the *Revue de Paris*, Feb. 1, 1921; in *Variété* (1924). Tr. by Malcolm Cowley, *Variety* by Paul Valéry (New York: Harcourt Brace, 1927); in part, by Louise Varèse, *Selected Writings* of Valéry (New York: New Directions, 1950).

17. "*Trackless delight*":"délice sans chemin." Valéry cites the phrase from Mallarmé's poem *Autre Eventail*.

21. *Il ne voit presque pas:* "He hardly sees the water he gazes on."

22. *Baudelaire said: "twin mirrors"*: "Dans nos deux esprits, ces miroirs jumeaux": "In our two minds, those twin mirrors" in his poem *La Mort des amants*.

23. *Vainement pour les dieux*: "No matter to the gods that it [time] flies with a light step."

Il est temps de passer: "It is time to come to that unhappy moment/When sorrowing Venus must leave her lover."

24. *Leurs fers après les miens*: "After mine, their bonds are unworthy of you."

25. *Jours devenus moments*: "Days that are but moments, moments strung on silk."

Moments pour qui le sort: "Moments that fate makes you sigh for in vain,/Delightful moments, you will return no more!"

26. *From one of them, not among the best known . . . the charming tale of the Beau Pécopin*: Valéry doubtless refers to a borrowing from chapter LI (lvi) of Binet's *Essai des merveilles de nature* (1621), which Hugo used in chapter X of his "La Légende du Beau Pécopin et de la Belle Bauldour," *Le Rhin* (1842). Etienne Binet (1569–1639) was a Jesuit rector and author of religious works. For the discovery of this borrowing, see: G. Dottin, "Le Rhin et l'Essai des merveilles de nature," *Revue d'histoire littéraire de la France*, X (1903); E. Philipot, "Etienne Binet et Victor Hugo," ibid., XVI (1909); J. Giraud, "Victor Hugo et 'Le Monde' de Rocoles," ibid., XVII (1910). Valéry may have been acquainted with the first of these source studies, but the whole question is far more complex than he indicates.

Master Verderer though he is: La Fontaine held the title of Maître des Eaux et Forêts at Château-Thierry.

27. *On y voit arriver*: "Stout-hearted Bronte arrives upon the scene."

28. *The horses of Hippolytus:* Valéry doubtless has in mind Théramène's long speech in Racine's *Phèdre*, V, vi.

29. *Nisus, ayant cherché:* "Nisus, having sought his safety in a tree,/Laughs to see this hunter colder than marble."

Les nymphes, de qui l'œil: "The nymphs, whose eyes see things in the future,/Had made him lose his way over darkened roads./The sound of horns was gone, by a magic spell. . . ."

30. *Ses yeux d'un somme dur:* "His eyes weighed down and veiled in a hard sleep,/Still he lies, lost in the darkest night."

On ne voit plus l'éclat: "No longer the brilliant glow upon his mouth,/Only its lines are seen."

31. *Mon amour n'a donc pu:*

"My love, then, could not make you want to live?
You leave me, cruel one? At least, open your eyes,
Show that you are moved by my sad farewell;
See with what grief your beloved one is stricken!
Alas! My cries are vain: he is deaf to my complaint.
An eternal night compels him now to leave me. . . .

If I could but follow him to that dark place!
Why cannot I too wander among the shades!

I did not ask that cruel Fate should weave
Into their [my charms'] web an eternal punishment;
Far from having power to keep him from death,
I beg for one moment, which I cannot have. . . ."

The famous manuscript: La Fontaine wrote for it a lengthy dedication (not reproduced in the printed editions) to Nicolas Fouquet, finance minister under Mazarin. (See note for p. 244.) It was doubtless Fouquet himself who commissioned the manuscript, now in the library of the Petit

Palais, Paris. It was published in facsimile by the Société des Bibliophiles français in 1931.

   Acante: poetic name assumed by La Fontaine in his poem *Le Songe de Vaux*.

   32. *Nos deux époux:* "Our two spouses, as the story tells,/ Were not for a moment without disputing."

   33. *Dans l'Orient désert:* "In the desert East, vast was my ennui!" (Antiochus, in *Bérénice*, I, iv.)

   35. FUNERAL ORATION FOR A FABLE: "Oraison funèbre d'une fable," preface to La Fontaine's *Daphnis et Alcimadure* (Havermans, 1926); also in *Commerce*, No. 10 (1926); in *Variété II* (1929).

   36. "*Nothing any longer exists for me*": "rien ne m'est plus, plus ne m'est rien," lament attributed to Valentine Visconti (1370–1408), duchess of Orléans and mother of the poet Charles d'Orléans. She died of grief after her husband was assassinated by Jean sans Peur (1407).

   "*I never live but two years hence*": "Je ne vis jamais que dans deux ans." Valéry was fond of citing this remark of Napoleon's.

   Madame de La Mésangère: To this lady, Marguérite, marquise de La Mésangère, daughter of La Fontaine's patroness Madame de La Sablière, he dedicated the fable *Daphnis et Alcimadure* (1685); to her also Fontenelle dedicated his *Entretiens sur la pluralité des mondes* (1686).

   39. A FOREWORD: "Avant-propos," preface to *Connaissance de la Déesse*, poems by Lucien Fabre (Société Littéraire de France, 1920); in *Variété* (1924). Tr. by Malcolm Cowley, *Variety;* in part, by Louise Varèse, *Selected Writings* (see note for p. 8).

   42. "*Reclaim their own from Music*": Valéry's phrase is

"reprendre à la Musique leur bien." The idea is Mallarmé's; a statement of it is found in his letter to René Ghil, Mar. 7, 1885: "cet acte de juste restitution qui doit être le nôtre, de tout reprendre à la musique": "that act of just restitution which must be ours, to reclaim everything from music."

47. *M. Fabre:* Lucien Fabre (1889–1952), engineer, scientist, poet, and novelist—like Valéry, a native of southern France. They first met in Adrienne Monnier's bookshop in the Rue de l'Odéon, Paris. Without knowing that Valéry was from Sète, Fabre is said to have delighted him by identifying the "scene" in *La Jeune Parque* with the coastal rocks there. Valéry remained strongly attached to Fabre. (See further pp. 231 ff. and note.)

51. *L'ardente chair ronge:* "The burning flesh endlessly gnaws/At the hard vows it has sworn." (From Fabre's poem *La Vestale.*)

52. POETRY AND ABSTRACT THOUGHT: "Poésie et pensée abstraite," The Basil Zaharoff Lecture at Oxford, Mar. 1, 1939 (Oxford: Clarendon Press, 1939); in *Variété V* (1944). Tr. by Charles Guenther in *Kenyon Review*, spring, 1954; by Gerard Hopkins in *Essays on Language and Literature*, ed. by J. L. Hevesi (London: Wingate, 1948).

74. *Mère des souvenirs:* "Mother of memories, mistress of mistresses" (the first line of Baudelaire's *Le Balcon*).

Sois sage, ô ma Douleur: "Be quiet, O my Sorrow, and lie still" (the first line of Baudelaire's *Recueillement*).

82. PROBLEMS OF POETRY: "Questions de poésie," written as a preface to *Anthologie des Poètes de la N. R. F.* (1936); but appeared first in the *N. R. F.*, Jan. 1, 1935; in *Variété III* (1936).

88. *"All the rest is Literature"*: "Et tout le reste est littéra-

ture," the last line of Verlaine's *Art poétique* (1884). The phrase became a byword of the Symbolists.

100. MEMOIRS OF A POEM: "Fragments des mémoires d'un poème," in the *Revue de Paris*, Dec. 15, 1937; in *Paul Valéry*, by Emilie Noulet (Grasset, 1938); in *Variété V* (1944). Tr. in part, by Louise Varèse, *Selected Writings* (see note for p. 8).

103. *Palissy:* Bernard Palissy (*c.* 1510–*c.* 1590), father of ceramics in France.

I prefer Restif to Jean-Jacques: Restif de la Bretonne (1734–1806); Jean-Jacques Rousseau (1712–78).

M. de Seingalt: Giacomo Girolamo Casanova de Seingalt (1725–98), better known as Casanova.

115. *As the Code naïvely puts it:* the Napoleonic Code of French law.

122. *The famous contrast between the "mathematical" and the "intuitive" mind:* Pascal's distinction between *l'esprit de géométrie* and *l'esprit de finesse.*

127. *A contrario:* by counter imitation.

131. *The spirit blows where it will:* Cf. John 3:8. The King James version has "the wind bloweth where it listeth"; Mgr. Knox, "the wind blows where it will." Valéry's "l'esprit souffle où il veut" is the traditional French version of the Vulgate's "spiritus ubi vult spirat," but he has put his own imprint on the sense.

133. THE PRINCE AND 'LA JEUNE PARQUE': "Le Prince et La Jeune Parque," published first under the title *Comment je revins à la poésie*, in *Les Annales*, Apr. 15, 1927; under another title, *Retour à la poésie*, in *Poésie* (see note for p. 3); under a third title, as above, in *Variété V* (1944).

135. *Adolphe Brisson:* (1860–1925), editor of *Annales poli-*

tiques et littéraires; became known for his interviews with celebrities published in *Le Temps* under the title "Promenades et Visites."

Rachel: stage name of Élisa Félix (1820–58), the greatest tragedienne of her time.

136. *Gautier:* Théophile Gautier (1811–72), poet, novelist, and critic. (See note for p. 259.)

Janin: Jules Janin (1804–74), journalist and dramatic critic.

N'aurais-je tout tenté: "Could it be that all I have done is for a rival?" (Roxane, in Racine's *Bajazet*, III, vii).

137. *Va, cours, mais crains:* "Go, fly, yet beware, you may there meet Hermione" (Hermione, in Racine's *Andromaque*, IV, v).

Adrienne Lecouvreur: a tragedy by Scribe and Legouvé (1849), on the death of the great French actress of that name (1692–1730).

Marie Stuart: Schiller's *Maria Stuart* (1800), in French translation.

Malheur, malheur à vous: "Woe, woe to you, when one day Truth,/Snatching from you the cloak of austerity,/Shall turn full upon you its glaring torch!"

138. *Je voudrais assister:*

"Would that I could witness your final dawn,
   Watch your bleeding meteor sink in the waves,
   And alone on the shores of ocean, breathe the cool air
   Of eternal night."

140. CONCERNING 'LE CIMETIÈRE MARIN': "Au sujet du *Cimetière marin*," in the *N. R. F.*, Mar. 1, 1933; preface to *Essai d'explication du "Cimetière marin,"* by Gustave Cohen (1933); in *Variété III* (1936). Tr. by F. Codman and H. Baugh, *Southern Review*, summer, 1938.

144. *Jacques Rivière:* (1886–1925), critic and novelist; one of the earliest associates, then secretary, and finally editor (1919–25) of the *Nouvelle Revue française.*

153. COMMENTARIES ON 'CHARMES': "Commentaires de *Charmes,*" preface to *Charmes,* poems of Paul Valéry with commentaries by Alain (1929); in the *N. R. F.,* Feb. 1, 1930; in *Variété III* (1936).

   Alain: pseudonym of Emile-Auguste Chartier (1868–1951), philosopher and moralist; professor at the Lycée Henri IV in Paris.

159. ON SPEAKING VERSE: "De la diction des vers," speech given at a banquet of the *Revue critique,* May 27, 1926; in the literary supplement of *Figaro,* June 5, 1926; in book form (Emile Chamontin, 1926); together with *Lettre à Madame C.* (Chamontin, 1933); in *Œuvres,* Vol. E (1935). Tr. by Louise Varèse, *Selected Writings* (see note for p. 8). The Chamontin edition of 1933 had this preface:

In 1923, Madame Croiza and M. Paul Valéry together became interested in the problem of speaking verse. One evening at the Salle Erard, Madame Croiza sang, among some other pieces, three songs of Debussy with words by Baudelaire: *Harmonie du soir, Recueillement, Le Jet d'eau.* M. Paul Valéry greatly admired the manner in which these poems were at once sung and spoken. In congratulating Madame Croiza, he expressed his desire to read some poems with her, to hear her read, and finally, with her and through her, to put into practice certain ideas on recitation, or spoken song, which had engaged his mind for a long time. Madame Croiza, who was at the time preparing two important rôles—the Penelope of Fauré and another Penelope in Monteverdi's *Il Ritorno d'Ulisse in Patria*—was happy to hear his views. With him, she studied some poems of Ronsard.

On March 3, 1925, the friends of Madame Croiza were gathered at a dinner in her honor. M. Paul Valéry, unable to be present, sent his regrets in the form of the letter printed here. [See pp. 167 ff.]

The ideas it contains were later applied, in preparing a performance of *Bajazet* to be presented by the Petite Scène. M. Paul Valéry was consulted on how Racine's verse should be spoken, and the advice which he gave on that occasion he later put into more finished form for the address delivered in May, 1926, at the banquet of the *Revue critique*. This was the talk "On Speaking Verse" published here.

163. *Madame Croiza:* stage name of Claire Connolly (b. 1882 in Paris), French concert and opera singer, interpreter of Debussy, Fauré, Chausson. (See note for p. 159.)

167. LETTER TO MADAME C.: "Lettre à Madame C." (Collection "Les Amis des Cahiers Verts"; Grasset, 1928); in *Pièces sur l'art* (1931). (See note for p. 159.)

169. THE POET'S RIGHTS OVER LANGUAGE: "Les Droits du poète sur la langue," a letter dated Nov. 19, 1927, to Léon Clédat, editor of the *Revue de philologie française;* in the first number of that review for 1928 (Vol. XL); in *Pièces sur l'art* (1931).

    Your Dictionary: Léon Clédat, *Dictionnaire étymologique de la langue française* (Hachette, 1912).

170. *Thérive:* André Thérive (b. 1891), literary critic and novelist.

    La nation chérie: "The beloved nation has broken faith." (Racine's *Esther*, I, iv.)

172. *Naturae non imperatur nisi parendo:* "Nature can be controlled only by obeying her."

173. A POET'S NOTEBOOK: "Calepin d'un poète," first published in *Poésie* (see note for p. 3); in *Œuvres*, Vol. C (1933).

184. PURE POETRY: "Poésie pure," published first in English translation by Malcolm Cowley, *New York Herald Tribune*, Apr. 15, 1928; the French text, as part of "Calepin d'un poète," in *Poésie* (see note for p. 3); in *Œuvres*, Vol. C (1933).

There is a great stir in the world: i.e., the literary debate that began in 1925 on the question of "pure poetry." See Henri Bremond, *La Poésie pure* (Grasset, 1926).

A few years ago, in a preface I wrote . . . I happened to use these words: The preface referred to is "A Foreword" (see p. 39). For the "two words: *pure poetry*," see p. 46.

193. CONTEMPORARY POETRY: "La Poésie contemporaine," published, as a reply to an inquiry, in *Figaro*, May 22, 1925. The French text has not been reprinted.

196. REMARKS ON POETRY: "Propos sur la poésie," lecture given at the Université des Annales, Dec. 2, 1927; in *Conférencia*, Nov. 5, 1928; in *Œuvres*, Vol. K (1939). Tr., anonymous, *Forum* (New York), Apr., 1929.

216. THE NECESSITY OF POETRY: "Nécessité de la poésie," lecture given at the Université des Annales, Nov. 19, 1937; in *Conférencia*, Feb. 1, 1938; in *Œuvres*, Vol. K (1939).

Francis Vielé-Griffin: (1864–1937), born at Norfolk, Virginia; one of two Americans who became well-known French Symbolist poets. The other was Stuart Merrill (1863–1915), born at Hempstead (Long Island), New York.

217: *Thrène:* "Threnody":

> "If I should say to you: 'Master!
> Day is breaking;
> Here is another dawn, just as pale;
> Master, I have opened the window,
> Dawn is coming again through the eastern door,

A day is about to be born!'
I could almost hear you say: 'I dream.'

If I should say to you: 'Master, we are here,
Living and strong,
As yesterday, at your door;
We have come laughing, we are here,
Expecting your smile and strong embrace,'
Someone would answer: 'The Master is dead.'

Flowers on my terrace,
Flowers, as in the leaves of a book,
Flowers, what for?
Here is a little of ourselves, a quiet song
That turns and falls,
As the leaves are turning and falling,
Here are the shame and the rage at being alive
And speaking words—against your tomb."

220. *The Lamoureux Concerts:* the series founded and conducted by Charles Lamoureux (1834–99), who popularized Wagner in France and performed Russian and new French music. Mallarmé and his disciples were regular attendants. (See "At the Lamoureux Concerts in 1893," in the present edition, Vol. 12.)

222. *The French Academy is a kind of registry:* The Academy's first duty has remained the care of the language through the Academy Dictionary (1st edn., 1694; 8th edn., 1932).

231. NOTES ON TRAGEDY AND A TRAGEDY: "Notes sur un tragique et une tragédie," written in the spring of 1944; appeared posthumously in the weekly *Opéra*, June 12, 19, and 26, 1946; preface to *Dieu est innocent*, a play by Lucien Fabre (Nagel, 1946). (See note for p. 47.)

238. *As I once wrote: "What must be said"*: in "Concerning *Adonis*" (see p. 23).

Ruy Blas: a verse drama (1838) by Victor Hugo.

239. *By dint of shocks:* The "regrettable expression" in French is *à coups de chocs.*

242. THE POETRY OF LA FONTAINE: "La Poésie de La Fontaine," written in June, 1944, for the *Dictionnaire des lettres françaises, 17ième siècle* (Arthème Fayard, 1954); but previously published in *Vues* (La Table Ronde, 1948).

244. *The Fouquet affair:* Nicolas Fouquet (1615–80), finance minister under Mazarin, amassed a fortune through the corrupt use of his office. Louis XIV, at the insistence of Colbert, had him arrested in 1661. His trial, which lasted four years, was conducted in so scandalous a manner, through the interference of Colbert and the King, that popular opinion turned largely in his favor. He was finally condemned, despite the loyalty of powerful friends, and died in prison. (See note for p. 31.)

246. *"Letter to Mme de La Sablière"*: Valéry doubtless refers to the *Discours à Madame de La Sablière*, near the end of Book IX of the *Fables.*

247. *Doux trésors, se dit-il:*

> "Sweet treasures, he said, dear pledges that never
> Brought upon yourselves lying and envy,
> I take you up again: let us go from this palace
> As one would wake from a dream."

248. *Prends ce pic et me romps:* Valéry misquotes. The line is "Prends ton pic, et me romps ce caillou qui te nuit": "Take your pickax and break me that boulder that troubles you." (From *Le Chartier embourbé:* "The Cart Driver Stuck in the Mud," Fable XVIII, Book VI.)

248–49. *Nuls traits à découvert:*

> "No naked features here will find a place;
> All will be veiled, but with gauze, and so well
> That nothing I think will be missed.
> Whoever thinks subtly and expresses himself with grace
> Can say anything. . . .
> You make no one blush
> And everyone understands. . . ."
> (From *Le Tableau*, in *Contes et nouvelles*, IV.)

249. *Le roi de Naple:* "The king of Naples had, at the time, a daughter,/The honor of her sex, the hope of her family. . . ." (From *Belphégor*, in *Contes et nouvelles*, V.)

250. . . . *Et, pleurés du vieillard:* "And, [they] bewept by the old man, he engraved on their tombs . . ." (From *Le Vieillard et les trois jeunes hommes:* "The Old Man and the Three Youths," Fable VIII, Book XI.)

251. VICTOR HUGO, CREATOR THROUGH FORM: "Victor Hugo, créateur par la forme," broadcast from Radio-Paris, May 25, 1935, as part of a celebration of the 50th anniversary of Hugo's death; published in *Les Cahiers de Radio-Paris*, Aug. 15, 1935; in *Vues* (see note for p. 242).

257. *Madame Simone:* stage name of actress and novelist Pauline Benda (b. 1880).

Cirque de Gavarnie: a spectacular amphitheater of mountains in the French Pyrénées.

259. *Passons, car c'est la loi:*

> "Let us go, for that is the law; none can escape it;
> All things decline, this great age with all its glory
> Enters the immense darkness to which, all pale, we
> fly.

Ah! what a brutal sound they make in the twilight,
The oaks they are felling for the pyre of Hercules!
The horses of death are beginning to neigh
And are happy that this brilliant age is to end;
This proud century that tamed the opposing wind
Is dying. . . . O Gautier! Thou, their peer and their
    brother,
Thou goest too, after Dumas, Lamartine, Musset.
The ancient spring is dry where we grew young;
As the Styx is no more, no more is the Fountain of
    Youth.
The grim reaper with his great blade draws near,
Pensive, with slow steps, for the rest of the grain;
My turn has come; night fills my clouded eyes,
And they, alas! guessing the future of doves,
Weep over cradles and smile toward the tombs."

(From the poem *A Théophile Gautier*, in the posthumous collection of Hugo's poems *Toute la lyre*, 1888.)

260. VICTOR HUGO'S FINEST STANZA: "La Plus Belle Strophe de Victor Hugo," published, as a reply to an inquiry, in *Figaro*, Sept. 1, 1934. The French text has not been reprinted.

262. FOUNTAINS OF MEMORY: "Fontaines de mémoire," preface to a volume of poems with this title, by Yvonne Ferrand-Weyher (Le Divan, 1935); in *Pièces sur l'art* (1936).

264. *Chant Royal:* one of the fixed forms invented by French poets of the Middle Ages, an elaborate and stately kind of ballade.

269. A SOLEMN ADDRESS: "Allocution solennelle," delivered Sept. 4, 1939, from the stage of the Théâtre Français,

Paris; published as *Notre plus grand poète: La France*, in *Caval-cade*, Apr. 12, 1946; in *Vues* (see note for p. 242).

    The Comédie Française: the official name of the two state theaters; the one in question here is the Théâtre Français, situated beside the Palais-Royal in Paris.

    273. *Théroulde:* Turoldus, the 12th-century author or scribe (which one is unknown) who signed the *Song of Roland.*

    275. AN AFTER-DINNER SPEECH: "Discours au PEN Club," a toast delivered at the banquet of the international PEN Club, Paris, 1925; in *Les Nouvelles littéraires*, June 6, 1925; in *Œuvres*, Vol. E (1935).

    278. *"The world," he used to say:* Mallarmé's phrase is "le monde est fait pour aboutir à un beau livre" (from "Sur l'Evolution littéraire").

    279. SPIRITUAL CANTICLES: "Cantiques spirituels," pref-ace to *Les Cantiques spirituels de St. Jean de la Croix*, translated into French verse by Father Cyprian (Louis Rouart, 1941); in *Variété V* (1944).

    285. *A l'ombre d'une obscure Nuict:* The following quota-tions in verse are taken, by permission of Harvill Press, from *The Poems of St. John of the Cross*, translated by Roy Camp-bell (London: Harvill Press, and New York: Pantheon, 1951):

> "Upon a gloomy night,
> With all my cares to loving ardors flushed
> (O venture of delight!)
> With nobody in sight
> I went abroad when all my house was hushed."

    287. *A l'obscur, mais hors de danger:*

> "In safety, in disguise,
> In darkness up the secret stair I crept,

(O happy enterprise)
Concealed from other eyes
When all my house at length in silence slept.

Upon that lucky night
In secrecy, inscrutable to sight,
I went without discerning
And with no other light
Except for that which in my heart was burning."

Dans mon sein parsemé de fleurs:

"Within my flowering breast
Which only for himself entire I save
He sank into his rest. . . ."

Morte bise arreste ton cours:

"Cease, then, you arctic gale,
And come, recalling love, wind of the South. . . ."

288. *Allons . . ./Au mont d'où l'eau:*

"By mountain-slope and lea
Where purest rills run free
We'll pass into the forest undetected. . . ."

290. *Henri Bremond:* (1865–1933) *abbé*, historian, and literary critic; member of the French Academy from 1928. His *Histoire littéraire du sentiment religieux en France*, 11 vols. (Bloud and Gay, 1916–33), is an inquiry into the forms of French Catholicism from the end of the sixteenth century, and particularly into the various expressions of mysticism in France.

In regio aerario praefectus: "intendant of the royal treasury."

In saeculo fortunam constituisse videbatur: translated in the preceding phrase.

292. *Combien suave et plein d'amour:*

"What peace, with love enwreathing,
You conjure to my breast
Which only you your dwelling place may call."

En solitude elle vivoit:

"In solitude she bided,
And in the solitude her nest she made:
In solitude he guided
His loved one through the shade."

294. *Art Catholique:* a publishing bookshop in Paris; same as "Louis Rouart" (see note for p. 279).

295. VARIATIONS ON THE 'ECLOGUES': "Variations sur les Bucoliques," preface to *Traduction en vers des Bucoliques de Virgile*, limited edition, illustrated by Jacques Villon (Société de Bibliophiles *Scripta et Picta*, 1953); trade edition, without illustrations (Gallimard, 1956). Both editions have the following introduction—here slightly condensed—by A. Roudinesco:

I had the good fortune to persuade Paul Valéry, during the Occupation, to make a verse translation of Virgil's *Eclogues*, for an edition to be illustrated by Jacques Villon.

Many people had shown surprise at my extravagant presumption in asking this of him, and had predicted the most humiliating refusal. But I was received with the simplicity that great worth confers.

"What is this you're asking of me?" said Valéry. "I'm no Latinist, I haven't opened my Virgil since my school days. Get a scholar, he will do you a good translation."

"There's no lack of translations," I said, "but I want more than a mere translation; I want a transposition, I want some Valéry, I want beautiful lines like those in *La Jeune Parque*."

"And rhymes too? I'll need a hundred years! Why do you want rhymes? Virgil hasn't any. It was St. Ambrose who devised that calamity."

"I want to make a handsome book; I need impeccable typography, and a beautiful layout. I need the same number of French lines as Latin—the two texts will be printed facing."

"What you're asking is awfully difficult. Latin uses far fewer words than French. I promise nothing, but I will reread my Virgil. Come back day after tomorrow."

I came back, not very hopeful.

"I have reread the *Eclogues*. They're rather juvenile. And those shepherds seem to practice a very odd kind of love. But I have a little free time at present; I'll have a try, and telephone you."

"Are you still determined to have no rhymes? But will your verse *sing* without rhyme?" I dared ask him.

"Oh, I can promise you that," he said.

He telephoned me a month later and read me the first Eclogue.

"Do you like it? You see, it does sing. I told you rhymes were of no use!"

Indeed it was enchanting. . . . In less than a year, all the Eclogues were translated. . . .

After reading and rereading the original, Valéry had changed his mind. "That flatterer, Virgil," as he liked to call him, "is deeper than he looks at a first glance."

. . . .

I now wished to have a preface that would reveal to the reader the true sense of these poems. I hoped to get it from Valéry.

"I'm no historian," he answered. "My translation will set the grammarians and the philologists on me. Now you want me to quarrel with the historians. Ask Carcopino to do the job, he knows all about the matter."

. . . .

I waited patiently. A few months later, I received the preface,

"Variations on the Eclogues." It was dedicated to me: "To my dear doctor A. Roudinesco, in memory of our affectionate, and sometimes medical, collaboration (August 20, 1944)." I hoped for ten pages . . . he had written twenty-two. This invaluable preface may be considered Valéry's last testament in poetics.

299. Πρὸς Χάριν: one of Valéry's favorite mottoes; translated in the preceding phrase. (See Vol. 4, *Dialogues*, p. 195.)

312. *Ludere quae vellem:* "He has allowed me to play what I will on my rustic flute." *Erit ille semper deus:* "He will always be a god." (Both lines are from the first Eclogue.)

314–15: ON LITERARY TECHNIQUE: "Sur la technique littéraire," in *Dossiers I* (July, 1946). Valéry submitted this very early essay (1889) to *Le Courrier libre* (Paris), which had published poems of his. With it went this note: "I have taken the liberty this time of sending you a little article, 'A Literary Chat'—on various technical matters—thinking that it may interest your readers, who are more or less all writers. I hope the piece does not look too long!" The review ceased publication before the article could appear. Henri Mondor wrote, in connection with its first publication (1946): "This is doubtless Valéry's first article." This and its rarity are reasons for including the French text here.

318 *La Genèse d'un poème:* the title given by Baudelaire to his translation of "The Philosophy of Composition."

PAUL VALÉRY was born in 1871 in Cette and studied law at the University of Montpellier. There, influenced by a visit from Loüys and Gide, he decided to go to Paris and devote his life to writing. Leon Daudet commissioned him to do "Introduction to the Method of Leonardo da Vinci" for his *Nouvelle Revue,* and the following year *Centaur* published "An Evening With Mr. Teste." In 1900 he married Jeanne Gobillard. For the next seventeen years he published almost nothing until Gide asked him to collect his earlier scattered poems, which were finally published as *La Jeune Parque.* Suddenly, at the age of forty-six, Valéry found himself famous and started work on his renowned *Graveyard by the Sea.* By 1925, as the foremost poet of France, he was elected to the French Academy, where he occupied the chair of Anatole France, Thiers, and Malesherbes. When he died in 1954, in Paris at the age of seventy-three, he left behind him hundreds of notebooks of unpublished writings with instructions that they might not be consulted for fifty years. C. M. Bowra maintains that Valéry wrote for the few, but for them his work "is representative of the age in which it was written, scientific and sceptical of transcendental hypotheses but willing to admit that in the varied pattern of life there is much that calls for wonder."

This colophon was chosen from a number of drawings by Paul Valéry of his favorite device.

VINTAGE FICTION, POETRY, AND PLAYS

VINTAGE HISTORY
AMERICAN

A free catalogue of VINTAGE BOOKS will be sent to you at your request. Write to Vintage Books, Inc., 457 Madison Avenue, New York 22, New York.

VINTAGE WORKS OF SCIENCE
AND PSYCHOLOGY

VINTAGE RUSSIAN LIBRARY

VINTAGE BIOGRAPHY AND AUTOBIOGRAPHY

A free catalogue of VINTAGE BOOKS will be sent to you at your request. Write to Vintage Books, Inc., 457 Madison Avenue, New York 22, New York.

VINTAGE HISTORY
EUROPEAN

A free catalogue of VINTAGE BOOKS will be sent to you at your request. Write to Vintage Books, Inc., 457 Madison Avenue, New York 22, New York.

VINTAGE BELLES-LETTRES

A free catalogue of VINTAGE BOOKS will be sent to you at your request. Write to *Vintage Books, Inc., 457 Madison Avenue, New York 22, New York.*

VINTAGE HISTORY AND CRITICISM
OF LITERATURE, MUSIC, AND ART

A free catalogue of VINTAGE BOOKS will be sent to you at your request. Write to Vintage Books, Inc., 457 Madison Avenue, New York 22, New York.